WITNESSES
of
CHRIST

**Messages of John Paul II
on Consecrated Life**

Compiled and Indexed
by the
Daughters of St. Paul

ST. PAUL EDITIONS

Reprinted with permission from *L'Osservatore Romano*, English Edition.

ISBN 0-8198-8206-2 cloth
0-8198-8207-0 paper

Cover credit: DSP

Printed in the U.S.A., by the Daughters of St. Paul
50 St. Paul's Ave., Boston, MA 02130

The Daughters of St. Paul are an international congregation of religious women serving the Church with the communications media.

CONTENTS

Religious and the Apostolate of the Family

From "Familiaris Consortio"

The contribution that can be made to the apostolate of the family by men and women religious and consecrated persons in general finds its primary, fundamental and original expression precisely in their consecration to God. By reason of this consecration, "all Christ's faithful religious recall that wonderful marriage made by God, which will be fully manifested in the future age, and in which the Church has Christ for her only spouse" (PC 12), and they are witnesses to that universal charity which, through chastity embraced for the kingdom of heaven, makes them ever more available to dedicate themselves generously to the service of God and to the works of the apostolate.

Hence the possibility for men and women religious, and members of secular institutes and other institutes of perfection, either individually or in groups, to develop their service to families, with particular solicitude for children, especially if they are abandoned, unwanted, orphaned, poor or handicapped. They can also visit families and look after the sick; they can foster relationships of respect and charity toward one-parent families or families that are in difficulties or are separated; they can offer their own work of teaching and counseling in the preparation of young people for marriage, and in helping couples towards truly responsible parenthood; they can open their own houses for simple and cordial hospitality, so that families can find there the sense of God's presence and gain a taste for prayer and recollection, and see the practical examples of lives lived in charity and fraternal joy as members of the larger family of God.

I would like to add a most pressing exhortation to the heads of institutes of consecrated life to consider—always with substantial respect for the proper and original charism of each one—the apostolate of the family as one of the priority tasks, rendered even more urgent by the present state of the world.

Christ Is the Light of Human Life

On February 2, 1982, the Feast of the Presentation of the Lord in the Temple, the Holy Father blessed candles during a Liturgy of the Word held in Saint Peter's Basilica. He delivered the following homily.

1. *Lumen ad revelationem gentium.*

These words resounded for the first time in the very place of the temple of Jerusalem where the rite of purification of mothers after the birth of their firstborn was observed.

They were spoken by the old man Simeon, who was a prophet.

They were spoken in the presence of Mary and Joseph, who had brought to the temple the Baby born in Bethlehem.

Although these words resounded in only one place, the truth proclaimed in them filled the whole temple: the entire place dedicated to the God of Israel in expectation of the Messiah.

These words filled the temple of Jerusalem with the light of their destiny conceived from eternity:

"a light for revelation to the Gentiles, and for glory to your people Israel"

(Lk. 2:32).

THE SIGN OF CHRIST

2. Today we enter the Basilica of St. Peter repeating the words of Simeon.

We walk in procession, holding candles: the sign of the light "that enlightens every man" (Jn. 1:9). The sign of Christ born in Bethlehem. The sign of Christ presented in the temple. The sign of contradiction (cf. Lk. 2:34).

We confess Christ in this sign.

Didn't His contemporaries often contradict Him? The children of the people to whom He had been sent? Yes. It is so. They contradicted Him. To put out the Light, they inflicted death on Him.

Simeon prophesies this death when he says to His Mother: "And your own soul a sword shall pierce" (Lk. 2:35).

Death on the cross did not extinguish the light of Christ. He was not crushed by the burial stone.

Here we are—we enter this basilica carrying the light: the sign of Christ crucified and risen.

In the cross and resurrection the prophecy of Simeon is fulfilled completely: a sign of contradiction—a sign of light.

AGE OF CONTRADICTIONS

3. Did not Christ enter with this sign into the history of man? Does He not emerge before us from the various stages of human history? A period does not exist in which He has not been

contradicted. And in this contradiction the light to enlighten man has been revealed anew each time.

Is not our century, too, the age of a multiple contradiction with regard to Christ?

And in this very century is He not perhaps revealed again as the light to enlighten men and peoples?

"Lumen gentium cum sit Christus..." with these very words the text of the main document of the Church of our times begins.

The luminous sign in which we today profess Christ—the Son of Mary—Christ born in Bethlehem, presented in the temple—Christ crucified and risen—is a sign that is simple, yet at the same time so rich. Rich as life—since in fact "the life was the light of men" (Jn. 1:4).

Christ is the light of human life. He is the light because He dispels the darkness. He is the light because He makes life's mysteries clear. Because He answers questions that are at once basic and definitive. He is the light because He gives meaning to life. He is the light because He convinces man of his great dignity.

In the sign of this light we have come today to this Roman temple of St. Peter, as once Mary and Joseph went up to the temple of the ancient Covenant, which awaited the Messiah.

4. We are here to live anew the mystery of the presentation of the Lord. The presentation in the temple, which became a model and a source of inspiration.

It is also the light that enlightens human life. We live in Christ with the light of the presentation.

Through the heart of man, in which man offers "spiritual sacrifices," is not the whole world transformed into a gigantic temple of the cosmos?

Is it not transformed into a large Christocentric space of the created spirit, in which the Holy Spirit operates?

Oh, how much the little human heart can do when it lets itself be penetrated by the light of Christ and becomes the temple of the presentation!

LET YOUR LIGHT SHINE

5. I am speaking precisely about you, dear brothers and sisters, sons and daughters of the Church, members of so many religious orders and congregations.

I am speaking of everyone—of the whole People of God whom Christ "has made a kingdom of priests for our God" (Rv. 5:10)—but I am speaking especially of you.

Of you who are here today carrying in your hands the light of Christ—and of all of your brothers and sisters in the whole world. In particular I am speaking of all who carry the heaviest crosses!

May the light of the holy presentation, which through the grace of Christ has been kindled in your hearts through religious profession, burn always in each and every one of you!

As it burns, may it shine before others!

Do not hide this light! Do not take its simple evangelical splendor away from it!

You are so necessary for the whole messianic People of God in their pilgrimage towards the eternal Light.

6. Christ in the temple of Jerusalem! Renew us all in the mystery of Your presentation—allow us, through the intercession of Your Mother, to continue with perseverance towards Him who "lives in inaccessible light" (1 Tm. 6:16).

Amen.

Commitment of Perfect Charity

Men and women religious of Nigeria met the Holy Father at the Seminary of Ibadan on February 15, 1982. The Holy Father addressed them as follows.

Dear brothers and sisters in Christ,

1. I am overjoyed to have this meeting with you, men and women of the different dioceses in Nigeria, who are living the religious life of

consecration to Jesus Christ. Through your commitment of perfect charity you express the hope of the Church and become her crown and glory. You are a comfort for her. You are ambassadors for her. This encounter could not be omitted.

Having been already consecrated to God by Baptism, you give special witness to Christ in the Church and in the world by your renunciation—for the sake of the kingdom of heaven—of marriage, earthly possessions and the doing of your own will. Through your vows you make this sacrifice freely, out of love for God and your fellowman, in a spirit of dedication and service.

Consecrated chastity has great witness value in a world rampant with selfishness and the misuse of sex. In addition, in Nigeria and throughout Africa the sacrifice of fatherhood or motherhood is no small matter. Poverty calls people to give up attachment to money and what money can buy. And obedience swims against the world current of revolt, pride, vanity and oppression. As the Second Vatican Council says, the religious state is a proof that the kingdom of Christ and its overmastering necessities are superior to all earthly considerations (cf. LG 44).

Even more important than the various works which you carry out is the life which you live: in other words, what you are. You are consecrated persons striving to follow Christ with great intensity of love.

2. Your love of God and union with Him in prayer expresses itself in the activities of the apostolate. In many ways you are called to collaborate in the cause of evangelization. Through a multiplicity of works you strive to communicate Christ and to offer service in His name. Through a whole network of ecclesial initiatives you pursue the definitive aim of catechesis: "to put people not only in touch but in communion, in intimacy, with Jesus Christ" (CT 5). Wherever a child is in need, wherever someone is suffering, wherever a brother or sister feels alone or rejected, the religious has the opportunity to work for the kingdom of God. But prayer and union with God always remain the soul of your apostolate. Without Jesus we can do nothing.

3. I appreciate your efforts for the *continuing theological* and *spiritual formation* of your members, your initiative of post-novitiate training centers, the regular meetings of your major superiors, and the area meetings which involve every religious. Through such activities you are able to reflect more deeply on religious life, grow in an understanding of charity and the meaning of your mission, consolidate unity among yourselves and coordinate your apostolate. Having been refreshed and renewed in faith and love, you will be in a position to give

yourselves with ever greater availability to the service of the local and the universal Church.

4. I wish to make a particular mention of *religious brothers* and to praise them and to encourage them. Your vocation, my dear brothers, is not an easy one, especially because the spirit of the world does not appreciate evangelical poverty and humble *service*. You are called to follow Christ in a life of total self-giving which does not generally bring public acclaim.

Many people cannot understand your vocation because they cannot grasp how Christ's invitation, when accepted, can truly bring joy and deep fulfillment: "If any man would come after me, let him deny himself and take up his cross and follow me" (Mt. 16:24). The Christ who emptied Himself is your model and your strength. You yourselves, then, must never begin to doubt your own identity. Your understanding of your vocation, your transparent happiness and infectious peace, and your zealous commitment to your apostolate and to the good of the people whom you serve are an eloquent *witness* to the power of Christ's grace and to the primacy of His love.

5. All religious, both brothers and sisters, must be aware that *temptations* will not spare them. Your three vows will sooner or later be tested in the crucible of problems, crises and

dangers. Your intense love of Christ and His Church will teach you how to remain faithful.

In particular, you will have to seek ever more authentic ways to live lives of evangelical poverty in a country in which the gap between the rich and the poor is widening all the time. In the Nigeria of today you are also expected to be a leaven in society through a spirit of humble service, exercised particularly among the poor. This type of consecrated service is the opposite of complacency, arrogance and privileged position.

In planning its apostolate and the professional training of its members, each congregation should take full account of the *local Church* or diocese. The diocese is a spiritual family of which the bishop is the father and head, and religious must avoid the temptation of running programs parallel to those of the diocese. Rather the entire diocese—priests, religious and laity— should coordinate its apostolic plans and strategy and give corporate witness to Christ.

CLOISTERED RELIGIOUS

6. I wish to add a special word to the *monks and cloistered nuns* of Nigeria, because of the specific contribution which their way of life makes to the Church and the nation. You rightly

place particular emphasis on divine worship, on prayer and contemplation. The Church herself ratifies your vocation because of her conviction that apostolic fruitfulness is a gift of God. By assiduous prayer you are associated with Jesus, who is "living for ever to intercede for all who come to God through him" (Heb. 7:25). United with Jesus in His intercession, you are thus able to obtain graces for the active apostolate and for the whole world. I personally rely on your help.

You live lives of real self-sacrifice. You thereby give to all Christians, and indeed to all people, a silent but eloquent testimony of God's sovereignty and of Christ's primacy in your lives. By the work of your hands and by your intellectual endeavors, you show the close relationship between work and prayer. At the same time you express your solidarity in work with all your brothers and sisters throughout the world.

Through monastic silence you help create an atmosphere for enabling people to listen to God and to receive His inspirations. It is no wonder that priests, religious and laity flock to your monasteries and convents for the sacred liturgy, prayer, spiritual retreats, recollection days, advice and even simply rest. In such ways you can help promote the maturity of your people in the Paschal Mystery of Christ's death and resurrection.

LIVE YOUR VOCATION
FAITHFULLY

7. And to all of you, beloved religious of Nigeria, I wish to express my deep affection in Christ Jesus. I am very grateful to you for your lives of consecration and for all your generous service to the Church. I ask your continuing prayers for the intentions of the Apostolic See and for the needs of the universal Church. May our Blessed Mother Mary, our model of love for Jesus and of dedication to Him, help you to live out faithfully your vocation of love and faith, of joy and hope. For, in the words of St. Peter, without having seen Jesus "you love him; though you do not now see him, you believe in him and rejoice with unutterable and exalted joy." Dear brothers and sisters, "set your hope fully upon the grace that is coming to you at the revelation of Jesus Christ" (1 Pt. 1:8, 13).

Personal and Community Witness of Detachment and Availability

From the meeting of the Holy Father with the clergy, religious, and catechists in St. Mary Cathedral at Libreville on February 19, 1982, we print the part of his discourse directed particularly to religious congregations working in Gabon.

In preparing my pastoral journey I noticed that many religious congregations work in Gabon and that those who are here longest—the Holy Ghost Fathers, the Sisters of the Immaculate Conception of Castres, and the Brothers of St. Gabriel—have made a singular contribution to the building of the Church in Gabon and to the human development of the country. In the name of all of you, I must offer special thanks to the Little Sisters of St. Mary of Gabon for their courage, their simplicity and their closeness to the people of Gabon. But it is to the eighteen institutes which have come to serve you that I offer my congratulations and encouragement.

Dear brothers and sisters, take account of what you are and of what you do! You are Christian men and women in the midst of others. You have had the grace of understanding the call to the radical practice of the Gospel, a call characterized today as yesterday by the vows of poverty, chastity and obedience. It is a radical practice which, year in and year out, brings you to a state of openness towards the Lord and towards your human brothers and sisters, who feel challenged by it. Personal and community witness of detachment and availability should harmonize with and reinforce one another. This is what society needs, as people are tempted to shut themselves up in a practical materialism which often puts on the mask of the idolatry of power, money and sex. If this witness seems to you sometimes difficult and limited, go back, I pray, to the spirit of your founders, who were aflame with the love of Christ and His Church.

What you actually do must also be considered. Many teach in schools and colleges, many collaborate in parish or diocesan pastoral work in the fields of catechetics, liturgy, apostolic movements, the continuing formation of young people and adults, works of charity, etc. I am very glad about this and I congratulate all of you in the name of the Church. Perhaps the time has come for greater collaboration between you, the religious of various congregations, and for greater collaboration with the diocesan leaders of joint pastoral action. Planned joint action often allows economy in personnel, technical and financial means, and gives new energy and effectiveness to efforts which are too diffuse.

At this point, I should like to say a word of encouragement concerning the efforts being made by the episcopal conference to foster

priestly and religious vocations. I know that the
results to date are hardly encouraging. However, the increasing numbers in several seminaries and novitiates give cause for confidence
and hope. In the reports you sent me during the
past weeks, I saw that many youth movements
and youth centers give new signs of hope. I read
too that many young people, disillusioned by the
consumer society, were looking for the absolute
or at least new reasons for living. The various
sections for the pastoral care of vocations are
very conscious of this complex phenomenon
which one sees today in our affluent society.
This could be for some the way towards a radical
commitment to the following of Christ. It seems
to me also that communities of priests, religious
men and women, imbued with a true Gospel
spirit and giving proof of a disinterested welcome and openness to young people and to their
parents as well, have a part to play in this
apostolate. Some of them, and several Christian
communities also, are happy to receive young
people, who may have thoughts of a vocation,
for a period of reflection and cooperation. This is
a real convergence of initiatives which are
prudent, updated and constant and which will
help the Gabonese Church to find in her own
membership a good number of the workers she
so greatly needs. I promise to continue my
prayers for this intention.

Obedience and Trustful Availability to the Loving Gesture of Christ's Vicar

On February 27, 1982, the Holy Father received in audience in the Consistory Hall the Jesuit provincials and the assistants and councillors of the General Curia who had been meeting at Grottaferrata at the invitation of the Pope's Delegate, Fr. Paolo Dezza. Also present at the audience were the Superior General, Fr. Pedro Arrupe, and Fr. Dezza's Coadjutor, Fr. Giuseppe Pittau.

After hearing Fr. Dezza's address of homage, John Paul II addressed them as follows.

1. I am particularly pleased, dearest brothers in Christ, to welcome you today in this special meeting! I warmly greet my delegate for the Society of Jesus, Fr. Paolo Dezza, and his Coadjutor, Fr. Giuseppe Pittau, and especially the revered Superior General, Fr. Pedro Arrupe, and all of you assistants and councillors of the General Curia, and the 86 provincials who represent before my eyes the 26,000 Jesuits, who, scattered all over the world, are pledged "to serve the one Lord and the Church His Bride, under the Roman Pontiff, the Vicar of Christ on earth."

To these sentiments of sincere joy for your presence there should be added a due sentiment of recognition and gratitude, which—following in the steps of my Predecessors—I wish to express to the whole Society of Jesus and to its individual members, for the historic contribution of apostolate, of service, of fidelity to Christ, to the Church and to the Pope, given over the centuries with an unwearying generosity and an exemplary dedication in all fields of the apostolate, in the ministries, in the missions. It is a recognition which I express today in the name of the whole Church to you, worthy heirs of these religious, who for four centuries and a half have taken as their motto and ideal "the greater glory of God."

This gratitude and appreciation acquire a special significance in the present circumstances which appear and objectively are delicate for the government of your well-deserving order. It is well known that after the very dear Father Arrupe had been stricken by illness, I deemed it opportune to appoint my personal delegate, and his Coadjutor, for the government of the order and for the preparation of the General Congregation. The situation, undoubtedly singular and exceptional, suggested an intervention, a "trial" which—and I say it with deep emotion—was received by the members of the order in a genuinely Ignatian spirit.

The attitude of the Very Rev. Superior General, especially in such a delicate situation, has been exemplary and moving. He edified me and you by his complete availability in regard to the directions from above, by his generous "fiat" to the exacting will of God manifested in the sudden and unexpected illness and in the decisions of the Holy See. Such an attitude, evangelically inspired, has yet again confirmed that total and filial obedience, which every Jesuit should show towards the Vicar of Christ.

To Fr. Arrupe, present here in the eloquent silence of his infirmity, offered to God for the good of the Society, I wish to express, on this occasion particularly solemn for the life and history of your order, the thanks of the Pope and of the Church!

I should also publicly express a sentiment of appreciation to my personal delegate, Fr. Paolo Dezza. In a spirit of perfect Ignatian obedience, he accepted the burden and the task, particularly difficult, heavy and delicate. But his deep spirituality, his vast cultural preparation, his consummate religious experience are and will be for the Society a guarantee of faithfulness in continuity. I express similar sentiments to his Coadjutor, Fr. Giuseppe Pittau. For many years he worked in Japan, in that noble nation in which Fr. Arrupe, especially after the Second World War, had poured out the treasures of his apostolic fearlessness and priestly generosity.

ATTITUDE OF OBEDIENCE
AND AVAILABILITY

2. It is my duty to express keen satisfaction for the similar attitude of obedience and trustful availability shown in practice during this period by the assistants, the councillors of the General Curia, as well as by the Jesuits of the whole world. Public opinion, perhaps, expected from the Jesuits a gesture dictated solely by human logic; but it received, with admiration, a reply dictated instead by the spirit of the Gospel, by a spirit profoundly "religious," by the spirit of the fine, genuine Ignatian traditions.

This attitude of obedience and availability has been the conscious reply on the part of the Society of Jesus to the *gesture of love* in its regard by the Holy See and the Vicar of Christ.

Yes, beloved brothers! The decision taken by the Holy See had its profound motivation and true source in the *special love* which it had and has for your great order, well deserving in the past and protagonist of the present and the future of the Church's history.

On my part, this love is dictated by a special relationship of the Society of Jesus to my person and to my universal ministry. But it also springs from my priestly and episcopal experience in the Archdiocese of Krakow, as well as from the hope and expectations for what concerns the carrying out of post-conciliar and present-day tasks of the Church.

In such a climate of serene welcoming of God's will, you are reflecting in meditation and prayer during these days on the best way to respond to the expectations of the Pope and of the People of God, in a period of polarizations and contradictions which mark contemporary society. The object of your reflections, inspired by Ignatian "discernment," are the fundamental problems of the identity and of the ecclesial function of the Society: the *"sentire cum Ecclesia";* the apostolate; the quality of Jesuit religious life; formation; what the Church expects from the Society of Jesus.

YOUR GLORIOUS HISTORY

3. During this meeting of ours, as I look on your qualified group of the Sons of St. Ignatius, there is offered to my consideration the vision of your order and of its glorious history.

It is known to all those who are familiar with the history of the Church, how and to what extent the Society of Jesus, founded at the time of the Council of Trent, effectively contributed to the implementation of the directives of that Council, and to the vitality engendered by the Council.

However, it is opportune to reflect on your order's past in order to grasp the fundamental marks of this process and the richest and most positive aspects of the way in which the Society contributed to it. They will be like guiding lights or beacons to indicate what the Society of today, impelled by the dynamism typical of its founder's charism, but genuinely faithful to it, can and must do to foster what the Spirit of God has brought about in the Church through the Second Vatican Council.

As one looks back over the four centuries and a half of its history, certain elements of genuine value emerge. They are those which characterize the life and mission of that body which, by the will of Ignatius, is the Society of Jesus.

The first concern of Ignatius and of his companions was to promote an authentic *renewal of the Christian life*. The state of society and of the Church were such that only the work of men of God could have an influence and supply sanctifying vitality.

Following the example of Jesus who went about "all the cities and villages, teaching in their synagogues and preaching the gospel of the kingdom" (Mt. 9:35), the first companions, sent out under obedience, went their pilgrim way to various cities, spreading the Good News and bringing a breath of saintly life. That was the beginning of those missions to the people which were destined to be of service to the Christian faithful, to instruct them in the Faith and to lead them to a consistency of life. These missions to the people were subsequently to have a flourishing development and a vast influence for good.

The *Spiritual Exercises* of St. Ignatius which imprinted an indelible mark on the history of spirituality, proved to be a particularly efficacious means for a deeper renewal of the Christian life. The first companions and their successors were formed by the exercises, and with the exercises they became the spiritual guides of innumerable faithful; they helped them to discover their vocation according to God's plan and to become genuine, committed Christians, whatever their state in life might be.

CONCERN FOR TRUE CATHOLIC DOCTRINE

4. Besides spiritual direction, the Society had a solicitous concern for spreading the true Catholic doctrine among the learned and the unlearned, from the young to the oldest. The two Jesuit Doctors of the Church, St. Peter Canisius and St. Robert Bellarmine, were the authors of two celebrated catechisms for the young and they were, both of them, masters held in admiration—the former engaged in the

theological discussions of the Council of Trent, and the latter a defender of the Faith in the universities of Louvain and Rome.

For a similar reason St. Ignatius, and after him the Society, took pains with the education of youth. They founded and multiplied colleges in which, following a new system of teaching—the famous *"Ratio studiorum"*—they aimed at providing an integral formation of the human person, in order to mold men who, while being eminent in study and in every profession, would also be outstanding Christians.

All this happened at a time when the world, and particularly Europe, were in a state of change, indeed at a decisive turning point in the literary and scientific field. In this process Jesuit scholars and men of science played a forceful part by performing a pioneering work *"ad maiorem Dei gloriam,"* that is to say, by fostering that Christian development of man which, when achieved, is to the glory of God.

VALUABLE CONTRIBUTIONS OF THE ORDER

5. Looking then at a sector of vital importance for the Church, St. Ignatius and the Society after him were concerned about seminaries and higher centers of learning for the formation of the clergy. To St. Ignatius is due

the founding of the Roman College, later to become the Gregorian University; and likewise the founding of the Germanic College, which was followed, often with the collaboration of so many Jesuits, by the other national colleges in Rome, to prepare for the Church a flow of priests endowed with sound doctrine and solid virtue. These became zealous apostles in their own homelands, and not infrequently martyrs for the Faith.

In connection with these centers of learning the Society has made a most valuable contribution in the field of the sacred sciences and has given a numerous band of Jesuit theologians, biblical exegetes, patrologists, Church historians, moralists and canonists, and scholars of so many other sciences connected with sacred studies.

But St. Ignatius's vision opened on still wider horizons, as broad as the world, which, following upon the then recent geographical discoveries, had assumed larger dimensions. It is the yearning for Christ which throbbed in the heart of the saint and in the hearts of those who, sharing his spirit, offered themselves entirely to "our Lord, eternal King," whose "will is to conquer the whole world" (Spiritual Exercises, no. 95).

The group of Ignatius's first companions was small; yet the saint sent St. Francis Xavier to the East, the first of that uninterrupted band of Jesuit missionaries who were "sent" to the East and the West to announce the Gospel. On fire with apostolic zeal, they were ready to give their life as a witness to their Faith, as is attested by the numerous martyrs of the Society. While the primary scope of their mission was to communicate the Faith and the grace of Christ, they made every effort at the same time to raise the human and cultural level of the peoples among whom they worked, to promote a more just social life and one more in keeping with God's plans—because of which the famous *Reducciones* of Paraguay [unique autonomous communities of Christian Indians run by Jesuit missionaries in the 17th and 18th centuries— *Editor's note]* are still remembered in history.

The generosity and the spirit of the missionaries attracted new recruits; the letters of St. Francis Xavier touched the hearts of the university students of Paris. The life and writings of so many other well-known apostles of Christ's kingdom had a similar effect. To them must be added a nameless host of holy religious who sacrificed their life in humility and in secret, in isolated mission lands.

Among so many Jesuit missionaries I would like to mention one, because his memory is particularly topical today. I refer to Fr. Matteo Ricci, for we are about to celebrate the fourth centenary of his arrival in China. To go to that great country was the dream of St. Francis Xavier who died thirty years earlier on Sancian Island, at the threshold of that China which was, and again wishes to be, a privileged field of the Society's apostolate.

Thus in the course of history the Society of Jesus, in every part of the world where it fought for Christ and for the Church, has been present with its finest sons, on fire with zeal, fortified with virtue, endowed with doctrine, and faithful to the directives of their head, the Vicar of Christ, the Roman Pontiff.

This is the Society of Jesus which history places before our eyes; the Society of Jesus which the enemies of Christ persecuted until they obtained its suppression, but which the Church has made to rise again, realizing the need of such valiant and devoted sons. Popes have trusted in them in the past, and the Pope wishes to place his trust in them in the future.

YOUR APOSTOLIC AND MISSIONARY VOCATION

6. If I have spoken about the Society of Jesus of the past, so as to bring together the distinctive features of its life and mission, that is because I am thinking of the Society as it is today and what the Church expects from it at the present and in the future.

Whoever considers the contribution that your order has made to the Church and to the world and appreciates its main objectives, cannot but see what was for St. Ignatius one of the most characteristic features of the order founded by him under the impulse of the Holy Spirit.

In fact, the Society of Jesus has always throughout its history, in all its many and varied forms of apostolic ministry, distinguished itself by the mobility and vigor which its founder infused into it, and which have made it capable of understanding the signs of the times and of being in the forefront of the renewal desired by the Church.

In view of the apostolic and missionary vocation which is yours, the members of this chosen body that you constitute, by the will of St. Ignatius and the Church, are—as Paul VI said to you—"in the first line of the profound renewal which the Church, especially since the Second Vatican Council, desires to bring about in this secularized world. Your Society is, so to speak, a test of the Church's vitality throughout the centuries; it is in some sense a crossroads where, in a very significant manner, difficulties, temptations, efforts, undertakings, the durability and the successes of the entire Church all meet together" (Paul VI, Allocution to the Fathers of the 32nd General Congregation, December 3, 1974).

As my venerated Predecessor already told you, the Church today wants the Society to implement effectively the Second Vatican Council, as, in the time of St. Ignatius and afterwards, it spared no effort to make known and apply the Council of Trent, assisting in a notable way the Roman Pontiffs in the exercise of their supreme Magisterium.

DEVIATIONS HARMFUL TO THE ENTIRE CHURCH

7. Allow me to insist once more and solemnly on the exact interpretation of the recent Council. It was and still is an ecclesial renewal under the guidance of the Holy Spirit. On this most important point the conciliar documents are absolutely clear (cf. LG 4, 7, 9; cf. GS 21, par. 5, and 43, par. 6).

This renewal of fidelity and fervor in all sections of the Church's mission—matured and expressed in the collective heeding of the Pentecostal Spirit—must be welcomed and lived today according to the same spirit and not according to personal criteria or psycho-sociological theories. That is why, the better to accomplish this work in the bosom of the Church, contemplatives and religious who live the apostolic life have been called by the same Council to renew their evangelical life.

The decree *Perfectae caritatis* (nos. 2 and 3) expressed clearly and fervently these criteria of renewal. Where there is fidelity, there is no room for deviations which are certainly harmful to the vitality of communities and of the entire Church. It seems to me that the Society of Jesus, ever more imbued with the spirit of true renewal, will be ready to play its part fully today as in the past and always: to be able to help the Pope and the Apostolic College to advance the whole Church along the great road marked out by the Council, and to convince those who are tempted, alas, by the ways of either progressivism or integralism, to return with humility and joy to unsullied communion with their pastors and brothers who suffer from their attitudes and their absence.

This patient and delicate task is surely the work of the whole Church, but faithful to Saint Ignatius and all his sons, you must rise like one man for this mission of unity in truth and charity.

The fourth vow of the Society was understood by St. Ignatius precisely as the living and vital expression of the awareness that Christ's mission continues in time and space in those who, called by Him to follow and share His works (cf. *Spiritual Exercises*, nos. 91-98), make His sentiments their own and thus live in intimate union with Him and therefore with His Vicar on earth.

That is the reason why St. Ignatius and his companions, wishing to share in Christ's mission which continues in the Church, decided to place themselves without reserve at the disposition of the Vicar of Christ, and to bind themselves to him by "a special vow, so much so that this union with the Successor of Peter, which is the specific characteristic of the members of the Society, has always assured your communion with Christ, of which it is the sign; for Christ is the first and supreme Head of the Society, which by definition is His—the Society of Jesus" (Paul VI, Allocution to the Fathers of the 32nd General Congregation, December 3, 1974).

PRIESTLY MINISTRY IN ALL ITS AUTHENTIC FORMS

8. Because of this distinctive and characteristic feature of your order, the Church first of all requires you to adapt the different forms of traditional apostolate which even today retain all their effectiveness, and to work for the renewing of the spiritual life of the faithful, the education of youth, the formation of the clergy, of religious men and women, and missionary activity.

This requires catechesis, proclamation of the Word of God, the spreading of Christ's doctrine, Christian penetration into the culture of a world trying to establish division and opposition between science and faith, pastoral activity for those on the fringe of society, exercise of priestly ministry in all its authentic forms, not forgetting the new means of apostolic works provided by modern society, such as the press and the other media, while bringing to perfection the use which the Society has already made of them during recent times.

Besides this, the Church wishes the Society to interest itself still more in the initiatives which the Second Vatican Council has particularly encouraged:

—*ecumenism*, in order to reduce the scandal of division among Christians. It is now more than twenty years since the Church instituted the Secretariat for Christian Unity. In a world becoming less Christian, collaboration between those who believe in God and in Christ is needed.

—*the deepening of relations with non-Christian religions*, carried out by the Secretariat for Non-Christians, and the presentation of Christian life and doctrine in a manner adapted to the different cultures which tactfully keeps in mind their different characteristic traits and the richness of each one.

—studies and initiatives concerning the disturbing phenomenon of atheism. These studies are being encouraged by the Secretariat for Non-Believers, remembering the behest of Paul VI to "resist atheism vigorously and as strongly as possible" (Allocution to the Fathers of the 31st General Congregation, May 7, 1965).

There is still one point to which I wish to call your attention. Today we feel with ever growing urgency the need to promote justice in the Church's evangelizing action. When we think of the demands of the Gospel and at the same time of the influence of social conditions on practical Christian living, we easily understand why the Church considers the promotion of justice to be an integral part of evangelization. It must be understood as an important sphere of apostolic action. In this domain not all have the same function, and as far as the members of the Society are concerned, it must not be forgotten that *this necessary concern for justice must be exercised in conformity with your religious and priestly vocation.* As I said on July 2, 1980, in Rio de Janeiro, priestly service, "if it is really to be faithful to itself, is essentially and par excellence spiritual. This must be even more emphasized in our times against the many tendencies to secularize the priest's work by reducing it to a purely philanthropic function. He is not a medical doctor, a social worker, a politician, or a trade unionist. In certain cases, no doubt, the priest can help, but in a supplementary fashion—as in the past priests have done with remarkable success. Today, however, these services are admirably rendered by other members of society, while our service is always more precisely and specifically spiritual. It is in the realm of souls, of their relation to God and their attitude towards their fellowman that the priest has an essential function to fulfill. That is where he should use his talents with the people of today. Certainly, whenever there is need, he must also give material assistance through works of charity and by upholding justice, but, as I have said, in the last analysis, this must be a secondary service which must never obscure the principal service which is to help souls to discover the Father, to be open to Him and to love Him in all things."

The Second Vatican Council has already clarified the apostolate of the laity and has exhorted them to play their part in the Church's mission; but the role of priests and religious is different. They are not meant to take the place of the laity, and still less should they neglect the duty that is specifically theirs.

PROLONGED SOLID FORMATION OF FUTURE MEMBERS

9. Your Constitutions lay down clearly those prerequisites which are necessary if the Society

of Jesus is to contribute efficaciously to the implementation of the Conciliar Decrees as the Church expects it to do.

First there is the prolonged, solid formation of the future apostles of the Society. In the very Formula of the Institute, after describing the way typical of the Society, Ignatius writes: "By experience we have learned that the path has many and great difficulties connected with it. Consequently we have judged it opportune to decree that no one should be permitted to pronounce his profession in this Society unless his life and doctrine have been probed by long and exacting tests" (*Formula of the Institute of the Society of Jesus*, no. 9).

You must not yield to the easy temptation of watering down this formation which has such importance in each and every one of its aspects: spiritual, doctrinal, disciplinary and pastoral; the ensuing damage would outweigh by far any results which could perhaps be achieved right away.

Remember that even in the days of your founder, the Society was faced with the anguishing problem which faces you today. Even then there were too few apostles, apt and ready, to cope adequately with the pastoral needs.

OUTSTANDING
FOR INTIMATE UNION WITH GOD

10. However, you must bear in mind that this long and exacting preparation has as its primary aim the formation of men who are outstanding because of their intimate union with God. In fact, Ignatius was convinced that all apostolic activity has value and is efficacious only if it flows from that "union between the instrument and God" of which he so often speaks. The primacy of the interior life is the very foundation of Ignatius' vision and spirituality; it constitutes the inner core of an authentic apostolic life, because the true apostle lives out his mission in total dependence on God and in union with Him.

Your founder and with him his first companions were indeed men of God; in answer to the freely-given call of the eternal King *(Spiritual Exercises,* nos. 91-98), and having understood interiorly the Spirit which animated Jesus Himself, the One sent by the Father, they lived as the Lord asked His Apostles to live, when He said to them: "Abide in me, and I in you. As the branch cannot bear fruit by itself, unless it abides in the vine, neither can you, unless you abide in me. I am the vine, you are the branches. He who abides in me, and I in him, he it is that bears much fruit, for apart from me you can do nothing" (Jn. 15:4-5).

Yet again, in virtue of what is the richest element in the spirit of your founder, I beg you to reflect on the deepest meaning of the "Contemplation for Obtaining Love," by which the apostolic man lives in the awareness of the reality that "all gifts and benefits come from above. My moderate ability comes from the Supreme Omnipotence on high, as do my sense of justice, kindliness, charity, mercy and so on, like sunbeams from the sun or streams from their source..." *(Spiritual Exercises, no. 237).* Such is the spirit of the true apostle who lives his mission in total dependence on God and in union with Him.

For this reason in apostolic religious life of which St. Ignatius, under God's impulse, was one of the great founders, there should be no separation between the interior life and the apostolate. These are the two essential and constitutive elements of this life: they are inseparable, and they mutually influence and compenetrate each other.

11. Together with solidity of virtue, your Constitutions insist on a *solidity* and *soundness of doctrine,* such as is essential for an efficacious apostolate. Consequently, "the Jesuits were universally considered to be a support for the doctrine and discipline of the whole Church. Bishops, priests and lay people used to look upon the Society as an authentic nourishment

for the interior life" (Letter of Cardinal Villot to Fr. Arrupe, July 2, 1973). The same should remain true in the future by means of that loyal fidelity to the Magisterium of the Church, and in particular of the Roman Pontiff, to which you are in duty bound.

ESSENCE OF IGNATIAN CHARISM

12. In fact, a special bond binds your Society to the Roman Pontiff, the Vicar of Christ on earth. As I have already mentioned above, St. Ignatius and his companions, having spiritually grasped the true meaning and value of the mission of Christ, and how it is prolonged in history, attached capital importance to this bond of love and service to the Roman Pontiff, so much so that they wished this "special vow" to be a characteristic element of the Society. While describing their own interior disposition, and what they expected of those who would later be admitted to the professed body of the Society, they wrote those words which are, and must remain, engraved in the heart of every Jesuit worthy of the name: "For the sake of our greater devotion in obedience to the Apostolic See, of greater abnegation of our own wills, and of surer direction from the Holy Spirit, in addition to that ordinary bond of the three vows, we are obliged by a special vow to carry out whatever

the present and future Roman Pontiffs may order which pertains to the progress of souls and the propagation of the Faith; and to go without hesitation or excuse, as far as in us lies" *(Formula of the Institute of the Society of Jesus,* no. 3). It is evident that here we are touching upon the essence of the Ignatian charism, and upon what lies at the very heart of your order. And it is to this that you must always remain faithful.

The Roman Pontiff to whom you are linked by this special vow is, in the words of the Second Vatican Council, "the Supreme Pastor of the Church" (CD 5). As such he has a particular ministry of service to exercise for the good of the universal Church, and in which he willingly accepts your loving, devoted and time-tested collaboration. But the same Roman Pontiff also accepts the collaboration that you offer him in his role as head of the Episcopal College (cf. LG 22), united with his brother bishops in a collegial ministry of discernment and harmony, which, in virtue of a distinctive charism, coordinates in docility to the Holy Spirit the other roles of ecclesial service (cf. MR 6). For this reason you are likewise linked to the members of the College of Bishops by a bond that calls you to be united with them in pastoral charity and in close practical collaboration. Precisely because of your special availability to the call of the Roman Pontiff, you are able to work ever more effectively with the College of Bishops and with its individual members, who in the Successor of Peter find their perennial and visible source and foundation of unity (cf. LG 23).

POPE'S GRATITUDE FOR COLLABORATION

As the Second Vatican Council explained, the Roman Pontiff also employs the departments of the Roman Curia in the exercise of his service to the universal Church (cf. CD 9). This fact itself requires a loyal collaboration between the Society of Jesus and these departments. Because of the exigencies of your vows and the reality of my ministry, it could not be otherwise. Some of the special tasks assigned to the Society of Jesus and other important works that it has assumed in the postconciliar period correspond to the programs of the Apostolic See that are coordinated by some of its new departments. Through collaboration with these various bodies, the Society of Jesus can find its rightful orientation in a number of issues and at the same time make an enormous contribution to the universal Church.

On his part the Roman Pontiff offers you, in the name of Christ, whose Vicar he is, the full measure of his grateful love for your collaboration with him personally, with the College of Bishops, and with the whole Roman Curia, which the Society of Jesus has been generously assisting in so many ways for years.

THE BEST PREPARATION FOR THE GENERAL CONGREGATION

13. I shall not delay any longer these reflections, because I know that during these days you are considering, together with Father Delegate, the wishes that I have expressed regarding the Society, and that in a spirit of faith and of fraternal collaboration, you are seeking the most suitable means of putting them into practice.

My only task is to encourage you to continue in this work which, while being of special importance for the good of your Society, will also be of great benefit for the whole Church which looks to the Society with a special interest and appreciation.

The exemplary nature of your religious life, the spiritual atmosphere of your communities, the austerity of your mode of life, and your fervor in apostolic works will be a cause of edification for the whole People of God, and will attract ever more numerous vocations to your Society—generous young people who aspire, not to mediocrity in the following of Christ, but to a radical consecration to Him.

In this way you will prepare in the best possible manner for the General Congregation. I am confident that this preparation will proceed in such a manner that it will be possible to convoke the General Congregation within this year. The Congregation as you know will have to provide a new Superior General for the Society, according to the wishes expressed some time ago by the revered Fr. Arrupe. At the same time it will have to communicate to the whole Society a new stimulus to carry out its mission with renewed enthusiasm in accordance with the hopes of the Church and of the world.

I shall accompany you in this work with my good wishes and my prayers that the Lord, through the intercession of her whom you are in the habit of invoking as Queen and Mother of the Society of Jesus and of your many saints and blesseds, may bless your work and make it fruitful.

To these saints and blesseds, already elevated to the honors of the altar, it is consoling to add also so many of your brothers who because of their outstanding virtue are awaiting the Church's official recognition of their sanctity. In this regard it is a pleasure for me to recall that precisely on the eleventh of February of this year, I had the joy of declaring heroic the virtues of the humble and well-beloved coadjutor brother, Francis Garate, who died some fifty years ago, a native of that land which saw the birth of your holy founder, Ignatius of Loyola.

The life of these religious of the Society as also of so many excellent Jesuits who live and work throughout the whole world in a spirit of faith filled with love and with a dedication to the service of man that is truly exemplary, is a clear proof that even in our times holiness continues to flourish in the Society.

It is a proof also of the continuing validity of the vocation of the coadjutor brothers in the Society. Through their complete dedication to the service of the Lord in the carrying out of the various offices, these brothers really cooperate with the Fathers in that priestly ministry which is proper to the Society.

With these sentiments I impart to you with all my heart my apostolic blessing, and through you I extend it to all the members of the Society as a pledge of divine gifts.

Be "Other Christs" as Francis Was!

On March 12, 1982, the Holy Father delivered the following message to priests, religious, and representatives of lay movements from the dioceses of Assisi and Nocera-Umbra, Gualdo-Tadino, assembled in the Cathedral of San Rufino in Assisi.

Beloved confreres in the priesthood, dear men and women religious!

1. Coming to Assisi to take part in the work of the extraordinary assembly of the Italian Episcopal Conference, how could I have neglected to have a meeting, however brief, with you priests and religious in this historic cathedral dedicated to the martyr Rufino, the first bishop and principal patron of the city? This morning's concelebration with my brother bishops, far from dispensing me, rather invites me and urges me to address to you a special greeting that may be a memento of my presence today in the local Church, and at the same time an encouragement to all of you to carry out your pastoral work within it.

I cordially greet you, and with you I greet the qualified lay people who have come here as representatives of the Catholic movements in the dioceses of Assisi and Nocera-Umbra, Gualdo-Tadino. A special thought, with deep gratitude for the words addressed to me, goes to Mons. Sergio Goretti, to whom both these communities are entrusted, and from this moment I give him and you the task of extending my greeting, as a sign of blessing and good wishes, to the faithful of all the parishes and all the centers scattered in the plains and mountains of this choice portion of Umbria.

CENTENARY YEAR

2. The theme of this talk appears to me easy and obligatory—at least by choice. So fine and strong is the connection between Assisi and Francis that it lends itself, especially on the occasion of the centenary year, to timely and salutary considerations: in this city he was born; with the bishop of the city, Guido—*his* bishop—he had relationships of homage, obedience and friendship; here, for the most part, he marvelously worked in the not-long journey of his earthly existence; from here he irradiated the example of his virtues and his message of brotherhood and peace, which, almost in the form of seeking wider and wider avenues, spread into the surrounding region, into the neighboring areas of Tuscany and Lazium, and then into Italy, Europe, and the world.

The figure of St. Francis, the "poor and humble," dominates still, well beyond the geographical limits of this land of his. Why? It is a legitimate question that everyone can ask; but especially you, you who are his fellow citizens and countrymen, must ask yourselves this question. And since you are priests, or rather consecrated persons, take care to collect within the folds of your answer those elements and aspects that really touch the mind of Francis and as such are not only true and genuine, but also more valid and indicative for you and for your work in the sacred ministry.

IDEAL LOFTY CALL

3. Eight centuries from his birth, the world —even so far removed from and indifferent to religious values—looks admiringly at Saint Francis, because it sees in him an authentic, faithful, and therefore credible, copy of Jesus Christ. This is the answer in a nutshell! He is *alter Christus,* but not merely in words, not only *de iure* (as whoever professes to be Christian must basically be): he is such even and above all in the reality of his life.

At a certain point, as you well know, when he was a brilliant young man in lively medieval Assisi, he made a radical and generous choice: stripping himself of everything, renouncing his father's inheritance, naked and set apart, he decided to follow totally, irrevocably, the Lord Jesus, from His birth in the cave of Bethlehem right up to Calvary. He remained faithful to this "fundamental option," carrying out an effective following, step by step, in the footsteps of the Redeemer, right up to the stigmata of Verna, right up to death on the bare ground, down there in the plain below this city....

How can one deny, beloved confreres, that such a line of perfect correspondence and consistency between Francis and Christ is clearly and sharply placed before each one of you again through the similar choice that, although in different ways and circumstances, you have made with regard to the following of Christ? Is not the priest also an *alter Christus?* He is and he must be, through the sacramental character imprinted on his soul by priestly ordination; he is and he must be, through the role as the legitimate representative of Christ, to which he has been raised; he is and he must be, through the unbroken daily relationships which, by virtue of his ministry, he enters into with Christ present and living in the Eucharist, in the treasure of His Word, in the person of His brothers and sisters.

You see, then, how that rapid and essential response, which gives us the degree of the greatness of Francis, can be profitably applied, as the ideal lofty call and authoritative teaching of life, to each one of you. The priest is an *alter Christus;* as Francis, so you too!

A TIME OF CRISIS TODAY

4. If limited time prevents me from developing the numerous and precious examples of virtue that Francis, who remained always a deacon, offers to one who has attained the order and dignity of the priesthood, I cannot, however, omit another fact of particular relevance which, easily singled out in his biography, can also inspire the action of the priest in the modern world.

One day on his way back from Rome, he got into a discussion with his companions as to whether he would retire into solitude and seclusion for contemplation and prayer, or whether he would rather "spend his life among the people" to preach the Gospel and save his brothers and sisters through a direct apostolate. After praying, he immediately found the answer, and it was a new choice perfectly in line with that fundamental choice of following Christ (cf. *Legenda Maior* IV, 1-2). As He had traveled the countrysides of Palestine calling to repentance and proclaiming the Gospel of the kingdom (cf. Mk. 1:14-15), so Francis and his brothers would do, developing an itinerant ministry of contact, word and witness in the society of their time. In an era of crisis spread through the great changes which after the eleventh century were already verified in the various nations of Europe and which could not but concern the Church, the meditated choice of the Poverello of Assisi gave a determining contribution to the fortunate religious-moral renewal. He and his disciples worked tirelessly to bring Christ back into society, and they did this, not in opposition to or in polemics against the legitimate authority of the Church (as some heretical sects of the time), but in perfect obedience and in fulfillment of an apostolic mandate (cf. *Regula non Bullata* XVII; *Regula Bullata* IX).

The second lesson I wish to propose to you—as you can well understand—is this: it is in the effort, following the example of Francis, that the priest must make in the present age which is approaching the year 2000. Today too is a time of crisis—the time of the decline of values and of generalized secularization. What must be done, then, to bring Christ and His Gospel back among men? At the end of the last century, when with the advent of the first industrial society some sign of crisis began to be noticed, it was said that it was high time for the priests to "come out of the sacristies" and go meet the people. And today? Today all this seems to be imposed with more serious urgency and already finds a significant "precedence" and an emblematic model in the behavior of Francis and his disciples, who went through the streets of the world according to the programmatic mandate of the Lord Jesus:

"Go: behold, I send you as lambs in the midst of wolves; carry no purse, no bag, no sandals.... Whatever house you enter, first say: 'Peace to this house....' Whenever you enter a town and they receive you,...heal the sick and say to them: 'The kingdom of God has come near to you'" (Lk. 10:3-8; cf. 9:1-6; Mt. 10:5, 9-10; Mk. 6:7-13).

Here is the style of the evangelical worker: it is his going through the streets of the world with courage, in total detachment from the things of earth, as a bearer of peace and a proclaimer of the coming of the kingdom. Today, even more than in the past, we must go to proclaim to men the good news of the merciful love of God, and with it, the duty to respond to this antecedent and prevenient love; we must go to promote the whole good of men; we must go without opposing the commitment to the service of God and that of our brothers and sisters; we must go and coordinate in a balanced harmony the so-called vertical dimension upward towards God, and the horizontal one in the direction of men.

As the two arms of the cross are a symbol of this twofold dimension, so Francis, who followed Christ right to the cross and could with good reason repeat the words of St. Paul: "I have been crucified with Christ" (Gal. 2:20; cf. 6:17), reminds all of us priests of the twofold orientation to which we must look in taking on and exercising the sacred ministry. The "man of God" is first of all, essentially, the priest, but at the same time, without denying this quality, he is appointed for the good of men (cf. 1 Tm. 6:11; Heb. 5:1).

THE SPIRIT OF FRANCIS

5. I have no doubt that these brief references, obviously valid for everybody, have a special efficacy, and I would say a greater driving force, for you who are sons of this land and are therefore almost naturally "harmonized" with the spirit of Francis, which was—I am happy to repeat—an apostolic and evangelical spirit.

Priests *or* religious, priests *and* religious, beyond the legitimate differences and canonical distinctions, there is an objective convergence in what you do, according to your respective assignments, within each community, as in the sphere of the diocese and in the universal Church. Work, therefore, in fraternal harmony; work in the union of charity; work in collaboration among yourselves and with the bishop for the building up of the one and undivided Church of Christ. From this will benefit not only the necessary coordination and organization of pastoral work, but also and above all the credibility of that one and immutable message which all of you are called to announce.

Especially you priests, in the wake of your great fellow countryman, who always paid bishops and priests a singular respect and honor, be more careful and alertly aware of the incomparable gift received from God (cf. Jn. 4:10). In this way you will be able daily to confirm and strengthen your commitment to evangelical works, in union with the bishop, with your confreres, and with your religious and lay collaborators.

In the name of the Lord, under the patronage of St. Francis, I heartily bless you all.

How Important You Are for the Life of the Church

Message given by the Holy Father to the nuns in the Monastery of St. Clare on the occasion of his visit to Assisi, March 14, 1982.

This visit is a source of great joy to me. It was not planned, but then an unknown protector of yours said to me: "A visit should be made to the Poor Clares." I accepted the suggestion, because it is really difficult to separate these two names: Francis and Clare; these two phenomena: Francis and Clare; these two legends: Francis and Clare. It is true you are not celebrating this year an anniversary of St. Clare; when you do, it should be celebrated with great solemnity.

It is difficult to separate the names of Francis and Clare, these two phenomena, these two legends of sanctity. In them we find something profound, something which can be comprehended only according to the criteria of Franciscan, Christian, evangelical spirituality. The two names, Francis and Clare, are a reality which can be understood only when considered according to the Christian, spiritual categories of heaven; but they are a reality of this earth, this city, this Church. And it all took place here. They were not spirits, but human beings, persons with spirit.

In the living tradition of the Church, of all Christianity, of humanity, there remains more than the legend. There remains the way in which Francis saw his sister; the way in which he espoused Christ; he beheld himself as an image of her, spouse of Christ, mystical spouse with whom he formed his sanctity. He saw himself as a brother, a poor man in the image of the sanctity of this authentic spouse of Christ in whom he found the image of the most perfect Spouse of the Holy Spirit: Mary most holy. So it is not merely a human legend, but a divine one which deserves to be contemplated according to divine categories, to be contemplated in prayer.

This is the place where for eight centuries
so many pilgrims have come to contemplate the
divine legend of Clare beside Francis. This
certainly has had great influence in the life of
the Church, in the history of Christian spirituality. It has been one of the decisive moments.
The life totally dedicated to the Lord by Francis
and by his sister Clare, and by so many of their
brothers and sisters in countless parts of Europe
and the world, has outlined a way for vocations.
For many years I myself lived near a monastery
of Poor Clares in Krakow, and I know many
other places in my native country where the
living tradition of St. Clare and St. Francis
continues to echo down through the centuries of
the Church and the world.

I am not making an official address; but I
want to mention something on my mind. In this
circumstance, my dear Poor Clares, sisters of
St. Clare, I want to share with you my concern,
which I have clearly stated also to the bishops. I
speak to you more directly: I am disturbed, and
so are all of us bishops in this country, and those
in other lands also, because vocations of women
to religious life are growing scarce. It would
appear that women of today, especially young
women, do not feel drawn to this vocation.
Hence I invite you to pray; I hope you can
repeat in these our times the miracle of St. Francis and St. Clare, so that we may again see

girls, young women of today, in this vocation, in this mission, living this splendid charism, hidden indeed, but certainly not without external attractiveness, so profound, so feminine! A real spouse. Indeed the feminine soul is capable of complete, undying love for an invisible Spouse. It is true He is invisible, but so visible! Among all the spouses in the world certainly Christ is the most visible of all who are visible; He is always visible, but He remains invisible and visible in the soul consecrated to God. Saint Francis discovered God a first time, and then with new vigor with Clare beside him he discovered God again.

In our day the discovery of St. Clare, so important for the life of the Church, must be repeated. You do not know how important you hidden, unknown nuns are in the life of the Church, how many problems, how many things depend upon you. It is necessary to rediscover that charism, that vocation, the divine legend of Francis and Clare.

One final item. That friend of mine who made the suggestion, in fact obliged me to come to visit you Poor Clares—you know him—also mentioned that St. Clare is the heavenly patron of the means of social communications. Consequently, I commend these to your prayers. As such they are, I would say, mysterious structures, natural rather than supernatural. Like all things, like all natural structures they are at the same time a passive subject which may receive supernatural realities. If the human thought and word is transmitted by social communications, why not the divine Word, the evangelical Word? Cannot the divine Word work effectively through such technical means as social communications? The decree on social communications begins with the words *"Inter mirifica"*—"among the marvelous things." Hence I recommend to you this *"Inter mirifica"* and all those—some here present—who dedicate themselves to social communications.

Your Poverty Constitutes the Riches of the Church

During his pastoral visit in the church of the Most Holy Cross at Forte Bravetta, on March 15-16, 1982, the Holy Father spoke to some representatives of the congregations of sisters serving in the parish.

There are many sisters in this parish. You consider yourselves poor. Yes, this is true: you are poor, but nonetheless you are riches; precisely in your poverty lie the riches of the Church. It is necessary to pray that this your vocation, your charism may never be lacking in the Church.

These young girls, these novices with you, must strive to find the way to the religious vocation in total consecration of the person, of the human heart, to the Lord. This constitutes your riches and for this reason in every parish you are the riches of the Church.

You have divers apostolates by reason of your consecration. Being spouses of the Lord you want to do all you can so that He can be the Spouse of all: because the Redeemer is always Spouse. And because He is Redeemer and Spouse He loved the Church, He gave Himself for the Church, that is, for all. You strive to bring all, especially the sick, the suffering, the abandoned, the youth and children to our Redeemer, Spouse of your souls. Therein lies your riches. You are on that account rich, while being poor; and for this reason you are the riches of the Church.

I hope and pray that you preserve this spirit of poverty and riches: the spirit of the vows, of the evangelical counsels.

Be Docile Instruments of the Lord To Save Modern Society

After the meeting and dinner with the workers of the Solvay factory in Rosignano on March 19, 1982, Pope John Paul II left by helicopter for Montenero, the hill on which the major Marian shrine of Tuscany is situated. There he met the priests, religious and sisters of the diocese of Livorno and delivered the following address.

Dearest brothers and sisters,

1. I have come here to this hill as a pilgrim to venerate the image of Our Lady of Montenero, together with you, priests, religious and sisters, whom I greet with deep affection, each and every one. I address a grateful thought to Bishop Ablondi for having given me the joy of this pilgrim meeting with brothers and sisters close to the Mother of Jesus and Mother of the Church.

I cordially greet the fathers of the monastic Congregation of Vallombrosa who, as custodians of the Montenero Shrine, have for two centuries welcomed with love and dedication the ever-more numerous pilgrims coming from various parts of Italy.

All of us are on our way through the paths of the world towards our ultimate destination, which is our heavenly homeland. Down here we are only passing through. For this reason nothing can give us the profound meaning of our earthly life, the stimulus to live it as a brief period of trial and at the same time of enrichment, as much as the interior attitude of seeing ourselves as pilgrims.

Marian shrines throughout the whole world are like milestones that have been placed to mark the stages of our itinerary on earth: they allow a rest stop on the journey in order to give us again the joy and certainty of the way, along with the strength to go ahead; like the oases in the desert, put there to offer water and shade.

PATRONESS OF TUSCANY

2. In the wake of the Pontiffs, from Innocent II to Pius IX, who have preceded me on this earth, I have come to this Shrine of Our Lady of Montenero, whom my venerated Predecessor, Pius XII, proclaimed the "Principal Patroness of all Tuscany before God," and which is the goal of so many pilgrimages.

In the land of Tuscany, where art and poetry have reached their height—art and poetry inspired for the most part by religious values, especially by the Mother of God—there could not fail to be on this hill a shrine dedicated to Mary. Here, through a marvelous painting of nature, the clear blue sky, painted by Giotto and admired by Dante, meets the sea with its many routes which since far-off times have brought the Tuscan people to every known continent. For her kindness towards men of the sea, Our Lady of Montenero is called also the "Star of the Sea."

So here, in direct contact with nature, the soul is spontaneously brought to contemplation, to conversation with God, to a study of the meaning of our earthly pilgrimage, to rising from the level of our daily concerns, in order to place ourselves closer to the reality of the values that never fade.

VENERATED
AS OUR LADY OF GRACE

3. The Virgin of Montenero is venerated as Our Lady of Grace, and the Gospel on her feast is the canticle of the Magnificat. "My soul magnifies the Lord, and my spirit rejoices in God my Savior, because he has regarded the humility of his handmaid.... The Almighty has done great things in me and holy is his name."

Dear priests, religious and sisters of the diocese of Livorno, in this meeting of ours, we too, like Mary, in giving thanks to the Almighty, whose name is holy, want to raise together the hymn of our exultation, because he has regarded the humility of his servants.

The holy Virgin intones the Magnificat, aware that in order to fulfill His plan of salvation for all men, the Lord wished to associate her, a humble girl of His people. Following Mary's example, we are here to intone our Magnificat, knowing that we are called by God to a service of redemption and salvation, notwithstanding our inadequacy.

The greater the work to be accomplished, the poorer are the instruments chosen to collaborate in the divine plan. As it is true that the power of God's arm is emphasized by the weakness of the means employed, so too, the smaller the human persons who are invited to serve, the greater the things that the Almighty, through us, is disposed to accomplish.

It is for this reason that the rich are sent away empty-handed, the proud are confounded in the thoughts of their heart, while on the other hand, the lowly are exalted and the hungry are filled with good things. To accomplish the mission and render our service, what is asked of us is not so much a patrimony of material or human gifts, such as money, intelligence, culture, the talent for organization or efficiency, but rather the sense of our own uselessness and generous commitment in confident and complete abandonment to the love of the Almighty. The salvation of mankind, in which even man is called to collaborate, is an eminently divine work, of such greatness that it surpasses the limits and possibilities of human powers. Therefore it can be achieved only if the human collaborators accept and develop the covenant with the omnipotence of God.

This is the meaning of the canticle and the Marian message that we want to accept and meditate on today. Our poverty is filled with the richness of God, our weakness with His strength, our "nothingness" by Him who is "everything."

"The Almighty has done great things in me," Mary states. She is fully aware of the greatness of her mission. But at the same time, seeing herself and remaining a "lowly hand-maid," she attributes all credit for it to God the Savior. The grandeur of the redemptive mission is achieved in Mary with the perfect accord between divine omnipotence and humble human docility.

NEED TO EVANGELIZE
AND REEVANGELIZE

4. Dear priests, religious and sisters, these considerations arising from meditation on the essential contents of the Magnificat take on a significance of urgent moment if we pause to establish a relationship between the spiritual needs of modern society, of the universal and local Church, and the availability of collab-orators' arms.

Certainly the work of salvation continues ceaselessly in the world, today as yesterday, and as it will tomorrow. And today too we must repeat with Jesus: "The harvest is great, but the laborers are few."

In our modern society there is so much to be done to evangelize or reevangelize, even within the confines of your ecclesial community. The task is difficult, complex, and not of short duration. And it cannot be the result of mere human efforts. It is the work of God, even if God asks men's cooperation.

But God wants to save modern society, whatever be the nature of the social or ideological difficulties. God can do all things. He is not forgetful of His mercy, and the power of His arm is not weakened. And when He calls human collaborators to comply with His plan of evangelization and salvation, He wants them in an attitude of humility and docility, like Mary.

Brothers and sisters, God has called you too, or rather He continually calls you. Since the time when the Lord's glance was cast with love on each one of you personally and you said "Yes," you became apostles of the Gospel in permanent service.

Associating you in the work of salvation, God intends to accomplish "great things" through you. Things that certainly are impossible to man, but not impossible to Almighty God. Entrusting to you a portion of His vineyard, the Lord intends, together with you, to evangelize the modern world, your cities, your countries, of sea or mountain, all buffeted by ideological atheism or by the practical materialism of well-being.

If the difficulties are many, have no fear. God is with you.

You will fulfill your mission worthily, you will carry out your service, if, like the holy Virgin, your dedication is total; if, placing yourselves in the attitude of humble and docile servants, you do not put your confidence in your own personal abilities, in the sciences or technologies of men, in the use of economic means, in the search for public acclaim, even if the wise use of human means can offer its contribution. May your human insufficiency not frighten you. Keep your glance constantly fixed on the mercy and the power of God, who can raise up His children even from hearts apparently as hard as stones. Seek the kingdom of God. The rest will be given besides.

LABORERS TOO FEW

5. The harvest is great, in the world, in Europe, in Italy, in Tuscany, in your diocese of Livorno. And the laborers are few. Looking at the group of diocesan priests, and from the statistical point of view, comparing it with the spiritual needs of the population and with the

percentages in other dioceses, the Gospel image of the small flock immediately comes to mind. But I know, dear priests of the diocese, that urged on by zeal for souls and pastoral concern for the faithful, you try to compensate for insufficiency of number with multiplication of yourselves, with intensification of activities. Yet, reminding you of the words of the Magnificat which we have just meditated on, I am sure of your personal conviction that external activity must not be detrimental to your interior life. The priest, if he does not want to become an empty, clanging cymbal, can find time for meditation and prayer. He also can find time for necessary updating, because the new problems, for which he must have clear ideas and correct lines of solution, are many; and if he does not take the step, he risks remaining behind, with danger of the same thing happening on the pastoral level.

I therefore recommend to you the interior life and updating. Then try to compensate for the scarcity of numbers also with the formation of nuclei of good catechists who will be in a position to alleviate your work, substituting for you in many activities.

You religious in particular, without losing the characteristics of the original charism of your foundation, are called to lend a strong hand to the diocesan clergy, to become involved in the local Church, to give your substantial contribution to the development of the one Church.

In a special way, you sisters, so numerous at this meeting and so solicitous and ready in so many areas of diocesan life, have before you irreplaceable and appointed tasks to be fulfilled. I congratulate you very much for the precious help you offer the overall apostolate.

Dear brothers and sisters, may the Lord shower upon all of you, each one of you, the abundance of His graces. May the Virgin Mother be an example and an incentive for you; and may my special blessing be a sign of divine favor.

Blessed Luigi Guanella's Vast Program of Charity

At the end of his visit to the Don Guanella Institution on Via Aurelia Antica on March 28, 1982, Pope John Paul met with the Servants of Charity and the Daughters of St. Mary of Providence, who staff the Don Guanella homes. Following is the prepared text of the address that the Holy Father decided to set aside in order to speak to the religious extemporaneously.

Dearest sons and daughters of Don Guanella,

1. Having completed the long tour of this city of love and pain, we are now gathered here for this brief but significant meeting reserved

especially for you who have most closely followed the footsteps and the ideals of him who dedicated his whole life to loving and helping the suffering.

You, religious "Servants of Charity," and you sisters, "Daughters of St. Mary of Providence," who this year are celebrating the first centenary of your founding, must rejoice to be able to imitate the example of your blessed founder, continuing to carry out the works of charity inspired and initiated by him.

Don Guanella, from his boyhood, strongly felt this call to love for the poor and abandoned. Ordained a priest in Como (May 26, 1866), he already had his very clear plan of work and apostolate. A man extremely sensitive to the condition of those who are set aside, of the handicapped, orphans, the elderly, invalids, of persons without home or affection, he wanted to be always and for everyone the Good Samaritan of the Gospel, and he dedicated his life completely to works of mercy. You well know how much he had to suffer to be able to realize this sublime torment of his. Intelligent, ingenious, industrious, rich in courage and generosity, with an intellectual training and a sure and solid asceticism, simple and of vast horizons, he was undoubtedly an extraordinary personality who, despite innumerable and continuous difficulties, oppositions, humiliations, persecutions, calumnies and suspicions, succeeded, with his tenacious and total confidence in God, in carrying out his vast and heroic program of charity.

2. In the address at his beatification, Paul VI stated that "the adventurous, complicated and feverish experiences of the prodigious life" of this man of God were always sustained by a "great piety, assiduous prayer, a striving for continuous communion with God" (*Insegnamenti di Paolo VI,* vol. II, 1964, pp. 611f.). He wanted to be only a faithful servant, a manifestation of divine goodness, a sign of divine Providence. From this arose his apostolic anxiety, first as a priest in the care of souls, then, from 1882 onward, as founder and builder of homes and centers for the care of the most marginal, beginning with Pianello Lario and then in Como, and subsequently in other areas of the diocese, in Italy, in Rome, in America. Consoler of the afflicted, he used to say to you, his spiritual sons and daughters, and he still says: "The whole world is your homeland.... You cannot stop as long as there are poor to be cared for and needy to be provided for." And he used to add: "It is not enough to relieve misery, you must go find it." But he also emphasized that "the soul and secret of the work is confidence in the Lord." Paul VI exclaimed with burning enthusiasm: "The work of Don Guanella is the work of God!

And if it is the work of God, it is marvelous, it is beneficial, it is holy!" *(Insegnamenti, ibid.)*

3. We must listen to and accept the message of the saints! They, especially enlightened by the Most High, with their life and their intuitions, are the answer to our questions and our problems. From the saints we can understand that the one thing that counts is the love of God for men and vice versa, and that in particular, they build up the history of the Church and live it day by day, embodying before the world the teaching of the Gospel. The specific message that Don Guanella left is that of God's "paternity," that is, His love, His providence, His affection and mercy present in the vicissitudes of men. "It is God who does it. Everything is of God," he used to state, "even if the Lord wants everything down here to follow common ways." "How can God not think of what He has willed?" And making use of all the devices and means of foresight and human providence, Don Guanella was convinced that to be authentic "Servants of Charity" means to be above all and always "Servants of Truth." For this reason we do not find empty rhetoric in him: he prayed and he acted; he caused to pray and he caused to act! Firm in the perennial doctrine of the Church, faithful to the solemn Magisterium of Pius IX, Leo XIII, and Pius X, his great friend, he passed unharmed through the

insidious storm of positivism, rationalism and modernism. He was a writer and a clear and persuasive apologete, and in that very era, buffeted by terrible pains and marked by so many tears, he wanted to be a concrete and living proof of God's love. Darkness exists only that light may shine; evil and pain remain in human history only that everyone may love, feeling nostalgia for God and a happy eternity! So he used to say, "They want us in everything as victims, they want us especially as victims conformed to the great Victim of Calvary, to raise up towers of salvation for souls." A servant of truth in order to be truly a servant of charity, Don Guanella understood that in order to love in a concrete and effective way, it was necessary to focus on the Eucharist and the anticipation of eternal life. So he exhorted his sisters, "You need not list the hardships of life, illness and death! Make yourselves victims for God and for the work of God...." "You must decay in prayer and concealment, like the grain that gives bread to everybody."

It is certainly an austere and sometimes heroic message, this message of Blessed Luigi Guanella; it is also as relevant as ever. Divine goodness wants to be present and visible today too, through our love: this is the charge that Don Guanella has left.

4. I entrust to the most holy Virgin, to the "Madonna of Work," as she was invoked by him, your intentions, your works, all your fellow brothers and sisters scattered throughout the world, and especially vocations to your two congregations. May they always be chosen and numerous in order to continue with courage and confidence the witness of God's love in the world. May the intercessory apostolic blessing accompany and comfort you.

Theological and Cultural Preparation

On April 18, 1982, in St. Peter's Cathedral in Bologna, the Pope met with the clergy, religious and sisters of the Archdiocese of Bologna and of all the dioceses of Emilia-Romagna. John Paul II addressed the gathering as follows.

Beloved brothers and sisters!

1. It is a great joy for me, which each time is freshly renewed, to be able during the course of my pastoral visits to meet with those who have given themselves to Christ in the fullness of their spiritual and physical energies, welcoming without reservation His call to a commitment to the coming of the kingdom of God.

Therefore, I express to you my affectionate greeting, priests, religious and members of the secular institutes in Emilia-Romagna, who have gathered together in this ancient Basilica of St. Peter to express your affection and your devotion to his humble Successor, called by Christ to the tremendous task of "feeding my sheep, and tending my lambs" (cf. Jn. 21:15-17). Borrowing the words of the Apostle Paul, I wish to repeat to you today with deep feeling: "My love is with all of you in Jesus Christ" (cf. 1 Cor. 16:23).

I know the noble traditions of active zeal which have always distinguished the clergy and religious of this land in which St. Apollinaris sowed the seed of the Word of God many centuries ago, beginning a spiritual breaking of ground which was to produce precious fruits of Christian life. Beside him and after him, a glorious array of evangelical workers bent over this fertile ground, bathing it with the sweat of inexhaustible apostolic dedication and at times watering it with the blood of supreme witness.

Even today, in times which from a certain point of view are no less difficult, other generous souls have taken out of the hands of those preceeding them the torch of the proclamation of the Gospel, assuming the task of carrying the light of Christ to the present generation, often attracted to and misled by the illusory flames of false ideologies. These generous souls are you, priests and religious, working in the noble Churches of Emilia-Romagna. They are you, members of the secular institutes who in new ways, dictated by the needs of the times, follow the same ideal, that of being the evangelical yeast, placed in the dough "till it was all leavened" (Lk. 13:21). They are you, the cloistered of the forty-six monasteries of the region, spiritually present here with your prayers and with the offering of your lives.

AN INVITATION TO FAITH

2. To each of you I wish above all to address an invitation to faith. Christ is risen! The glorious announcement, which the Easter liturgy has made echo once again during these days, is the confirmation of a reality on which the history of humanity lives. Christ kept the promise made to His disciples: on the third day after His death, He rose again and entered eternal life. He lives and will live forever!

More than that: He rose again not only for Himself, but also for us. Every man who believes in Him is introduced into the sphere of life hereafter which He—"first-born among many brethren" (Rom. 8:29)—opened for us. The Paschal Mystery not only concerns Him, Son of God and Son of Man; it also concerns us, sons of men, who in Him have become sons of God. The power of His resurrection already works in the world as a victorious force which urges those who accept it on faith towards the supreme goal of full life beyond death.

What a current of optimism flows out of such a message! Life, for whoever has faith, anticipates a radiant landing beyond the dark abyss of death at the end of human vicissitudes. Good bears in itself the assurance of the final victory over evil. Happiness is heralded as a realizable aspiration and in a measure surpassing what our hearts cannot even conceive (cf. 1 Cor. 2:9).

And what urging to generosity and commitment does not stem from such a pronouncement to those who wish to make their own contribution to the progress of humanity! They know they can depend on the Spirit, whom the risen Christ gave to the Church (cf. Jn. 20:22), in order to raise from the earthly and mortal city the heavenly and immortal one, encouraging and supporting the dedication of those who strive to direct the temporal order towards freedom and justice, towards unity and harmony, towards reciprocal love and active peace.

Let yourselves be permeated, my dear ones, by the joy which flows from the Easter message so that it may radiate from your every word and from your every attitude.

WITNESSING BY YOUR WORDS AND LIFE

3. This is precisely the second word I wish to entrust to you today: be witnesses. Witnesses to the hope that is rooted in faith. Witnesses to the invisible in a secularized society which too often excludes every transcendental dimension.

Yes, dear priests and religious, consecrated souls: in the midst of men of this generation, so immersed in the relative, you must be voices which speak of the absolute. Have you not perhaps thrown, so to speak, all of your resources on the scale of the world so that it may happily tip towards God and the blessings promised by Him? Yours has been a decisive choice in your life; you have opted for generosity and the gift in the face of greed and shrewdness; you have chosen to count on love and grace, challenging those who, because of this, regard you as being ingenuous and ineffective. You have placed your every hope in the kingdom of heaven when many around you make every effort to ensure themselves a comfortable place on earth.

It is up to you now to be consistent, in spite of every difficulty. The spiritual destiny of so many souls is bound to your faith and your consistency.

You must be the constant reminder of that destiny, which takes place in time but has eternity as its goal, witnessing by your words, but even more with your lives, the necessary direction towards Him who is the inevitable destination of our existential course. Your vocation places you as chosen forerunners of mankind on its journey. In your prayer and your work, in your joy and suffering, in your successes and in your trials, mankind must be able to find the model and anticipation of that which it is also called to be, in spite of its burdens and its compromises.

ESSENTIAL MISSION

4. In this context, I would like to say a particular word to those whose sacred ordination commissions them to a specific mission in the plan of salvation. There have been many discussions during recent years about the nature of the priesthood and the role which it fulfills in the Church. Not a few priests have consequently suffered an "identity crisis" which has restrained their commitment. It is now time to rediscover the grandeur of the gift which Christ made to the Church by instituting the ministerial priesthood. It is time above all to regain the generous enthusiasm in answering His call and welcoming

from His lips the charge: "Go into all the world and preach the Gospel to the whole creation" (Mk. 16:15).

This is indeed the essential mission of the priest. He is the proclaimer of the Word of God, which resounds ultimately and definitively in Jesus Christ. He is the Word of God's love for all men, called by Him to form a single family; a Word which asks to be translated into concrete action and also in new and better social institutions. Nevertheless, these innovative social consequences will not be up to the priest to deal with: in fact, this commitment is the specific mission of the laity (cf. LG 31; AA 7; AG 21).

And also, the Word of the Gospel message entrusted to the priest is the Word of pardon which frees from the alienation of sin and rekindles hope in the heart. There is no doubt that it has a healing influence on the wounds which guilt may have left on the psyche of whoever holds himself responsible. Nevertheless, it will not be the priest who must assume the burden of a specific psychological therapy which aims at resolving the traumas which are the result of mistaken past actions (cf. Admonition of the Holy Office of July 15, 1961, no. 3: *AAS* 1961, vol. 53, p. 571).

The Word that the priest proclaims reaches its highest point in the Eucharistic Sacrifice in which the bread, which is the body of Christ, is "broken" and "given" to men. Who does not see in that gesture a clear invitation to share all the other blessings that the Creator has placed on the "altar" of the earth for men, who are all equally His children? Nevertheless, the concrete commitment to a more equal distribution, among individuals as well as nations, of available resources is the task which directly involves not the priest, but those responsible for the economic and political lives of the city, of the nation and of the whole world (cf. LG 36; AA 14; GS 69).

Is this perhaps a timid and renunciatory speech? Must there be recognized in it a flight from concrete commitment? The only one who can think so has not measured in all its fullness the personal involvement which the mission entrusted to him to "proclaim the Word" demands of the priest. If he must renounce certain tasks, it is only in order to carry out to the fullest the task that is specifically his: that of being the bearer of a message which is not identified with any particular role, but which every role judges and recalls to the radical seriousness of the supreme norm: "Love one another as I have loved you" (Jn. 15:12).

In order to be able to proclaim the "message of salvation" (Acts 13:26) with the greater freedom which comes from not being "an interested party" in the tensions present in the community and in the world, the priest must exercise constant self-control and must also face the hardship of feeling misunderstood, or even contested and rejected. Generous dedication to his own task will not fail to obtain from God that "boldness" (cf. Acts 4:21, 29; 28:31) which allowed the first Apostles to face a still totally pagan world and transform it.

PROCLAIMING THE WORD

5. "Proclaim the Word": this is your specific mission, dear priests. Here is the root of your daily incentive, here is the inexhaustible source of your most authentic joy. As ministers of the Word, however—this is the last thought that I leave with you—you must know both the content of the message which is entrusted to us as well as the mentality of the persons to whom it is destined. This means that you must force yourselves to be men of culture and, in particular, true theologians.

It pleases me to recall this task here in a region which has as its center a city such as Bologna which, with regard to culture, has shone throughout the centuries as a beacon of brilliant light. Yours is the pride of being faithful to such a noble tradition, both looking after the constant updating of the central and peripheral educational structures, as well as personally committing yourselves to reflecting more deeply on the Word of God in the context of the questions arising from experience, which is the soul of every good theology.

It will be thanks to such an effort that you will avoid being either colorless reciters of formulas that are right in themselves, but not applied to today's problems, or heedless innovators who, yes, are able to sense the mood of the moment, but do not know how to evaluate it with mature "discernment" (the *diakrisis* Saint Paul spoke of: cf. 1 Cor. 12:10) in the light of the supreme criterion which is, and will always remain, the Word of God. The risk of being childishly "tossed to and fro and carried about with every wind of doctrine" (Eph. 4:14) is not only a thing of the past, but strikes every period in history, not excluding ours.

Consequently, it is necessary to "dedicate oneself to reading" (1 Tm. 4:13), deepening one's knowledge of the Scriptures which are able to "instruct you for salvation through faith in Jesus Christ" (2 Tm. 3:15), and then to proclaim with fidelity what is proposed in it, not limiting the proclamation to what is pleasing to one's own heart, perhaps still too "hardened," or limiting it to what one thinks may meet the approval or at least the benevolent welcome of the surroundings. Today, too, in fact, just as yesterday and always, it remains true that the Gospel of the cross is "a stumbling block to Jews and folly to Gentiles, but to those who are called...the power of God and the wisdom of God" (1 Cor. 1:23, 24).

6. Beloved, in taking leave of you I wish to renew the call to confidence and optimism with which I began. Wasn't it repeated in the liturgy just today that in our faith lies "the victory which overcomes the world" (1 Jn. 5:4)? Have faith, therefore, even though you "have not seen" (Jn. 20:29), and every problem will be resolved and overcome in the end.

May the holy Virgin, who is the insuperable model of such courageous faith, be with you with her constant help and may she accompany you along the road of your ecclesial service, that you may, from full hands, sow in the souls of so many brothers and sisters the seed of the hope which "does not disappoint" (Rom. 5:5). In her name, I impart to all of you with all my heart my apostolic blessing.

Our Era Demands
the Courage of Faith

On May 8, 1982, in the Throne Room of the apostolic palace, the Holy Father received in audience more than a thousand of the religious of the Congregation of the Sons and Daughters of Charity (Canossians) coming from every part of Italy to celebrate the 150th anniversary of the foundation of the male branch of the religious family. The group was led by the Superior General, Father Modesto Giacon and by the Mother General, Sister Filomena Annoni.

The Holy Father gave the following address.

Beloved brothers and sisters in the Lord!

1. You have been waiting for this meeting with the Pope for some time, and today your wish, which is also mine, can finally be satisfied!

Indeed, you are an active part of the Church, and I willingly open my heart to you and, in memory of your foundress, Blessed Maddalena di Canossa, I extend my respectful and affectionate greeting to the Superior of the Sons of Charity, to the Mother General of the Religious of Canossa, and to all of you present, collaborators and those in positions of responsibility, to the priests, to the brothers, to the clerics, to the sisters, to students and friends, and to the benefactors of your various works. I wish to extend my cordial greeting to all the members of the two congregations, expressing at the same time my gratitude for this act of fidelity, of homage, of love for the Vicar of Christ and his mission as universal Pastor.

ROOTED ON CALVARY

2. You have wished to underscore in a solemn and fervent way the 150th anniversary of the founding of your institute and the consignment to the religious of the new constitutions, approved by the Sacred Congregation last December 23. Therefore, this is a moment of particular reflection upon your spirituality and upon your ideals, which will permit you to take up again with increased ardor your journey in the spirit and along the path of your foundress.

Meditating on the happenings of the past and considering the many tribulations and obstacles which had to be encountered and overcome, first by Blessed Maddalena of Canossa for the foundation of the two religious branches, and then by her successors for their realization and growth, we must first of all thank the Lord for His constant help and His favor. The desire expressed by the foundress came to pass: "I wish that the Institute be rooted on Calvary, between the cross and Our Lady of Sorrows and be aflame with charity, even while remaining in the humility and obscurity of the cross." The spirituality and works of Maddalena of Canossa have now passed the century mark, and today we too can repeat what God's servant, Fr. Giovanni Calabria, said to Cardinal La Fontaine, Patriarch of Venice, in 1923, at a crucial moment for the male institute: "The work of the Canossians must remain, because *digitus Dei est hic!*" (The finger of God is here!) The two congregations also spread abroad in witness to Christ and in the exercise of charity: "servants of the poor," as the fearless marchioness wished, placing herself at the service of the most humble and underprivileged. The city of Rome must also be grateful to the Canossian Religious for the two parishes which they look after.

3. In the homily given on the occasion of the beatification of your foundress, December 7, 1941, Pius XII stated, "The events in the lives of the saints, if they are the training ground of their virtues, become for us a lesson and warning: God raises up saints so that their example may shine as a light and incentive to our steps" (*Discorsi e Radiomessaggi di Sua Santità Pio XII*, III, pp. 291-292). I would like to draw a directive and a resolution from the life of Blessed Maddalena of Canossa to propose to all of you as a remembrance and as a particular consignment of this important meeting, that they may help you to continue your journey with perseverance and fervor.

She was truly a strong and courageous woman.

She was a mystic in action who, from the strength of a faith contemplated and lived with inner joy, found the courage of her charitable action. Today is precisely the period in which the courage of Christian faith is demanded! This is the directive which I suggest to you in her name: be courageous and fearless, firm in the certainty that only Christ is salvation, only He is the truth, the light, the cornerstone: "Who shall separate us from the love of Christ? Shall tribulation, or distress, or persecution, or famine, or nakedness, or peril, or sword?... For I am sure that...not anything else in all creation will be able to separate us from the love of God in Jesus Christ our Lord" (Rom. 8:35, 38, 39).

Putting into perspective the historical events of the period, Pius XII said this in the same talk: "Dauntless and generous, Blessed Maddalena knew all the political and social crises which, from the beginning of the French Revolution in 1789 up to the final fall of Napoleon in 1815, overwhelmed Europe with twenty-five years of popular upheavals and continual wars." We must not fear the historical crises which continuously follow each other; only Christian faith gives meaning to life and offers true salvation. A biographer could well write, when speaking of the meeting which took place between the marchioness and Napoleon Bonaparte in Verona, "Those two personalities facing one another...

represented two greatnesses. Without diminishing the political and administrative merits of the man, it is certain that they were accompanied by appalling wars which bled Europe, while that frail creature waited to rebuild where illness and wickedness had destroyed. Quick judgment places great conquerors on a pedestal, but a more profound judgment cannot but place the great benefactors there" (Igino Giordani, *Maddalena di Canossa,* Brescia, 1947).

CHARITY TO THE POOR

4. Closely related to this apostolic courage is a characteristic that is typical of Blessed Maddalena of Canossa: her assiduous commitment to religious instruction. Her ideal and principal activity were surely charity towards the poor, orphans, and the sick, but she wanted it to be always accompanied by doctrine, to the point of composing a catechism, writing a commentary on the Sunday Gospels, and dictating pedagogical rules. Indeed, she stated that "God was not loved because He was not known." A truly intelligent and farsighted woman, in this she also showed herself to be modern and up-to-date. Therefore, following in the footsteps of your foundress, dedicate yourselves with love and conscientiousness to the teaching of Christian doctrine through constant and up-to-date preparation, always safeguarding the purity

of the Faith, obedient and respectful to the Church's Magisterium, as was Blessed Maddalena. This is the resolution that I heartily suggest, for the good of the Church, for your sanctification, for an increase in vocations in your well-deserving congregations.

IMPORTANT LETTER

5. On December 10, 1825, the young priest Antonio Rosmini wrote from Rovereto a very important letter to the Marchioness Maddalena of Canossa in which he sketched the first outline of the institution which in his heart he hoped to found. In the letter he expressed himself as follows: "How much I like the concept that I have often heard from your lips, that it is necessary to have a great heart, that our Lord is great, and that the Christian wrongs his Lord by making Him look smaller!"

Beloved! You also must have "a great heart" which knows how to understand, love, give of itself; which is not frightened by evil or error; which courageously embraces brethren and is totally dedicated to charity in the name and with the power of Christ! May you be granted it by Mary most holy, Mother of the crucified and risen Christ, to whom I entrust you while I willingly impart to you and to all the members of the congregations my intercessory apostolic blessing.

St. Augustine and the Church, Exemplary Communion of Life

After his meeting at the Augustinianum on May 8, 1982, the Holy Father went to the Generalate of the Augustinian Fathers where, in their chapel, he addressed them as follows:

Reverend Prior General and dear confreres of the Augustinian Order!

1. *"Ecce quam bonum et quam iucundum habitare fratres in unum!"* ("Behold, how good and how pleasant it is when brothers dwell in unity!") (Ps. 133[132]:1)

After the meeting a short while ago in the beautiful seat of the Patristic Institute, I am truly happy to be now among you who, as members of the General Curia, visibly represent the entire spiritual family of St. Augustine. And I am also happy for the fact that this second meeting is taking place inside the chapel, almost to signify—I would say in the same style of the saint—a symbolic route from the external to the internal, from the didactic-formative activity to its central inspiration, which is prayer; from the origin of such an important ecclesial work to its source of nourishment, which is contact with God.

The greeting, therefore, which I now address to each of you here present, and which through you I wish to extend to all the religious of the order spread out in more than forty countries, is according to this list of priorities in the name of God the Father and His Son Jesus Christ. *"Gratia vobis et pax"*—I repeat to you along with St. Paul—*"a Deo Patre nostro et Domino Iesu Christo"* ("May the grace and peace of God our Father and the Lord Jesus Christ be with you") (1 Cor. 1:3).

I wish the Lord, who finds us united here, to confirm our spirit in peace and grace, letting us taste the joy of that living together in the bond of brotherly communion whose spiritual and strengthening fruitfulness your Master and at the same time the great Doctor of all the Church, Augustine, celebrated in so many pages of his prestigious works. Guided by his example and his teaching, all of us here wish to experience the indescribable joy of this communion: *"Ecce quam bonum et quam iucundum habitare fratres in unum."*

UNIQUE ORIGIN OF YOUR ORDER

2. But I also have a debt of gratitude to fulfill: gratitude for the not only hospitable and courteous, but also so warm and intimately familiar, way with which I have been welcomed today during my visit to the three institutions which make up this unified complex; gratitude for the loving and respectful words which the Superior General just now directed to me in

his welcoming address; gratitude, above all, for the multiple services which your order gives to the Church and to the Holy See, beginning with the hard work which is done and encouraged in this Curia, and with the ministry of the Augustinian religious at the General Vicariate of Vatican City and at the Pontifical Parish of Santa Anna.

Called to rule the Church during this historical period, I cannot forget the unique origin of your order, which was born in the very heart of the Middle Ages through the initiative of my Predecessors Innocent IV and Alexander IV. For that reason it differs from other religious institutes, taking shape as the type of the vast range of the diverse forms and canonical structures for the profession of the evangelical counsels. In reference to the letter and to the spirit of the Augustinian *Regula*—in the very high title of nobility the very name of the saint gives it—through its juridical institution your order has holy Mother Church as its Foundress.

3. Augustine and the Church, therefore: two great names serve to define, beloved brothers, your particular features as religious. The heredity of the one and the very reality of the other (and Augustine—it is superfluous to recall here—remains an unsurpassed master of that reality through the depth of his ecclesiological intuitions) urge you to live in an intimate and

exemplary communion of life, to put it into practice and express it in ever more authentic ways, never to belie that which is rightly called the "Augustinian charism" of a community life made one by charity.

Act in such a way that what on a general level is the Church (as your father Augustine reminds and teaches you) will be verified through each of your communities. Know how to encourage in them such a togetherness of life so that the many who find themselves together there may become fused through charity and have "unity of mind and heart extended towards God" *(Regula* 1, 3). Then you will be able to fully understand the truth of the words quoted from the Psalm: *"Ecce quam bonum et quam iucundum habitare fratres in unum."* In fact, "so sweet is the sound of these words. It is as sweet as the charity which makes it possible for the brothers to live together.... Yes, these words of the Psalter, this sweet sound, this pleasant melody...also generated monasteries. The brothers who wished to live together paid attention to this sound; this verse was like a trumpet call for them" *(Ennarat. in Ps. CXXXII,* 1-2; PL 37, 1729).

Echoing such charming as well as authoritative calls, I invite you fraternally to always remain faithful—making the necessary sacrifices, respecting their intrinsic demands—to community life, generated and rooted in charity.

APOSTOLIC COMMUNITY

4. Know well that this life in no way means closing in on oneself and excluding others. So much less, I should say, could it mean this for you, sons of St. Augustine. Yours is and must be an apostolic community, that is to say, open and dynamic, extended—as I have already recalled —towards God, but precisely because of this, also extended towards your brothers. According to that approach, I refer to what the Prior General touched upon. And I approve the new initiatives which, in consistent continuity with all that has been done in the past by the Augustinian Order and has been written with singular honor in the golden list of ministerial and missionary activities of the Church, are begun and encouraged in the present "so that the Word of God may be spread and glorified" (2 Thes. 3:1). For this very timely and so promising work, with great confidence I offer my warmest encouragement, and implore for it the abundance of heavenly favors.

You who profess—and it is another title of honor for the order—a special devotion to the Mother of God and so often invoke her by the beautiful title of *Mater Boni Consilii* (Mother of Good Counsel), may you obtain from her help and comfort in the renewed resolution to strengthen the bonds of community life and project it, precisely because of this inner rooting, into the entire ecclesial community and even beyond. Above all, we can obtain from her that superior "counsel" which is discernment and wisdom in making decisions, but even more, the recognition of the increased spiritual needs of our age, vision of the human and social reality in the light of the Gospel and, as a result, also the courage to respond adequately to those needs and that vision.

Continue the Work of St. Anthony, Witness and Proclaim the Gospel

On May 12, 1982, the Pope met with a large number of representatives of the Franciscan family in Portugal and with the civil authorities of the city of Lisbon. Meeting in the Church of St. Anthony, situated next to the cathedral, the Pope addressed the group as follows.

Your Excellencies, Mr. President and Councilmen of the Municipal Council of Lisbon, Beloved children of St. Francis, my brothers and sisters,

1. Grateful for the distinguished presence of the Municipal Council and for yours, I greet everyone with Franciscan joy. And borrowing the words of the Apostle, I begin by saying to the beloved Franciscans: "First, I thank my God through Jesus Christ for all of you, because your

faith is proclaimed in all the world" (Rom. 1:8). And St. Anthony, whom we are honoring at this moment and in this place, has greatly contributed to this.

At the end of the twelfth century, here, in this house—transformed at the right moment into an oratorium by the municipal authorities of Lisbon—was born St. Anthony of Lisbon, also known as St. Anthony of Padua. According to the apt expression of my Predecessor Leo XIII, he is the "saint of the whole world." In this month of May, precisely the 30th, we shall commemorate the 750th year of his canonization, linked to which are well-known popular traditions.[1]

Also celebrated this year throughout the world is the eighth centenary of the birth of St. Francis of Assisi. Therefore, we have a double reason for rejoicing. And at this time I would like to borrow the words of Pope Pius XII, exclaiming: *"Exulta, Lusitania felix!"* (Rejoice, O happy Portugal!) In particular, rejoice, you Franciscans of Portugal! Rejoice, authorities and people of Lisbon! Be joyful, all you Portuguese spread throughout the world!

PORTUGUESE FRANCISCANS

2. The Franciscan movement—and it is cause for satisfaction to me to recall it on this occasion—has carved itself deeply into the souls

of Portugal's population, and not only the souls of the most humble and illiterate. As is well known, the Holy See often turned to the children of St. Francis to make them its intermediaries and spokesmen to monarchs and noblemen, to settle disputes and remind them, with humility but also with firmness, of their duties and obligations.

The missionary vocation of the Portuguese Franciscans, right after St. Anthony, is witnessed by Pope Innocent IV's sending to the Far East in the thirteenth century Fra Lorenzo of Portugal.[2] And it is known that the Rule of the Friars Minor includes an entire chapter on the missions.[3] It was this spirit which led them to Africa, India, Brazil, Ceylon and the Far East. So, the presence of the sons and daughters of St. Francis in Portugal, and in the Portuguese-speaking countries on the various continents, is rich in works of evangelization, aid, teaching and parish service.

I should like to emphasize here the importance of the small and humble cloistered convents in which the spirit of the founder and of St. Clare continues to live, rising from here in continuous prayer so that the multiple and active work of the other brothers and sisters "does not extinguish the spirit of prayer and devotion to which all other things are subordinate,"[4] as the Rule states. How I should like to have some time at my disposal to reflect with you upon this point! Prayer is always the soul of evangelization, the soul of the entire apostolate, our great spiritual strength.

BELOVED MIRACLE WORKER

3. Inspired by the glowing kindness of St. Anthony, praiseworthy initiatives in favor of youth began in Portugal, also among young people, especially during the last century, and they then spread to other parts of the world. May these Antonian commemorations serve as a stimulus to deepen Franciscan interest in youth, in accord with the directives of the universal Church and in the spirit of cooperation with the local churches, according to the directives of St. Francis and St. Anthony.

I should not like to leave the Third Order without a word of benevolence. I know it is active and renewed among you. It is the hope of the Church and the faith of the Pope that it be rejuvenated, well in harmony with the Second Vatican Council, with new strength and with the enthusiasm of those who feel they are "yeast in the dough" and sharers in Christ's mission.

4. The biographical profile of the universally revered Portuguese miracle worker, beloved sons and daughters of St. Francis, is well known to all of you. From the school of the cathedral next to us, to St. Vincent in Fuori, up

to Holy Cross in Coimbra, he was a traveler evangelically in love with God, in search of a greater internalizing and more intense way of living the religious ideal embraced in his youth among the cloistered monks of St. Augustine. After being ordained a priest in Coimbra, his anxiety for a more radical response to the divine call led him to develop the resolution of greater dedication to and love for God in his ardent desire to become a missionary and martyr in Africa. With this intention he became a Franciscan.

Nevertheless, Providence caused Friar Anthony to set off through the lands of Italy and France. During his first experiences as a Franciscan, he accepted the difficulties, faithful to the ideal, and joyfully responded to the divine plan in a total commitment to generous service, praying and teaching theology to the friars with a patient attitude, as the worker who waits for the early and the late rain to come, until the Lord in some way would make Himself known (cf. Jas. 5:7). What a wonderful lesson in living, brothers and sisters! His brief existence continued, leading him to serve, always with humility, as minister or superior general of the order. At his death at about age forty, the words from Wisdom could have been applied to him: "Being perfected in a short time, he fulfilled long years" (Wis. 4:13).

His teaching and ministry of the Word, just as his life as friar and priest, are distinguished by his love for the Church, instilled by the Rule.[5]

"Expert exegete in the interpretation of Sacred Scriptures; eminent theologian in understanding dogmas; distinguished doctor and master in treating the subjects of ascetical and mystical theology," as Pope Pius XII was to say,[6] he persistently proclaimed the Word (cf. 2 Tm. 4:2), moved by the evangelizing desire to "lead wrongdoers back to the paths of righteousness." He did so, however, with the freedom of the heart of a poor man, faithful to God, faithful to his response to God, in union with Christ and in conformity with the directives of the Church. True communion with Christ demands that a true harmony with the ecclesial community, guided by its legitimate pastors, be cultivated and put into practice.

HE STILL SPEAKS TO US

5. The Evangelical Doctor still speaks to men of our era, above all pointing out to them the Church—Christ's means of salvation. The uncorrupted tongue of the saint and his vocal organs, found marvelously intact, seem to attest to the perpetuity of his message. The voice of Friar Anthony, through his sermons, is still alive and strong: in particular, his guidelines contain a vivid appeal to the religious of our day, called by

the Second Vatican Council to bear witness to the sanctity of the Church, in fidelity to Christ, as collaborators of the bishops and priests.[7]

The letter of greeting from St. Francis to Friar Anthony is well known. He wrote: "I am happy that you read theology to the friars, trusting that, by such study, the spirit of prayer and devotion, as they are contained in the Rule, are not lost."[8] And a recognized theologian attests that the Evangelical Doctor knew how to remain faithful to this principle: "...Following the example of John the Baptist, he burned in the same way; and from so much ardor came light: he was a light which burned and shone."[9] For this, St. Anthony has remained in history as the precursor of the Franciscan School, permeated with a wise objective and the exercise of wisdom.

A FUTURE CATHEDRAL

6. Beloved brothers and sisters:

I know that the Cardinal Patriarch, the Municipal Council of Lisbon and the Franciscan Family are making every effort that a great temple be erected in this city, a future cathedral, dedicated to St. Anthony, and to perpetuate the devotion of the Portuguese communities spread throughout the world. A fine and praiseworthy initiative! If only it could gather all Portuguese around the great St. Anthony of Lisbon, in the unity of faith and harmony of hearts, for the glory of God.

But this material temple must be above all an expression of the fact that "you also are living stones built into a spiritual house" (cf. 1 Pt. 2:5) with the life, ministry and apostolic service which must always be bearers of evangelical values. May the example of St. Anthony penetrate deeply into your souls, so that you may continue his work as dispensers of Christ's salvation and goodness and as servants of His Church, by witnessing and proclaiming the Good News.

Your consecrated lives and your collaboration in spreading the Gospel are for me reasons for courage and joy in my mission as Pastor of the universal Church. May God help you and call many others to follow Christ in religious life, according to the spirit of the "Poverello of Assisi," as St. Anthony knew how to conform to it. Through his intercession, I implore "peace and good" for everyone with my apostolic blessing.

FOOTNOTES

1. Cf. Léon de Kerval, *Sancti Antonii de Padua Vitae duae* (Paris 1904) 116-117.

2. Cf. Antonino Franchi, *La svolta politico-ecclesiastica tra Roma e Bisanzio 1249-1254* (Roma 1981) 15, 16, 37, 74, 123, 127, 128, 161, 214.

3. *Regula Bullata*, cap. 12, *Regula non Bullata*, cap. 16, ed. Caietanus Esser, O.F.M., *Opuscula Sancti Patris Francisci Assisiensis* (Grottaferrata 1978) 237-238, 268-271.

4. *Regula Bullata*, cap. 5, ed. Esser. *Opuscula*, 231.

5. *Regula non Bullata*, cap. 17, ed. Esser. *Opuscula*, 271.

6. Pope Pius XII, Litterae Apost. *Exulta, Lusitania Felix, AAS* 38 (1964) 201, Lopes, S. Antonio de Lisboa, 296-297.

7. S. Antonii Patavini, O. Min. Doctoris Evangelici *Sermones Dominicales et Festivi*, Dominica II de Adventu (II, Patavi 1979) 478-491. Trad. Henrique Pinto Rema, O.F.M., *Santo Antonio de Lisboa. Obras Completas*, III (Lisboa 1970) 39-43.

8. *Epist. ad Sanctum Antonium*, ed. critica Esser. *Opuscula*, cap. IV, 95. Henrique Pinto Rema, O.F.M., *Santo Antonio de Lisboa. Obras Completas*, I (Lisboa 1970), XVII.

9. Cf. Francisco da Gama Caeiro, *Santo Antonio de Lisboa*, I (Lisboa 1967) 147-148.

Personal Witness: Best Form of Evangelization

The Holy Father's visit to Fatima on May 13, 1982, ended with the inauguration of the Paul VI Pastoral Center. In the amphitheater of the complex, the Pope met with priests, brothers, sisters, members of secular institutes, and seminarians, to whom he delivered the following address.

Dear fathers, brothers and sisters,

1. To you who are in God the Father and the Lord Jesus Christ, grace, mercy and peace, in the truth and love of the Holy Spirit who has been given to us! (cf. 1 Thes. 1:1; Rom. 5:4)

These words of the Apostle St. Paul express my sentiments and anticipate my wishes this afternoon at this meeting, which has a particular importance for me and, I think I can say, also for you. It is a great joy and it is beautiful to be together with you—priests, men and women religious of Portugal—and to be able to greet you and speak with you personally.

I feel full of joy, gratitude and hope when I can meet religious or those who are preparing for the religious life. It is for me a state of soul that has the intensity and vibration of a rare meeting—as though it could not be repeated again—with people very dear to me. I, too, by divine grace, am a priest of Jesus Christ; and every day my respect for the priesthood and for the religious life grows, because they represent and contribute to the mission, life and treasury of the Church, the Mystical Body of Christ. The Pope loves you in the Lord.

The communion of feelings that links me to you in brotherhood for life, at this moment makes me feel in a certain way the mysterious reality of the "Body" of our holy Church illuminated by the maternally affectionate gaze of our Lady. And here in Fatima, where she is so much loved and venerated, in greeting her with affection, I invite you to look to her stimulating example and, as your "older brother," in the name of all, I ask her maternal blessing, while praying: "Mother of mercy, show us Jesus, the blessed fruit of your womb!"

With her blessing and patronage, we confidently raise our hearts to God our Father in thanksgiving: for He loves us "and it was he who first loved us" (1 Jn. 4:10). It was neither we nor our parents who took the initiative, who chose to be created, baptized and made members of His Church. The initiative came from the "original love," the first principle, from whom proceeds the Holy Spirit through the Son. Yes, it was by the most liberal initiative of the love of God the Father, who wanted to give of His goodness, that we were created through His extraordinary and merciful kindness and then gratuitously called to share in His life and glory (cf. AG 2) in this ecclesial condition that is ours. Blessed be God.

RESPONSIBLE BEFORE CHRIST AND YOU

2. With our hearts in God, let us turn our attention anew to our Mother and let us imagine the tender blessing of her reply, when she says to us: "Jesus Christ? Look, and you can discover Him in His signs. And there are so many of these signs!" And at this moment perhaps she might add—to my confusion—"The sign is the Pope. He goes beyond his own person because he only lends his image to Him, to Jesus Christ." With this image, I want to say in all sincerity how limited I feel and at the same time how responsible before Christ and before you.

I see in my mind those moments of the Lord with "His own," with those whom from that moment He no longer called servants but friends (cf. Jn. 15:14), with whom He spoke in confidence heart to heart: of His sorrow for the multitudes, "like sheep without a shepherd," like "fields ready for the harvest," without arms to do the work *(ibid.,* v. 37); of the meaning of saying "yes" to this work—without material security (Mt. 10:9), personal capacities *(ibid.,* v. 20) or simple good will (Jn. 15:14)—with readiness, born of a simple heart, full of confidence in the power of God (Mt. 10:16), full of fear and courage *(ibid.,* v. 27). Finally He spoke to "His friends" frankly of the things closest to their hearts.

And today the Pope wishes to do the same, without overlooking the "sign" of the great "friend" of all of us.

CHOSEN BY GOD

3. You priests and religious consecrated your life to the service of the Gospel in a moment of generosity! You were "chosen" (Jn. 15:16); and today you are those "called" by God to whom He entrusted the marvelous gift of this special vocation, on behalf of the whole Church, "to go forth and bear fruit," a fruit that will last (cf. *ibid.*). You are God's gift to the Church in Portugal. I congratulate you and thank the Lord for your generous presence in

this always luxuriant "pasture" and for your
collaboration in serving and proclaiming the
Good News of salvation.

Look, God well knows the difficulties, the
"weariness of the day and of its heat"
(Mt. 20:12); and He, on His part, is faithful; the
graces necessary for perseverance and a happy
response to your vocation will never be lacking. On your part I am sure that docility and
generosity will never be lacking. And, it could
not be otherwise, after so many blessings received and so many others that we still await
from God, would we not be ashamed—a holy
bishop once asked—to deny the only thing
which He asks in return: love for Him and for
our neighbor? Could we dare to close our
hearts...to the Father and refuse to be truly
His sons and to serve others, our brothers?
(cf. St. Gregory of Nazianzus, *Sermones, De
Pauperum Amore*, 23: PG 35, 887).

CHRIST, THE ONLY WAY

4. I would like to linger with each one of
you and speak about your loving dialogue with
God; about that personal history, without doubt
a beautiful history, which began with Baptism,
up to the day when you "left all things" to follow
Christ, and then continuing along your road with
Him, as ones chosen by God. But since that is
not possible, I want to say to all of you, as if I

were speaking to each of you individually, Christ is the only way, the measure and scope of your life; He is the Christ of the good news and of the completeness of the gift of oneself "for the sake of the kingdom of heaven."

We could run through different adventures without being able to choose, but let us bring forward as an example the spirit of poverty. "Blessed are the poor in spirit for the kingdom of heaven will be theirs" (Mt. 5:3).

In a society which gives value only to having, in which a constant desire for personal well-being and comfort seems to rule, and which is so often fascinated with luxury—in direct contrast with evident misery; in this society, poverty—and especially the spirit of poverty—is a challenge. A challenge for all, for the rich and the poor in material goods, and a challenge especially for those who have made a "profession" of evangelical poverty.

Evangelical poverty is something more than the simple renunciation of material possessions; it is to abandon oneself, to "lose oneself" in God. Christ spoke one day about a merchant who chose a precious pearl and exchanged all that he had to buy it (cf. Mt. 13:46). He valued the choice of the higher goods, goods "of great value" given to those who can proceed with wisdom. Peter, after making this choice, dared to ask Christ about these "higher values," for which he had left everything to follow his Master; and he received the famous reply: a hundredfold in this life and life everlasting (cf. Mt. 19:27-29).

Thinking back to this exchange which we also make, in the light of the explanation obtained by St. Peter, could we or others hesitate to verify the fulfillment of the Lord's promise? Our internal attitude and external behavior which others see should always be that of serene possession of this "hundredfold" and of the hope of eternal life. Or will it more easily appear that we do not abandon everything—questions, "assumptions" without testing, human "security," "ties" which do not allow us to throw aside all risks, etc.—and receive nothing more than any other "non-chosen" who totally commits himself to living this present life?

WORTHY TO SUFFER

5. As you know, brothers and sisters, it is certainly not sufficient to abandon everything: it is necessary to follow Christ, with a continuous effort to identify oneself with Him and with His cause. We are in the world without being of the world, representing among men the signs of the truth and of the presence of Christ in the world. We give Him our whole being with its external features, that He may continue to exist, doing good (cf. Acts 10:38).

This offering of ours, this "giving up possessions," has marked us with a particular sign,
which has become our identity; with all our
dignity as persons "we are Christ's." All those
who see us must be able to recognize without
any difficulty this unique identity of ours. To
facilitate mutual welcome at gatherings and
meetings, it is current practice to display quite
visibly one's photograph and personal data; and
so without any embarrassment everyone is easily identified and called by name. It should
always be the same for us also; our attitudes and
external behavior should allow others to begin a
dialogue, private or open, with a priest, a male
or female religious, or with a seminarian, who
are all identified and called by name, as the
"chosen of God."

Just as it is difficult to live and to give
witness of evangelical poverty in a society of
consumerism and affluence, it is also difficult to
be recognized as religious, in the Absolute of
God, in an age of secularization. The tendency
toward leveling out, when it does not invert
values, seems to favor anonymity of people: to
be as most are, to go unnoticed. It is rather the
characteristic of being "salt" and "light" (cf. Mt.
5:13ff.) in the world that carries on Christ's call,
especially for those who are consecrated to Him.
Likewise there remains in force the promise:
"Whoever then will acknowledge me before

men, I will acknowledge him before my Father in heaven" (Mt. 10:32).

Beloved brothers and sisters: the "peculiarity" of the Master led Him to be called things that were hardly flattering (Mt. 10:24). And the disciples no less than the Master. The first disciples left us this testimony, showing themselves "full of joy that they had been found worthy of suffering dishonor for the sake of the Name" (Acts 5:42); and the present generation of the Church must be the bearer of this testimony.

INTERIOR AND SPIRITUAL FREEDOM

6. Fidelity to God and to men requires interior and spiritual freedom so that anyone can effectively share in the mission of Christ. Your vocation is a gift with regard to this mission. You are called to work for the kingdom of God. And now I would like to speak with you on this reflection: the apostolic and pastoral commitment.

The tasks of the Church and in the Church are various: from the ministry to the simple and hidden services and to works that require culture, together with people of different conditions; but they are always close to man. For this reason many initiatives have come forth, inspired by the Holy Spirit, to respond to the various calls and needs of times and places. A simple glance at this assembly already shows what a variety of forms there are to this service of the kingdom, while it shows the perennial vitality of the Church, with its constant solicitude, embodied in the founders of the religious families and by apostolic movements, each with its own role and merits.

But the common denominator, the first means and the most effective way to evangelization by participating within the Church in the mission of Christ, remains the individual with the witness of his life. The other means and ways are carried out in works and initiatives, of greater or lesser favor among those being evangelized. But what you are, priests and religious, must never go unnoticed, much less forgotten. Even when for good reasons you might have to perform secular tasks, let this remain auxiliary and subordinate to your primary condition and function.

Never diminish this identity and do not forget the precise goal of the ministry and apostolic service to which you have been called: to lead your fellowman in our day to communion with the most Holy Trinity. In these days there is a growing temptation to seek security in property, knowledge, prestige and power. With your fidelity to all the obligations assumed with Holy Orders and with your consecration to

Christ, generously alive in poverty, chastity and obedience, warn men against this false security; remember their eschatological dimension and point out the "kingdom of heaven" to which you consecrated your capacity to love.

7. The level of your pastoral and apostolic success will always be in proportion to the extent of your fidelity to Christ and your equal gift of love. It is this fidelity that frees the heart and inflames the spirit with total love for Christ and for His brothers and sisters in the world (cf. PC 1-12). And remember well that fidelity is achieved and maintained through union with the Lord, with the constant and profound renewal of prayer and the sacraments, so as to maintain the splendor of life in grace: "because without me you can do nothing" the same Lord says to us (Jn. 15:5).

Here, brothers and sisters, I would like to draw your attention to what is the fulcrum of my message to you today. If there is not a perfect balance between our life with God and our activity directed towards the service of men, we will compromise not only the work of evangelization to which we are committed, but also our personal condition as people who have been evangelized. Prayer is the very soul of your work for the kingdom: liturgical prayer centered in the Eucharist, received and lived with that purity of conscience that requires recourse to the Sacrament of Reconciliation, celebrated devoutly, for which there is no substitute; the Liturgy of the Hours, which signals the rhythm of continual adoration, in spirit and in truth, with the "beloved" presence of the Virgin in your prayers, the Handmaid of God and model of whoever wishes to serve the Lord.

UNITY IS BUILT IN TRUTH

8. With the need for the witness of one's life, likewise the duty to proclaim salvation through Christ must be included, as St. Peter said: "We cannot but speak of it" (Acts 4:20). There will always be the chance to sow; but the seed can be only true and good—just as it will prove fruitful—only if you have prayed and meditated on and studied the Word of God, according to the teaching of the authentic Magisterium.

Today wonderful means of communication inform us of everything, but not always freely and objectively; so there are many things that we must clarify, direct and help people in choosing. The heart is always inclined to share knowledge and adhere to the truth, which you have already identified in Christ (cf. Jn. 14:6); and with love, faithful to the truth, you adopted the rule of St. Francis of Assisi: to bring faith where there is doubt.

It is above all in truth that unity is built: the communion of minds is easily transformed into the union of hearts, in the convergence of intentions towards the same cause. A kingdom divided against itself cannot survive (cf. Lk. 11:17). The divided apostolate comes to nothing by itself. And we know that it will be divided if you give in to the temptation of exclusivism, contrary to the just diversity of gifts and charisms, or to the temptation of isolation, disinterest or a standstill regarding the work of others, without following a program or common pastoral plans.

If there is a diversity of gifts, services and operations, the source remains the same: "to each of us is given the manifestation of the Spirit for the common good" (1 Cor. 12:7).

UNDERSTANDING EACH OTHER BY SPEAKING

9. When I began to study your beautiful language, I was impressed by the popular saying, "It is through speaking that people understand each other." The union of the work forces of evangelization requires a goal; and this in its turn will be found through an authentic dialogue, which also has its affective elements. How beautiful and important it is for us to meet as brothers, on a deeper level than mere communi-

cation of concepts! To meet in friendship, to share spiritual gifts, in affirmation of human fullness, in voluntary and genuine poverty of spirit. Every time these meetings occur—your experience will certainly tell you this—with our brothers in the ministry, the common life or the apostolate, our sense of living and participating in the mission of Christ is strengthened. After all, it was the Master who told us: "By this will all men know that you are my disciples, if you have love for one another" (Jn. 13:35). And here would be the chance to broaden our considerations on the value of dialogue in charity and in regard to a whole series of life's situations. I will limit myself to two points:

—The case of old people (priests, men and women religious) in this International Year of the Aged, and of the infirm: to them I address a word of deep understanding and a warm greeting saying to them: You are important for the Church of Christ, today just as yesterday. With St. Peter Chrysologus I ask you: make an altar of your hearts, and with every confidence offer your body as an offering to God, with faith and generosity! The Pope loves you and blesses you!

—Relations with the coordinating authorities: here the dialogue, tranquil in docile and loyal cooperation and in obedience, achieves inestimable and mutual benefits which can be used for spiritual enrichment and for the treasury of the Church, and for the effectiveness of the work of evangelization.

Enlarging on the concept of dialogue, I would say that to avoid the danger of the gradual impoverishment of the priestly and religious life, through "difficulty" if not through atrophy, we must maintain contacts with the sources of our initial basic formation, we must continue that training. Likewise, for the adequate proclamation of the Good News, there must be a dialogue with the culture of our environment, in a constant commitment to our chosen activity in order to gather together the reasons for the hope that inspires us (cf. 1 Pt. 3:15) and to transmit them to others.

GIVE YOURSELF
WITH FAITH AND GENEROSITY

10. Something would be lacking in the joy of our meeting if we did not pay a brief visit in spirit to the brothers and sisters who have consecrated their lives to contemplation and live in silent meditation, personally offering themselves in the cloister "for love of the kingdom of heaven."

And what shall we say to them?

First of all, let us express our fraternal and joyful gratitude for what they are and what they represent for us, for the mission of the ecclesial community and for the world, placed as they are at the heart of the mystery of the Church. The contemplative life is absolutely vital for the Church and for humanity, which is always in need of the purifying and renewing oxygen of grace, breathed and distributed through these prayers and hidden immolations of our contemplative brothers and sisters.

But their silent immolation proclaims the Absolute of God and makes our fellowmen ask themselves about the meaning of life. The love expressed in their adoration and supplication is lavished in the history of these same men: those who already know, and those who do not yet know, the Lord of history and the salvation that He offers. They all must more and more build a world of justice and brotherhood according to divine plans.

And I would like to repeat something that I feel very strongly on this pilgrimage to Fatima, and which is always in my heart when I address contemplatives: pray and sacrifice for us and for all those who pray, for those who cannot pray, for those who do not know how to pray and for those who do not want to pray! And may the God of peace be with you always!

LOVE THE CHURCH

11. And to the new brothers—seminarians or those who are about to embrace the religious life—I also want to address to you a word of

deep affection, from my soul and with great confidence. You occupy a special place in the heart of the Pope, in the hope of the Church and, in a special way, in the Church of this country, with so many worthy traditions with regard to priestly and religious vocations. In you I see and greet all those who aspire to the priesthood or the religious life in all of Portugal. And I can tell you what nostalgia I feel for my days as a seminarian and what a joy it is to be with you today!

But on the horizon of this joy, even here in Portugal, there are clouds, which bring to mind spontaneously the exclamation of the Lord, "the harvest is ripe but the laborers are few" (Lk. 10:2). And with this memory there comes from my heart an appeal to all those who are interested in this problem—that is, all the People of God—to dedicate all their good will to the field of vocations: with constant prayers; with example, above all on the part of those already "chosen"; and with adequate pastoral action, starting with the family, then through the various communities and through the school, and finally at the level of the complete pastoral program. I know that you are already committed in this way and I want my words to comfort and encourage you.

Those in seminaries and houses of formation are giving the best of themselves to cultivate with the affection of Mother Church those plants destined to blossom into priests and men and women religious. I want to express all my esteem for you and repeat, even if you already know it: you are not alone in your generous and precious work; the whole Church is with you. Know that the Pope supports and appreciates you, as do your bishops and your religious superiors. May your work always be blessed by God!

And you, my young friends, cultivate high ideals; love this life and give it a noble scope. You are at a point in life when you must speak much to God about men, so that later you can speak to men about God. There is a phrase that you are sure to know, but which I would like to remind you of: "there are three 'much's' which three others can make up for: much study, much knowledge, much reflection—much wisdom, much virtue, much peace." Have courage!

Brothers and sisters:

The poor in spirit is the one who believes in the Gospel of the love and mercy of God and lives it every day. The consecrated one is he who affirms and lives in himself the absolute dominion of God, who wishes to be everything to all men (cf. 1 Cor. 15:28). The evangelizer is one who proclaims the Good News that he has in his heart and that transforms him interiorly and frees him spiritually. Be faithful to your sublime vocation!

And may the Virgin Mary, Mother of the Church—Our Lady of Fatima—be always present in your life, with her example and her protection; and may she give you the constant serenity, consolation and joy of her Son, Jesus Christ, in whose name I bless you with all my heart.

The World Needs Your Living Witness

At the Digby Stuart Training College in London, John Paul II met the religious men and women of England and Wales on May 29, 1982. During the meeting he addressed them as follows.

My dear brothers and sisters in Christ,

1. I wish to express my special joy at this meeting. You are here in such large numbers as representatives of all the religious of England and Wales. On the eve of Pentecost you are here to renew your religious vows. With the Pope, the Successor of Peter, you will proclaim before the whole Church that you believe in your consecration; that it is your call to follow Christ which inspires your joy and your peace. "Rejoice in the Lord always" (Phil. 4:4).

AMAZING REBIRTH

2. You worthily continue a tradition that goes back to the dawn of English Christian history. Augustine and his companions were Benedictine monks. The great monastic foundations of Anglo-Saxon and medieval times were not just the staging posts for evangelization; they were also the centers of learning and the seedbeds of culture and civilization. Places such as Canterbury, Jarrow, Glastonbury and Saint Albans are indicative of the role monasticism played in English history. Men like Bede of Jarrow, Boniface of Devon who became the Apostle of the Germans, and Dunstan of Glastonbury who became Archbishop of Canterbury in 960; women such as Hilda of Whitby, Walburga and Lioba, and many others—these are famous names in English history. Nor can we forget Anselm, or Nicholas Breakspear, born at Abbots Langley, who became Pope Adrian IV in 1154.

In Norman times this army of Christ reached new splendor with the foundation of monasteries of Cistercians, Dominicans, Franciscans, Carmelites and Augustinians.

Later, religious life suffered greatly. English religious communities were scattered and destroyed, or fled to foreign lands. It is impossible here to name all the men and women religious of this period who followed our Lord to the point of giving their lives in defense of their Faith. To that unhappy age belonged also an extraordinary Yorkshire woman, Mary Ward, who became a pioneer of the active unenclosed congregations for women.

The last century saw an amazing rebirth of religious life. Hundreds of religious houses, schools, orphanages, hospitals and other social services were established. Missionary congregations spread the Faith in distant lands.

In our own time the Second Vatican Council has addressed to you a call for appropriate renewal of religious life through a return to the original charism of each institute and through a healthy adaptation to meet the changed conditions of the times (cf. PC 2).

3. My brothers and sisters, we can see what the Church, and indeed society at large, expects from you today. The people of our time look to you and repeat what the Greek-speaking visitors to Jerusalem said to the Apostle Philip: "We wish to see Jesus" (Jn. 12:21). Yes, *in you the world wishes to see Jesus.* Your public profession of the evangelical counsels is a radical response to the Lord's call to follow Him. As a result, your lives are meant to offer a clear witness to the reality of the kingdom of God already present in the affairs of men and nations.

As you renew your religious consecration here this morning before God and the Church, in the sight of millions of your fellow countrymen, I wish to meditate with you on the greatness and dignity of your calling.

NEWNESS OF LIFE IN CHRIST

4. To most people you are known for what you do. Visitors to your abbeys and religious houses see you celebrate the Liturgy, or follow you in prayer and contemplation. People of all ages and conditions benefit directly from your many different services to ecclesial and civil society. You teach; you care for the sick; you look after the poor, the old, the handicapped; you bring the Word of God to those near and far; you lead the young to human and Christian maturity.

5. Most people know what you do, and admire and appreciate you for it. Your true greatness, though, comes from what you are. Perhaps what you are is less known and understood. In fact, what you are can only be grasped in the light of the "newness of life" revealed by the risen Lord. In Christ you are a "new creation" (cf. 2 Cor. 5:17).

At some time in your lives, the call of the Lord to a special intimacy and union with Him in His redemptive mission became so clear that you overcame your hesitations. You put aside your doubts and difficulties and committed yourselves to a life of total fidelity to the highest ideals of the Gospel. Your free decision was sustained by grace, and your perseverance through the years is a magnificent testimony of the victory of grace over the forces that struggle to tarnish the newness of your life in Christ. This "newness of life" is a gift of Christ to His Church. It is a proof of the Church's holiness, an expression of her vitality.

6. Through the profession of the evangelical counsels you are bound to the Church in a special way (cf. LG 44). Let me suggest to you, then, some of the aspects of your consecrated life that are especially significant in the present circumstances of the pilgrim People of God. Today there exists a widespread temptation to unbelief and despair. You, on the other hand, are committed to being men and women of deep faith and unceasing prayer. To you in a particular way may be addressed St. Paul's exhortation to Timothy: "Fight the good fight of the faith: take hold of the eternal life to which you were called when you made the good confession in the presence of many witnesses" (1 Tm. 6:12). Believe in the risen Lord. Believe in your own personal vocation. Believe that Christ called you because He loves you. In moments of darkness and pain, believe that He loves you all the more. Believe in the specific inspiration and charism of your institute. Believe in your mission within the Church. Let your faith shine before the

world, as a lamp in the darkness; let it shine as a beacon that will guide a confused society to the proper appreciation of essential values. May the spiritual joy of your personal lives, and your communal witness of authentic Christian love, be sources of inspiration and hope. Let your consecration be known. Be recognizable as religious men and women. The secular city needs living witnesses such as you.

COMPLETE DEDICATION

7. Today many people are tempted to live by a false set of values. You, on the other hand, are men and women who have discovered the pearl of great price (cf. Mt. 13:46), a treasure that does not fail (cf. Lk. 12:22-34). Through poverty voluntarily embraced in imitation of Christ—being poor in spirit and in fact, singly and corporately (cf. PC 13)—you seek freedom from the tyranny of the consumer society. Chastity practiced "for the sake of the kingdom of heaven" (Mt. 19:12) is a special gift to you from Christ, and from you to the whole Church. Virginity or celibacy is not only a preferential love of the Lord, but also a freedom for a total self-giving in universal service, without conditions and without discrimination. Your chastity, when it is marked by genuine generosity and joy, teaches others to distinguish between true

love and its many counterfeits. Through your obedience, which is a complete dedication of yourselves to the will of God, you seek to achieve the "mature measure of the stature of the fullness of Christ" (Eph. 4:13). Paradoxically, through self-renunciation, you grow to human and Christian maturity and responsibility. You show that many current ideas of freedom are in fact distorted. You help ransom society, as it were, from the effects of unbridled selfishness.

8. The witness of religious consecration has a special dimension for those of you who live the contemplative form of religious life. Your lives are hidden with Christ in God. In silence and through prayer and penance you praise Him. You call down His graces and blessings upon God's people (cf. PC 7). Many people have a vague idea of what you do, but very many more, including Catholics, fail to recognize the greatness of your special vocation and its irreplaceable role in the Church's life. Contemplative life imparts to God's people "a hidden apostolic fruitfulness" *(ibid.)*. Contemplative prayer sustains the Church in her struggle to bring mankind to a proper understanding of human dignity and spiritual values. In the name of the Church I thank you. I ask you to pray all the more for the pilgrim People of God and for the world. And to those who feel called to the contemplative life, I

repeat Jesus' invitation to two hesitant disciples: "Come and see." They came and saw and stayed with Him (cf. Jn. 1:39).

HIDDEN WITNESSES

9. The "hidden witness" of contemplatives is flanked by the vigorous apostolic thrust of the active religious communities. In the footsteps of the Master, with zeal for His Father's will, and confident in your own particular charism, you "show wonderfully at work within the Church the surpassing greatness of the force of Christ the King and the boundless power of the Holy Spirit" (LG 44).

Religious communities have a special responsibility to be sensitive to the signs of the times, and to try to meet such needs as are the proper concern of the Church's ministry. Imitate the faith and courage of your founders. Be ready to sacrifice yourselves as they did. Help the bishops in their pastoral ministry, with confidence in Christ's promise to protect and guide His Church.

10. Men and women religious, lift up your hearts! Give thanks to the Lord for your wonderful vocation. Through you Jesus wants to continue His prayer of contemplation on the mountain. He wants to be seen announcing God's kingdom, healing the sick, bringing sinners to conversion, blessing children, doing good

to all, and always obeying the will of the Father who sent Him (cf. LG 46). In you the Church and the world must be able to see the living Lord.

Do not be afraid to proclaim openly before the rest of the Church, especially the young, the worthwhileness of your way of life and its beauty. The Catholic community must be shown the high privilege of following Christ's call to the religious life. The young must come to know you more closely. They will come to you when they see you as generous and cheerful followers of Jesus Christ, whose way of life does not offer material rewards and does not accommodate itself to the standards of the world. They will be attracted by Christ's uncompromising, exciting challenge to leave all in order to follow Him.

11. In concluding, I wish to greet the religious of the Anglican Communion who are present here. You, too, are inspired by the evangelical call to an ever closer following of Christ. You have expressed a desire to welcome the Pope and to hear him speak. I thank you. I commend to your prayers the ardent desire of millions of Christians throughout the world: that we may be fully one in faith and love.

To all of you I express my gratitude and respect. I entrust all the religious of England and Wales to the loving protection of Mary, Mother of the Church, the loftiest example of discipleship. May the Holy Spirit fill your hearts with His gifts. Rejoice in the Lord always! Again, I say, rejoice! May the public renewal of your religious vows help bring about a new Pentecost in your lives and in the Church in this land.

Praised be Jesus Christ!

Love for Our Sacred Calling

Pope John Paul met the priests and religious of Scotland in Edinburgh Cathedral on May 31, 1982. In response to the greeting of Cardinal Gordon Joseph Gray, Archbishop of Edinburgh, the Pope spoke as follows.

My brothers and sisters in Christ,

1. As the Church celebrates Mary's great song of praise to God, the Magnificat, I am very happy to be with you in this cathedral dedicated to her name. I thank God for your love of Christ and your commitment to His Church.

You represent all the priests and men and women religious of Scotland. You are the closest collaborators of the bishops in their pastoral ministry. You are present in every area of the community's life, hastening the coming of the kingdom of God through your prayer and work. In you I feel the heartbeat of the entire ecclesial community. In your lives I read the history of the Church in this land, a history of much faith and love. I recognize the contribution made by priests and religious from other lands, especially from Ireland, who have helped to strengthen the Catholic community here. Your presence speaks of hope and vitality for the future.

During my pastoral visits to the various countries of the world, my meetings with the priests and religious are special moments of ecclesial significance. And today, once again, I am able to fulfill my task: to confirm you in the faith (cf. Lk. 22:31), and to remind you, with St. Peter, that you have been born anew to a living hope, to an inheritance that is imperishable (cf. 1 Pt. 1:4).

2. My greeting goes in the first place to the priests, both diocesan and religious, sharers in the one priesthood of Christ the High Priest, "appointed to act on behalf of men in relation to God, to offer gifts and sacrifices for sins" (Heb. 5:1). Your presence gives me great joy and fraternal support. In you I recognize the good shepherd, the faithful servant, the sower who goes out to sow the good seed, the laborer in the vineyard, the fisherman who launches his net for a catch. You are Christ's close friends: "I call you friends, not servants, for the servant does not know his Master's business" (Jn. 15:15).

As priests we must recognize the mystery of grace in our lives. As St. Paul puts it, we have this ministry "by the mercy of God" (2 Cor. 4:1). It is a gift. It is an act of trust on Christ's part, calling us to be "stewards of the mysteries of God" (1 Cor. 4:1). It is a sacramental configuration with Christ the High Priest. The priesthood is not ours to do with as we please. We cannot reinvent its meaning according to our personal views. Ours is to be true to the One who has called us.

The priesthood is a gift to us. But in us and through us the priesthood is a gift to the Church. Let us never separate our priestly life and ministry from full and wholehearted communion with the whole Church. Brothers in the priestly ministry, what does the Church expect from you? The Church expects that you and your brothers and sisters, the religious, will be the first to love her, to hear her voice and follow her inspiration, so that the people of our time may be served effectively.

3. As priests you are at the service of Christ the Teacher (cf. PO 1). A very important part of your ministry is to preach and teach the Christian message. In the passage that I have already mentioned, St. Paul describes his own attitude to this ministry: "We refuse to tamper with God's word, but by the open statement of the truth we would commend ourselves to every man's conscience in the sight of God" (2 Cor. 4:2). *We must not tamper with God's word.* We

must strive to apply the Good News to the ever-changing conditions of the world but, courageously and at all costs, we must resist the temptation to alter its content, or reinterpret it in order to make it fit the spirit of the present age. The message we preach is not the wisdom of this world (cf. 1 Cor. 1:20), but the words of life that seem like foolishness to the unspiritual man (cf. *ibid.*, 2:14). "In their case," Paul continues, "the god of this world has blinded the minds of the unbelievers, to keep them from seeing the light of the Gospel of the glory of Christ, who is the likeness of God" (2 Cor. 4:4). He goes on: "For what we preach is not ourselves, but Jesus Christ as Lord" (v. 5).

We should not be surprised then if our message of conversion and life is not always well received. Do everything in your power to present the Word as effectively as possible, believe in the power of the Word itself, and never become discouraged: "The kingdom of God is as if a man should scatter seed upon the ground and should sleep and rise night and day, and the seed should sprout and grow, he knows not how" (Mk. 4:26-27). Yet, in another sense, we do know how the seed grows: "God gives the growth" (1 Cor. 3:7). In this sense we are "God's fellow workers" (v. 6). How careful we must be about our preaching! It should be the continuation of our prayer.

4. We priests share in the priesthood of Christ. We are His ministers, His instruments. But it is Christ who in the sacraments, especially in the Eucharist, offers divine life to mankind (cf. PO 5). With what care, with what love must we celebrate the sacred mysteries! The sacredness of what takes place in our liturgical celebrations must not be obscured. These celebrations must be an experience of prayer and ecclesial communion for all who take part in them.

I know of the many efforts being made to ensure ecclesial renewal according to the directives of the Second Vatican Council. I encourage you to continue to develop among the laity a sense of shared responsibility for the liturgical and apostolic life of your parishes. Through their spiritual priesthood, the laity are called to take their proper place in the Church's life according to the grace and charism given to each one. Lead them in the Faith. Inspire them and encourage them to work for the well-being and growth of the ecclesial family; their contribution is extremely important. Encourage the young, especially, to "desire the higher gifts" (1 Cor. 12:31). Work closely with them, and also show them the challenge and attractiveness of the priesthood and the religious life.

5. To spend your lives in the service of the People of God through word and sacrament: this

is your great task, your glory, your treasure. But it is St. Paul again who reminds us: "We have this treasure in earthen vessels" (2 Cor. 4:7). The personal experience of each of us is that our joy and fruitfulness in the priestly life come from a full acceptance of our priestly identity. We must love our vocation and mission, but we must also *be seen* to love our priesthood. Let your people see that you are men of prayer. Let them see that you treat the sacred mysteries with love and respect. Let them see that your commitment to peace, justice and truth is sincere, unconditional and brave. Let everyone see that you love the Church, and that you are of one mind and heart with her. What is at stake is the credibility of our witness!

6. Brothers and sisters, members of the religious communities! How I wish I could greet each of you personally! To hear from each one of you the *"magnalia Dei,"* how the Holy Spirit works in your lives! In the depths of your hearts, in the struggle between grace and sin, in the various moments and circumstances of your pilgrimage of faith—in how many ways has Christ spoken to you and said: "Come, follow me"! Could the Pope come to Scotland and not say thank you for having answered that call? Of course not! So, thank you, on behalf of the Church. Thank you for the specific witness you give and for all the gifts you contribute.

Because you have carried your baptismal grace to a degree of "total dedication to God by an act of supreme love" in religious consecration (cf. LG 44), you have become a sign of a higher life—a "life that is more than food, a body that is more than clothing" (Lk. 12:23). Through the practice of the evangelical counsels you have become a prophetic sign of the eternal kingdom of the Father. In the midst of the world you point to the "one thing that is needed" (Lk. 10:42), to the "treasure that does not fail" (Lk. 12:33). You possess the source of inspiration and of strength for the various forms of apostolic work which your institutes are called to carry out.

7. Those of you who belong to contemplative communities serve the People of God "in the heart of Christ." You prophetically remind those engaged in building up the earthly city that, unless they lay its foundation in the Lord, they will have labored in vain (cf. LG 46). Yours is a striking witness to the Gospel message, all the more necessary since the people of our time often succumb to a false sense of independence with respect to the Creator. Your lives testify to the absolute primacy of God and to the kingship of Christ.

8. And you, brothers and sisters, whose vocation is active work in ecclesial service, you

must combine contemplation with your apostolic zeal. By contemplative prayer you cling to God in mind and heart; by apostolic love and zeal you associate yourselves with the work of redemption and you spread the kingdom of God (cf. PC 5). In your service to the human family you must take care not to confuse the *Regnum Dei* with the *Regnum hominis,* as if political, social and economic liberation were the same as salvation in Jesus Christ (cf. John Paul I, General Audience, September 20, 1978). Your prophetic role in the Church should lead you to discover and proclaim the deepest meaning of all human activity. Only when human activity preserves its relationship with the Creator does it preserve its dignity and reach fulfillment.

Your communities have been engaged in the process of renewal desired by the Second Vatican Council. You are trying to be evermore faithful to your role within the ecclesial community, in accordance with your specific charisms. Proceeding from the original inspiration of your founders and following the Magisterium of the Church, you are in an excellent position to discern the promptings of the Holy Spirit regarding the needs of the Church and the world today. Through appropriate exterior adaptation accompanied by constant spiritual conversion, your life and activity, within the context of the local and universal Church, become magnificent expressions of the Church's own vitality and youth.

In the words of St. Paul: "I thank my God through Jesus Christ for all of you, because your faith is proclaimed in all the world" (Rom. 1:8).

9. Brothers and sisters, there is one who walks beside us along the path of discipleship: Mary, the Mother of Jesus, who pondered everything in her heart and always did the will of the Father (cf. Lk. 2:51; Mk. 3:35). In this metropolitan cathedral dedicated to her, I wish to return to the thoughts and sentiments that filled my heart at Fatima on May 13. There I once again consecrated to her myself and my ministry: *Totus Tuus Ego Sum.* I reconsecrated, and entrusted to her maternal protection, the Church and the whole world, so much in need of wisdom and peace.

These are some of the invocations I addressed to the Immaculate Heart of Mary at Fatima:

"From famine and war, *deliver us.*

"From nuclear war, from incalculable self-destruction, from every kind of war, *deliver us.*

"From sins against the life of man from its very beginning, *deliver us.*

"From hatred and from the demeaning of the dignity of the children of God, *deliver us.*

"From every kind of injustice in the life of society, both national and international, *deliver us.*

"From readiness to trample on the commandments of God, *deliver us.*

"From attempts to stifle in human hearts the very truth of God, *deliver us.*

"From sins against the Holy Spirit, *deliver us, deliver us.*

"Accept, O Mother of Christ, this cry laden with the sufferings of all individual human beings, laden with the sufferings of whole societies.

"Let there be revealed, once more, in the history of the world the infinite power of merciful love. May it put a stop to evil. May it transform consciences. May your Immaculate Heart reveal for all the light of hope."

And to each priest and deacon, to each religious brother and sister, to each seminarian, I leave a word of encouragement and a message of hope. With St. Paul I say to you: "This explains why we work and struggle as we do; our hopes are fixed on the living God..." (1 Tm. 4:10). Yes, dear brothers and sisters, our hopes are fixed on the living God!

Today's Urgent Need for
the Values of Contemplative Life

On the occasion of the fourth centenary of the death of St. Teresa of Jesus, Pope John Paul II sent the following letter dated May 31, 1982, to the daughters of the great saint, the Nuns of the Order of Discalced Carmelites of Our Blessed Lady of Mount Carmel.

To the well beloved Sisters
The Nuns of the Order
of Discalced Carmelites
of Our Blessed Lady
of Mount Carmel

on the occasion of the IV Centenary of the death of St. Teresa of Jesus:

1. With profound joy and particularly deep affection I address you, the Discalced Carmelite Nuns, on the occasion of the Fourth Centenary of the blessed death of St. Teresa of Jesus, your foundress and Doctor of the Church, which took place at Alba de Tormes on October 15, 1582. You, her daughters, and the Discalced Carmelite Fathers have wished to prepare for this event by dedicating an entire year to the memory and honor of your venerated mother.

Right from the beginning of this "Teresian Year," I have encouraged the aims and projects of the sons and daughters of this great saint: with this in mind, on October 14, 1981, I addressed a letter, *Virtutis exemplum et magistra (AAS 73,*

1981, 692-700), to the Very Reverend Father Philip Sainz de Baranda, Superior General and, through him, to the entire order.

Now it is to you, daughters of St. Teresa, that I wish to address myself directly, because you are the firstfruits of her maternal care and of her work as reformer and, hence, you are very anxious to reap abundantly the spiritual fruits of this centenary. Moreover, by means of this letter of mine, I wish to respond to the numerous testimonies of obedience and fidelity to your contemplative charism, as well as your generous promise of prayer and sacrifice for my ministry as universal pastor, which continue to reach me, especially in this Jubilee Year, from all parts of the globe.

2. On this occasion, therefore, so full of significance for you, I want to express to you my heartfelt gratitude, while at the same time offering you a word of warm encouragement.

Yes, in the first place, I want to thank you, because I am aware of all you do for the glory of God and for the world by means of your life of prayer and sacrifice. With regard to this, I am pleased to recall to your minds the words of your holy mother who, referring to the need of saving souls, thus addressed her daughters: "This is why He—the Lord—has gathered you here together. This is your vocation. These must be the business matters you're engaged in.

These must be the things you desire, the things you weep about; these must be the objects of your petitions" *(Way of Perfection,* I, 5).

And with expressions still so very timely, she added: "The world is all in flames; they want to sentence Christ again, so to speak, since they raise a thousand false witnesses against Him; they want to ravage His Church" *(ibid.).*

Hence, for her the purpose of the reform and of the foundations was above all that of procuring the glory of God and the "good of His Church" *(Way of Perfection,* III, 6).

Only the Lord knows all that the daughters of St. Teresa, in the course of these four hundred years, have done in achieving this "good." Nevertheless, glancing over the chronicles of your monasteries and admiring the luminous examples of sanctity offered us in the past—for all let St. Therese of the Child Jesus, heavenly patroness of the missions, serve as an indication—as also the present-day witness to evangelical perfection offered by your religious families, we do succeed in obtaining a glimpse of this mysterious fruitfulness in the Church and for the Church. And so it is that I cannot refrain from expressing, in the name of Christ and of the Church, my gratitude to you, daughters of so great a mother, for all you have achieved and continue to achieve for the salvation of souls and the coming of the kingdom of God.

3. Hand in hand with these expressions of dutiful gratitude, I want to offer you my warm encouragement to continue always with ever greater conviction and success along the path traced out by St. Teresa, so as to offer the Church and the world all they expect from you.

The Second Vatican Council confirmed the legitimacy in the Church of institutes which, like your own, "are entirely devoted to contemplation, in such wise that their members attend solely to God *in solitude* and *in silence,* in *continual prayer,* and *intense penance...*"; the Council reaffirmed their utility for the Church herself, to which "they give increase by a mysterious apostolic fruitfulness," so that they constitute for her "a glory and a fountain of heavenly graces." At the same time, the fundamental conditions for this fruitfulness were indicated and attention was called to the fact that the work of updating of the said institutes be done "with respect for their separation from the world and for the exercises proper to the contemplative life" (cf. PC 7).

4. Now you will readily find in these Council norms the teaching and the directives of your holy mother. Was it not in order to obtain a life "entirely ordained to contemplation" that she undertook the reform?

She had in truth fully accepted the pressing call of the Lord: "I will have you converse now, not with men, but with angels" *(Life,* **XXIV,** 5), and she had dedicated long hours contemplating the example of Jesus who "teaches us to pray in solitude" *(Way,* **XXIV,** 4), so that she warned her daughters: "We have to separate ourselves from all so as to approach God interiorly" *(Way,* **XXIX,** 5).

Better than anybody else, your foundress knew that such solitude is only a means and, referring to this, she said: "It would in truth be a great pity if we could only pray in the little corners of solitude" *(Foundations,* V, 16). But at the same time, she knew by experience the importance of this means, and she was well aware that the desert is the place par excellence for meeting the Lord, as Sacred Scripture says: "That is why I am going to lure her and lead her out into the wilderness and speak to her heart" (Hos. 2:16). This explains her continual insistence on the observance of the enclosure, which is the concrete means for actualizing this contemplative solitude; an observance for which I also, in my address to the participants at the Plenary Session of the Sacred Congregation for Religious and the Secular Institutes, strongly recommended "appropriate austerity" *(AAS* 72, 1980, 211).

And together with enclosure and the external signs of which it is composed, the holy mother forcefully recommended all the other means which guarantee separation from the world, among which excel that silence which "highly facilitates prayer, the foundation of the monastery" (cf. *Way of Perfection,* V, 9).

5. Then as regards the "intense penance" indicated by the Council as a characteristic— together with prayer—of a purely contemplative life, more than by her exhortations, it is the very life and constitutions of St. Teresa which tell you of its importance or rather of its absolute necessity.

Hence, an updating that would lead to a lessening of penance, that is to say, to a less generous, less joyful, less complete sacrifice of yourselves, would certainly not be in keeping with the Council or with the charism of your holy mother.

In fact, fidelity to the practice of penance also promotes the exercise of fraternal charity, total detachment and authentic humility which remain the three hinges of the way of perfection *(Way,* IV, 4): at the same time, penance denotes that characteristic and essential element of Carmelite experience which St. John of the Cross, intrepid cooperator with St. Teresa in the reform of your order, has with masterly skill expressed in the absolute of the *todo-nada.*

I have no doubt but that the Carmelite nuns of today, no less than those of yesterday, tend with joyful hearts towards the attainment of this absolute, so as to offer an adequate response to the generous inspirations that are born of an exclusive love for Christ and of a total consecration to the mission of the Church.

6. Along this path, let the most Blessed Virgin be your help and your guide, since she is an incomparable example for all contemplatives and especially for you, daughters of an order which from the very beginning took an "entirely Marian" shape, in keeping with the motto of your Fathers of the Middle Ages: *Totus marianus est Carmelus.*

In her purpose of bringing back the order to its original fervor, your holy mother had as her one aim to work "for the Lord's service and the honor of the habit of His glorious Mother" *(Life, XXXVI, 6)*, and in founding the monastery of St. Joseph in Avila, her most burning desire was that "the rule of our Lady and Empress be observed with the perfection with which it was observed when initiated" *(Way)*. Our Lord Himself comforted her in this sense, when having achieved this foundation, "He thanked her for what she had done for His Mother" (cf. *ibid.,* no. 24).

Numerous other circumstances of her life witness to the extent to which the charism of Teresa of Jesus bore the sign of Mary. From her, in the year 1562, the great saint received, so to speak, her investiture of reformer (cf. *Life,*

XXIII, 14) and in her hands she once renewed her profession (Rel. 48). Hence, it does not surprise us to hear St. Teresa repeatedly calling her nuns "daughters of the Virgin" (*Life*, XXXII, 11, 14; XXXVI, 6, 24, 28; *Way*, XXII, 3; *Mans*. III, 1, 3; *Found.*, XIX, 5; XXIX, 23) and exhorting them with these words: "Imitate our Lady and consider how great she must be and what a good thing it is that we have her for our patroness" (*Mans*. III, 1, 3).

After the example of your reformer, meditating on the mystery of Mary whose heart, in virtue of her intimate union with Christ, is a fountain of life for the Church (cf. RH), you penetrate evermore deeply into the radiant light of your vocation, and of its demands for solitude, silence and total sacrifice, convincing yourselves, at the same time, of its secret fruitfulness, which appears to you all the more urgent today, in that, more so than four hundred years ago, "the world is on fire" and threatened by very grave dangers.

7. Dearly beloved daughters of St. Teresa and of the Virgin of Mount Carmel, while thanking you once again for all you do for the Church, for its bishops, priests and missionaries, of whom you are the hidden, silent but necessary helpers, I exhort you to live evermore generously this dimension of your vocation. May the "Teresian Year" help to deepen your

correct understanding of fidelity to the charism of your holy mother and obtain for you the indispensable graces for an ever greater commitment.

As a pledge of this, and as a sign of my special favor, I impart to all of you my apostolic blessing.

From the Vatican, May 31, Feast of the Visitation of Our Lady, 1982, the fourth year of our Pontificate.

Christ's Witness of Love and Peace Is Needed Today

The Holy Father's first stop in his visit to the Argentine capital of Buenos Aires on June 11, 1982, was the metropolitan cathedral, where he met the priests, religious and seminarians, and delivered the following message.

Beloved brothers and sisters,

1. I greet you cordially, priests, men and women religious, members of secular orders, seminarians and young people in the process of preparing yourselves for consecration to Christ.

I am with you in this cathedral of Buenos Aires, dedicated to the Holy Trinity, a few days after having celebrated the solemnity of the mystery of the Trinity and before the Feast of Corpus Christi.

This brings us to reflect upon the deep significance of the Eucharist in the vocation and life of the priest and of the consecrated soul.

St. Paul expressly places before our eyes the extraordinary ecclesial content which throughout our existence flows from the Eucharist: "Because there is one bread, we who are many are one body, because we all partake of this one bread" (1 Cor. 10:17).

We see outlined here in a few words the theological-existential foundation which, starting from the Eucharistic mystery, leads us to the reality of the Faith, of the ecclesial union, of the correspondence to this love which is at the basis of our consecration.

It is you who are consecrated to Christ and to the Church, to disinterested love for Him, to a kind of life based on faith—you are the ministers and witnesses of the Faith, the supporters of the Faith and the hope of others.

This marks you as persons who live very close to men and society, to their sorrows and their hopes. But it distinguishes you in the way you understand and live your own lives.

In fact, the priest is a consecration to God in Jesus Christ: "to serve...the multitude" (cf. Mk. 10:45). This consecration, as we well know, is an indelible sacramental gift conferred by the bishop, a sign and cause of grace.

For their part, the dedication of religious is a dedication of oneself accepted by the Church for its service. It constitutes a special consecration "which has deep roots in the consecration of Baptism and manifests it with greater fullness" (PC 5).

Or, in other words, one and the other dedication is more or less effective, in ourselves and in the communities we serve, according to the Faith to which we submit in living our lives, interior and exterior, in conformity with the gift received and the commitment accepted.

In order to understand and to faithfully live such dedication, the help of grace is necessary. Consequently, a priest or consecrated person must find the time to remain alone with God, listening to what He has to tell us in silence. It is therefore necessary to be prayerful souls, Eucharistic souls.

WE ARE BEARERS OF A MYSTERY

2. And since we are specially consecrated souls, we must be men and women who have a great understanding of the ecclesial unity which the Eucharist symbolizes and achieves. Living in the Church and for the real Church, we are not autonomous nor independent, nor do we speak in our own names, nor do we represent ourselves, but we are "bearers of a mystery" (1 Tm. 3:9) infinitely superior to us.

The guarantee of this ecclesial character of our lives is the union with the bishop and with the Pope. This union, faithful and ever renewed, can at times be difficult and even bring with it self-denial and sacrifices. But do not fail to accept one and the other when it is necessary. It is the "price," the "ransom" (cf. Mk. 10:45) which the Lord asks of us, for Him and with Him, for the good of the "multitude" *(ibid.)* and of you yourselves.

Therefore, if every priest, whether diocesan or religious, is bound to the episcopal body by reason of order and ministry, which relationship serves the good of the whole Church according to the vocation and the grace of each one (cf. LG 38), the religious for his part is also called to become part of the local Church by his own charism of love and respect for the pastors, and called to ecclesial dedication and to the mission of the Church itself (cf. PC 6).

3. These common bonds within the Church must lead to a close union among yourselves. The Eucharist, supreme fount of ecclesial unity, must make its constant fruits of communion felt, renewing it and reinforcing it more every day in the love of Christ.

And so, beyond the differences and peculiarities of each person, group or ecclesial community, may the Eucharistic Banquet be the perennial center of our communion in the same "body" (cf. 1 Cor. 10:17), in the same love, in the same life of the One who wanted to remain and renew His saving presence so that we may have His own life (cf. Jn. 6:51).

TRUE BROTHERHOOD

4. The concrete way to achieve that communion which the Eucharist demands must be the creation of a true brotherhood. Sacramental brotherhood, about which the last Council treats (cf. PO 8), addressing priests, and about which St. Ignatius of Antioch spoke earlier (*Ad Mag.* 6; *Ad Phil.* 5) is a requisite of the Catholic priesthood.

A brotherhood which must strengthen all those who share the same ideal of life, of vocation, and of ecclesial viewpoint. But a brotherhood which those having special titles among those who are "brothers," as the Gospel teaches (cf. Mt. 23:8), must feel in a special way.

A brotherhood which must become presence of life and of service to brethren, in the parish, in the university, in the school, in the priestly ministry, in the hospital, in the religious house, in the slums and in any other place.

A brotherhood translated into feelings, attitudes and actions in the reality of each day. So lived, it forms a part of our witness and credibility before the world, just as division and factions place obstacles in the paths of the Lord.

But we must be sure that this brotherhood, fruit of the Eucharist and of life in Christ, is not limited to the confines of one's own group, community or nation. It spreads and must include the entire universal reality of the Church, which, in every place and country, is present around Jesus Christ, who is salvation for those who make up the family of the children of God.

BECOMING RECONCILED

5. The need to establish such a climate of brotherhood logically leads us to speak of reconciliation within the Church and in society, particularly at the present delicate time which makes it much more necessary and urgent.

We all know the tensions and wounds aggravated by recent events, which have left their mark in Argentine society, and which we must try to overcome as soon as possible.

As priests, men or women religious, your obligation is to work for peace and for mutual upbuilding (cf. Rom. 14:19), seeking to create harmony of feelings with one another (cf. Rom. 12:16), teaching to overcome evil with good (cf. Rom. 12:21), and opening souls to divine love, primary fount of understanding and of change of heart (cf. Is. 41:8; Jn. 15:14; Jas. 2:23; 2 Pt. 1:4).

It is up to you to carry out the "ministry of reconciliation" (cf. 2 Cor. 5:18), proclaiming the "word of reconciliation" which has been entrusted to you (cf. *ibid.*). All this is not opposed to true patriotism, nor does it enter into conflict with it. Authentic love may lead to sacrifice; but at the same time it is necessary to take into consideration the patriotism of others, so that you may communicate with one another and enrich one another in a perspective of humanism and of Catholicity.

PRAYING TOGETHER

6. In this perspective is placed my present trip to Argentina, which has an exceptional character, very different from a normal apostolic-pastoral visit, which is postponed to another opportune occasion. The reasons for this journey I explained in my letter of last May 25th, which I addressed to the sons and daughters of the Argentine nation.

Today I come to pray with you during these important and difficult events which have been taking place for some weeks.

I come to pray for all those who have lost their lives, for the victims of both sides, for the families who are suffering, as I also did in Great Britain.

I come to pray for peace, for a dignified and just solution to armed conflict.

You who in this Argentine land are particularly considered to be men and women of prayer, raise your prayers to God with greater insistence, both individually and in community.

For my part, I wished to be here to pray with you, especially during these two days.

Let us concentrate our prayer during two particular moments: before the Mother of God in her sanctuary of Lujan, and during the celebration of the most holy body and blood of Christ.

GOOD RELIGIOUS SPIRIT

7. I know the good ecclesial and religious spirit which animates you. But you also represent the other priests or religious families in the country who constitute the leading vital strength of the Church in this beloved nation. I entrust to everyone this important intention, especially to the souls consecrated to God in the silence of the cloisters.

During these difficult and troubled days, the presence of the praying Church is needed in the Argentine nation; the Church which gives witness of love and of peace.

May this witness before God and men enter into the context of the important events of your modern history. May it raise hearts on high, since salvation history is also united to all events in human history.

May the witness of the presence of the Bishop of Rome and of your union with him give an impulse to the history of salvation in your homeland.

With these good wishes and with deep affection for each priest, man and woman religious, seminarian and member of the ecclesial institutes in Argentina, present and absent, I impart the apostolic blessing with all my heart.

A Fruitful Harvest for the Good of the Church

The Pope's letter to the Protoarchimandrite of the Basilian Order of St. Josaphat, July 1, 1982.

To the beloved son Isidore Patrylo, Protoarchimandrite and Superior General of the Basilian Order of St. Josaphat.

We are indeed glad to be able to greet both yourself and the delegates of the whole order from the provinces who have gathered in Rome for the General Chapter on the solemn anniversary day marking the centenary of the reform of the Basilian Order by St. Josaphat (called the reform of Dobromyl). Together with these we also greet the monks and religious of the Basilian Order, whom a variety of apostolic works detains in the different provinces both at home and abroad—those especially because of their blameless faith in Christ and their devotion to the Apostolic See—are a source of embarrassment.

The reform of Dobromyl, to refer to it briefly, has its origin and its *magna charta,* as it were, in the apostolic letter *Singulare praesidium* of our Predecessor, Leo XIII, issued on May 12, 1882 (cf. *Acta Leonis,* III, 58). This letter, certainly inspired by divine Providence, was so important that the order, which in bad times was on the decline and on the point of becoming extinct, was not only saved from so perilous a situation but also flourished in a proper way with a new increase of monks and institutes, and bore much fruit, resembling the first reform which took place in 1623. If you look at the matter from the historical point of view, the reform of Dobromyl was the second reform of the order.

It is well known that the monks of St. Basil the Great—whose work as a legislator on asceticism we praised in the apostolic letter *Patres Ecclesiae* (cf. *AAS,* 1980, 5-23)—were first brought in the 11th century to the Metropolitan See of Kiev by St. Anthony and St. Theodosius who founded the Monastery of the Caves in

Kiev itself (Kievo Pecerska Lavra). From this, as from a cradle, all the monasteries of the Slavs sprung.

Onto this spreading tree was grafted the earlier reform which St. Josaphat began in the monastery of the Holy Trinity at Vilna together with the Metropolitan Rutskyi in the year 1617 when the first monasteries were placed under the authority of one superior. This work of reform and renewed fidelity to the Apostolic See cost St. Josaphat his life. But from this very act, which was of such great importance, a rich harvest was reaped. So much so that in the year 1772 the order had 155 monasteries with 1,235 monks, 957 of whom were priests. In the annals that period is correctly considered to be the golden age.

Concerning the second reform, which our Predecessor Leo XIII began, it compares favorably with the first in splendor and vigor. And if the fierce wave of persecution destroyed the original headquarters and the provinces of the order extensively, there is no doubt that from that time it extended its territory and flourished everywhere after so great a destruction. Moreover, if at the first reform in the year 1623, all the members of the Basilian Order took an oath to be faithful unto death to the Church of Rome, in the second, your holy order *by a fourth vow* bound itself "to show fidelity and obedience to the Apostolic See and to the Successors of Peter." Again in the first reform the monks took an oath to preserve the Greek Rite and it is clear that they wanted this to be the distinguishing mark of your order as a proper characteristic to be perpetuated and to be seen as the happy sign of the unity of your Church.

This being so, what more suitable thing could we recommend to you on this solemn occasion than to keep these promises of yours made by your ancestors in the first and second reforms?

In his letter Leo XIII, our Predecessor, expressed the hope that your order "would flourish anew." Indeed, after he called it "great" and "distinguished," he added this: "With the flourishing of this order the Church of the Ruthenians flourished" *(ibid.,* no. 61). If we look to the past, what saying is more apt than this one, and if we look to the future, what saying has a more unifying force? For it is a property of your order, as of every monastic order, to give prominence to the evangelical life by a life of perfection. And if the order does this, it will once more be "a force and source of strength in the Church."

Besides, this picture of a fruitful harvest "for the good of the Church" seems to spring from the first beginnings of the Basilian Order of St. Josaphat, that is, as we have hinted, from

St. Basil the Great himself, who was "one of the greatest monastic pastors in the Church" *(Patres Ecclesiae,* II) and from St. Josaphat, who was himself a monk and a bishop.

Indeed from the episcopal office for the People of God (which is a priestly people), there arises that great concern which caused both Basil the Great and St. Josaphat the martyr to promote the Sacred Liturgy. This, according to the Second Vatican Council, is "the summit towards which the activity of the Church is directed and at the same time the fountain from which all her power flows" (SC 10). I wish that the Sacred Liturgy would inspire the whole of your apostolate!

But everyone knows how much St. Basil suffered and how hard he worked for the unity of the Church. He was wont to say that the dissensions of Christians obscured the truth of the Gospel and tortured Christ Himself (cf. *Patres Ecclesiae,* II), and he pointed out the way for the restoration of unity. This he placed in a renewed conversion of all to Christ and to His Word (cf. *ibid.).* Everybody knows that St. Josaphat shed his blood for the unity of the Church.

However, we cannot but express here the earnest wish that the Holy Spirit may water with the dew of His grace your way of life, your apostolate and your plans for unity. St. Basil used to invoke Him as "the Spirit of truth, the grace of adoption, the pledge of our future inheritance, the firstfruits of the eternal blessings, the life-giving power, the source of sanctification" *(Patres Ecclesiae,* III).

May Mary, the Blessed Virgin—whom Saint Basil praised in that Liturgy as "the most holy, the most pure, blessed above all others, the glorious, ever-virgin Mother of God, the woman full of grace and the joy of the whole world" *(ibid.,* III)—receive these wishes of ours.

While we invoke the help of St. Basil and St. Josaphat, your heavenly patrons, we lovingly impart the apostolic blessing to you, to all the members of your order, and to all those taking part in this celebration of yours as a sign of our fatherly benevolence and a pledge of the fullness of joy and perfection. From the Vatican, on the first day of July in the year 1982, the fourth of our Pontificate.

A Life Open to Universal Brotherhood

On July 5, 1982, in the Consistory Hall in the Vatican, the Holy Father received in audience the participants in the seventy-ninth General Chapter of the Franciscan Order of Friars Minor Capuchins. The religious, approximately one hundred fifty from all over the world, were led by Rev. Flavio Robert Carraro, Minister General.

In response to the address of homage by Father Carraro, John Paul II gave the following talk to the religious.

Beloved brothers!

1. I am happy to be here today with you who, as Chapter Fathers, not only represent all the Capuchins scattered throughout the world, but are carefully reconsidering your constitutions. This is taking place in the year of the eighth centenary of the birth of St. Francis, whose disciples you are and to whom I cordially commend you.

Therefore, this circumstance adds a further note of relevance and interest to our meeting, while I deeply thank you for having desired it.

FUNDAMENTAL REQUIREMENTS

2. In the Decree *Perfectae caritatis* from the Second Vatican Ecumenical Council, it is written that "the appropriate renewal of religious life involves the continuous return to the

sources of all Christian life and to the original inspiration of the institutes, and at the same time the adjustment of the institutes themselves to the changed conditions of the times" (no. 2). Of these two fundamental requirements—the return to the sources and the adjustment to the conditions of the times—during the years immediately following the Council, there was especially emphasized, and for understandable reasons, the second aspect, and that is the adjustment to what the conciliar text itself calls "the needs of the apostolate,...the requirements of a given culture, the social and economic circumstances" (no. 3). Along these lines, you Capuchins have also reviewed in various stages your constitutions and your life in order to make them correspond more closely to the requirements of the times and to the directives drawn up by the Church in the Second Vatican Council.

However, now that this effort to update has been brought to an end in its essential aspects, you too have felt the need—as also many other institutions in the Church—to address with renewed commitment that other primary requirement which the conciliar text calls the "continuous return to the sources," not in order to repudiate or set aside the legitimate adjustments and the new values discovered and tested during these years, but rather to give new life to them also, grafting them onto the living trunk of tradition, from which your order derives its character and strength.

Precisely to encourage such a balance between the two requirements, during your present General Chapter, after having elected the new superiors, you have wanted to review the constitutions in order to give them, now that the trial period is over, the form which—following the approval of the Apostolic See—should become definitive and permit your institute to undertake with renewed energy and without any kind of uncertainty a new stretch along its path in the service of the Church and of the world.

ORIGINAL INSPIRATION

3. You have rediscovered your "original inspiration" by reflecting with new sensitivity upon the very name received in legacy from your father St. Francis: that is, "Friars Minor." Indeed, within that name the saint included what is closest to the heart of the Gospel: "brotherhood" and "humility"; brotherly love and choosing for himself the last place, following the example of Christ, who came not "to be served, but to serve" (Mt. 20:28). In this is seen how the return to the sources is often the best way, even with the purpose of adapting to the expectations and signs of the times. A truly

fraternal life, lived under the banner of evangelical simplicity and charity, open to the meaning
of the universal brotherhood of all men and,
better yet, of all creatures, and in which each
person—young or old, learned or unlearned—is
accorded equal dignity and attention is, in fact,
perhaps the most up-to-date and most urgent
witness that can be given of Christian newness
to a society so marked as ours is by inequalities
and by the spirit of domination.

You have made a great effort to repropose
these two fundamental characteristics of your
Franciscan identity—brotherhood and humility—to the younger generations in the light of
the Capuchin tradition, which confers upon
them that unmistakable mark of spontaneity
and simplicity, of joyfulness along with gravity,
of drastic detachment from the world along with
great closeness to people, which have made the
Capuchin presence so effective and incisive in
the midst of Christian peoples and in the missions, and produced such an extensive array of
saints, among whom is St. Crispino of Viterbo,
whom I myself had the joy of adding to the roll
of heroic saints of the Church.

LIVE FOR GOD ALONE

4. Speaking of the first example of renewal,
which is a return to the sources, the Decree
Perfectae caritatis emphasizes that it is not only

a question of a return to the "original inspiration" of the institute itself, but it is necessarily also a "continuous return to the source of all Christian life," and that is to Jesus Christ, to His Gospel and to His Spirit. This is the meaning of the words with which all the religious of the Church, regardless of which order they belong to, are exhorted to consider as the supreme rule the following of Christ, to choose Him as the only thing necessary (cf. Lk. 10:42), in short, to live for God alone (cf. PC 5).

Aware of this, you have rightly reaffirmed in every way the primary place which prayer and, according to your most authentic tradition, especially contemplative prayer, must occupy in your lives, both personal and community. Of all the "roots," this indeed is the "mother root," that which absorbs mankind in God Himself, which keeps the branch joined to the vine (cf. Jn. 15:4) and assures to religious that constant contact with Christ without which—as He Himself states—we can do nothing (cf. Jn. 15:5), and with His Spirit of holiness and grace.

FOUNDER'S CENTENNIAL

5. The eighth centennial of the birth in the world of your founder, Francis of Assisi, with the extraordinary echo it has aroused, has shown

how much today's world is still sensitive to the call of the "Poverello," how much it needs and, one could say, misses him. It is up to you, in a very special way, to keep this hope always alive in the world and, what is more, to make it even more visible and recognizable. This will happen, as far as your order is concerned if, after having renewed with so much dedication and seriousness, each of you and each of your fellow religious feel urged to translate them into practice, in remembrance of those words spoken by Christ to His disciples: "Knowing these things, blessed are you if you do them" (Jn. 13:17).

Indeed, it now seems that the time has come for religious institutes to pass with resolution from the phase of discussion about their own legislation to that of putting into practice certain and fundamental values, from preoccupation with the letter to that of the spirit, from words to life, and this in order not to fall into that dangerous illusion that St. Francis himself denounces in one of his Admonitions when he writes that "those religious are killed by the letter who do not want to follow the spirit of the Holy Scripture, but want to know only words and explain them to others."

The due truthfulness and sincerity before God demands of an institute a renewed will for conversion and for fidelity to its own vocation in order for the image of itself which it has given to the Church and to the brethren by means of its own constitutions to be always as authentic as human weakness allows.

SIGN OF ESTEEM

6. Beloved brothers and sons, receive these words as a sign of my esteem for you. At the same time, be assured that you enjoy a special place in my prayers. I entrust you to the Lord, you and the entire praiseworthy family of the Friars Minor Capuchins. The holy Church and the world itself, which have already benefited greatly from your zeal, still expect from you a generous and intelligent contribution of shining evangelical witness.

May the Lord fill you with His graces, and in the spirit of St. Francis, may you continue, joyful and certain.

May you always be accompanied by my apostolic blessing, which I impart to you, Chapter Fathers, with special thought to your new Minister General, and which I extend to all the beloved members of your order.

Be the Salt of Your Land and the Leaven of the Ukrainian Community

On July 9, 1982, the Holy Father received in audience the participants of the General Chapter of the Basilian Order of St. Josaphat and the members of the Generalate. The religious were led by the Protoarchimandrite, Fr. Isidore Patrylo, who made a brief address in homage to the Pope.

Responding to the words of Fr. Patrylo, John Paul II gave the following address.

Praised be Jesus Christ!
Beloved brothers!

I am happy to greet you, Very Reverend Father Protoarchimandrite of the Basilian Order of St. Josaphat, along with the Fathers Consultors General and all the capitulars and the religious of the motherhouse. You have come from various parts of the diaspora: from Canada, from the United States, from Brazil, from Argentina, except, unfortunately, the homeland. Many of these countries have been visited by me, and your presence, so varied in its geographic origin, raises in my heart a flurry of recent and distant memories.

The celebration of a chapter is an important moment for a religious institute, but it becomes a unique event when it is also, as in your case, the centennial of the Leonine Reform of your "illustrious" order: 1882-1982! The reform is known as the Dobromyl Reform.

You remember and revere with good reason Leo XIII, the "reformer," one could say, of your order.

And it is, therefore, right that the centennial see you gathered not only in Rome but precisely around the Pope, who continues toward your order the benevolence and the concern of my great Predecessor. Nor can it be forgotten that with the Dobromyl Reform the order assumed a fourth vow: "that of fidelity and obedience to the Apostolic See and to the Successors of St. Peter," a vow which makes you particularly close to and dear to the Pope.

The reform of the order was a wise act on the part of Leo XIII, but it was also evidence of the generous spontaneity of the new incentives and the demonstration of the power that may be exercised by an ideal restored to the beauty of its origins.

In the apostolic letter of Leo XIII entitled *Singulare praesidium,* there is a sentence which resounds to the honor and encouragement of your order; it says: *"quo vigente, Ruthenorum viguit Ecclesia"* ("with the flourishing of this order the Church of the Ruthenians flourished") *(ibid.,* no. 61). The vigor of the Ukrainian Church always coincided with the vigor of your order.

This historical bond between the destiny of your order and the destiny of the Ukrainian Church is for all of you an invitation to be the evangelical salt of the earth, the leaven in the Ukrainian community.

We should like that the suffering and the tribulations of your brothers, called to bear witness to their faith and the union with the Apostolic See in harsh and often heroic conditions, may make more fruitful the apostolate of you who work for Christ in a climate of freedom.

May the Theotokos (Mother of God) give them holy perseverance and you an abundance of apostolic success!

In addition to St. Basil the Great, your order is also named after St. Josaphat, monk and bishop, who wore the martyr's crown.

May the witness of his blood be a treasure, an example and a comfort to your entire order.

Under the guidance of St. Josaphat, may your order flourish and become stronger, and may the intercession of the martyr hasten days of peace for the entire holy Ukrainian Church.

My heartfelt apostolic blessing to everyone.

Praised be Jesus Christ!

St. Francis—a Man Full of Joy, but Also One Who Worked for Peace and Universal Brotherhood

To the beloved sons John Vaughn, Minister General of the Order of Friars Minor; Vitale Bommarco, Minister General of the Order of Friars Minor Conventual; Flavio Carraro, Minister General of the Order of Capuchin Friars Minor; and Roland Faley, Minister General of the Third Order Regular of St. Francis, on the completion of 800 years since the birth of Saint Francis of Assisi.

Dear sons, health and apostolic blessing,

I

"He shone like a bright star in the night and like the dawn breaking over the darkness." In these words Thomas of Celano, who was his first biographer, praised St. Francis of Assisi.[1] We are pleased to repeat this commendation during the commemoration of the eighth centenary of the birth of this outstanding man. Actually on October 3, 1981, we broadcasted a message to the many members of the Franciscan families, to the religious sisters and others who in their way of life follow the Seraphic Father, as they were assembled in St. Peter's Basilica for the sacred vigil, and at the same time to the crowds of the faithful assembled in the Cathedral of Assisi under the leadership of the Bishop of Assisi. We did this to inaugurate the year set aside for the commemoration of the above-mentioned centenary. But now by this letter we propose to those following, as it were, this message, to highlight certain chapters of the Gospel teaching presented by him and to share with you, and through you with as many as possible, the message which he seems to give to the people of our time.

In the book known as *I fioretti di S. Francesco,* it is related that Brother Masseo, one of his first companions, once asked him: "Why is it that the whole world is coming to you?"[2] This question is still relevant after eight centuries have passed since the birth of St. Francis. Indeed, there is greater reason for asking it today. For not only has the number increased of those who have followed more closely in his footsteps by embracing the Rule composed by him as their norm for living, but also the admiration for and the enthusiasm about him far from diminishing with the passing of time— as happens in human affairs—have been more deeply impressed on men's minds and have grown more widespread. Signs of Francis' influence are to be found firmly fixed in all Christian activities, in art, poetry and all forms of Western culture. The Italian nation, which has had the privilege of giving birth to so great a man, has chosen him as its principal patron before God, together with its other outstanding daughter, Catherine of Siena. His fame has spread through the length and breadth of Europe to such an extent that the following words from the Gospel can be applied to him: "Wheresoever this Gospel shall be preached in the whole world, there also shall it be told what this man has done."[3]

Francis is the kind of man who has gained the unanimous approval of all those who have become familiar with his way of life for the example of humanity that he gave. Hence it seems relevant in this year dedicated to his memory to repeat the question put with such frankness by Brother Masseo: "Why is the whole world coming to Francis of Assisi?"

One can at least give a partial reply to this question by stating that people admire and love this saint especially because they see realized in him—and to an outstanding degree—those things which they greatly desire but which often they cannot attain in this life. These are joy, freedom, peace, harmony and reconciliation with men and with reality.

II

Truly all these things and others shine forth with singular splendor in the life of the Poverello of Assisi.

Joy especially predominates. Francis was recognized as a man who was full of joy. Throughout the whole of his life "his greatest and principal concern was to be careful always to have and preserve in himself interiorly and exteriorly spiritual joy."[4]

Often, as history relates, the urge to be joyful which comes from within cannot contain itself, so that like a wandering minstrel, imitating with pieces of wood those who play the musical instrument called the viola, he would sing the praises of God in French.[5] The joy which filled St. Francis came from the wonder with which in his simplicity and innocence of heart he contemplated all things and events. But above all it sprang from the hope which he fostered in his heart and which made him exclaim: "So great is the good that I am hoping for, that all suffering delights me."[6]

Although he hardly ever used the word "freedom," his whole life was really a remarkable expression of the freedom of the Gospel. Interior freedom of spirit and spontaneity, which makes charity the supreme law and which is very near to God, came through in all his behavior and his enterprises. One proof of this among many is the freedom in keeping with the Gospel which he gave to his brothers to eat whatever food was put before them.[7]

But the freedom which Francis sought and proclaimed is in no way opposed to obedience to the Church; much less is it repugnant "to all the people who are in the world,"[8] but on the contrary, it springs from this obedience. For the original perfect form of man according to which he is free and master of the universe shone forth in him in a special way.[9] In this also consists the extraordinary familiarity and docility which all creatures showed towards this Poverello of Christ. Hence it was that the birds would listen to him when he was preaching.[10] According to the well-known legend the wolf grew tame,[11] the very fire, lessening its heat, became *curialis*, that is, courteous.[12] So as his first biographer mentioned above states: "Walking along the road of obedience and embracing completely the yoke of submission to the divine will, he acquired in the obedience of creatures great dignity before God."[13] But above all the freedom of St. Francis sprang from his voluntary poverty. He was liberated from every worldly desire and anxiety so that he became one of those men who in the words of the Apostle are considered as "having nothing yet possessing everything."[14]

Apart from the fact that Francis was a man who was distinguished for his complete joy and his spirit of freedom, he did not cease to be respected as the pleasing lover of peace and universal brotherhood. But the peace which

Francis enjoyed and which he spread abroad is sought from God as from its source. Francis in his prayer spoke to God in these words: "You are gentleness, You are security, You are rest."[15] This peace takes on human form and force in Jesus Christ who is "our peace."[16] In Him, as Francis wrote, following St. Paul: "What is in heaven and what is on earth has made peace with and has been reconciled to the omnipotent God."[17] "May the Lord give you peace." Taught by divine revelation he greeted people with these words.[18] He was in fact "a peacemaker,"[19] or the promoter and author of peace—a man as such declared blessed in the Gospel—since "the whole substance of his words was directed to destroying enmities and laying the foundation for new pacts of peace."[20] He restored peace and concord to groups of citizens of the same town who were fighting among themselves to the point of bloody murder, and by his prayers he put to flight the demons who foster discord.[21] He brought peace to cities which were torn apart by discord, between the clergy and the people and even, it is said, between men and beasts. But Francis was convinced that peace is brought about by granting pardon. For this reason in order to persuade the mayor of Assisi and the bishop of the same town, who were at variance with one another, to make peace, he caused these well-known words to be added to the

Canticle of Brother Sun: "May You be praised, my Lord, because of those who forgive for love of You."[22]

Francis considered no one to be his enemy but looked upon everyone as his brother. Thus it happened that he broke down all the barriers which kept the people of those days apart and he preached the love of Christ even to the Saracens, sowing in their minds, as it were, the seeds of a disposition making one ready to talk and to establish ecumenism between people differing in character, culture, race and religion. These are some of the more splendid things to which our age has contributed. What is more, he extended this sense of universal brotherhood even to the inanimate creation, the sun, the moon, water, wind, fire and the earth. He called them, according to the gender of each noun, brothers and sisters, and he showed them a pleasing reverence.[23] In this respect we find the following written about him: "He embraced all things with his silent devotion, speaking to them about the Lord and exhorting them to praise Him."[24] Bearing all this in mind and out of a desire to comply with the wishes of those who are rightly concerned about the things of nature among which people live, in the Apostolic Letter of November 29, 1979, given under the seal of the Fisherman, we proclaimed St. Francis the heavenly patron of all those who foster ecology.[25]

But in this matter the example of Francis is at the same time a very clear proof that creatures and the elements are protected from unjust and harmful violation to the extent to which, in the light of the biblical teaching about creation and Redemption, they are seen as creatures towards which man has a certain responsibility, not as things which are left to his caprice, and also as things which together with him await and long "to be delivered from the bondage of corruption into the glorious liberty of the children of God." [26]

III

So far we have dealt with those matters about which mankind rightly boasts in relation to Francis of Assisi. Nor can we say that it has stopped admiring him for his joy, his freedom, his peace and universal brotherhood. But, if we were simply to stop here, it would be a question of a useless admiration which would have little or no influence in teaching the people of today how to attain these same benefits which have been mentioned above. It would be to act like someone who wants to gather the fruit while neglecting to care for the trunk and the roots of the tree.

Therefore, in order that the celebration of the eighth centenary of the birth of St. Francis may arouse people's consciences in these matters and have some lasting effect, it is necessary to return to the sources, to discover how the life of this seraphic man could produce such marvelous fruits. For indeed peace, joy, freedom and love were not natural endowments of Francis, nor did they come to him by chance, but were the result of a determined effort by the hard way. He sums this up in these words: "To do penance," just as at the beginning of his "Testament" he wrote: "The Lord granted to me, Brother Francis, to begin doing penance because being in sin it seemed too unpleasant a thing for me to look at the lepers. And the Lord Himself took me among them and I pitied them. And when I left them what had seemed horrible to me was transformed into something pleasing both to my mind and to my body. And after that I stayed a short while and then left the world." [27]

"To do penance" or "To live a life of penance"—these words occur very often in the writings of St. Francis, since they are an apt and brief summary of his life and preaching. When it was a question of rightly ordering his new life— which was very important at the time—opening the book of the Gospel he sought guidance from Christ and found there this reply of the Lord: "If any man will come after me, let him deny himself." [28] Then he modeled himself on this until his death. In fact, renunciation of self was the way in which Francis found his "spirit" or his life. He found joy in bearing hardships, freedom in obedience and the complete renunciation of himself, love for all creatures in hating himself, that is, as the Gospel teaches, in overcoming self-love.[29] One day while walking along the road he explained to Brother Leo that true joy is to be found in patiently bearing suffering and tribulation for the love of Christ.[30]

"To live a life of penance" for St. Francis was the same as recognizing sin in all its gravity, constantly treating with God in a spirit of repentance, translating into one's daily life this sense of compunction and sorrow by means of a strict asceticism. He made so much progress in this field that before his death, as if asking pardon, he confessed that "he had sinned greatly against his brother body" which during his life he had treated with such severity.[31]

This method, which Francis followed, is briefly summed up in the Christian word *cross*. He was and still is the herald and messenger through whom the Church is strongly reminded of the importance which the preaching of the cross should have, as if God, through His poor servant Francis, wanted to plant anew the wood of the cross "in the center of the city,"[32] that is, in the midst of the Church. For this reason when in this year dedicated to the memory of this saint, we went on pilgrimage to his tomb, we addressed this prayer to him: "The secret of your spiritual riches is contained in the cross of Christ.... Teach us, as Paul the Apostle himself taught us, 'to boast about nothing else except the cross of the Lord Jesus Christ.'" [33]

Christ crucified was for Francis his guide on his journey from the beginning until the end of his new life. Also on Mount Alverna He gave him externally the sacred stigmata so that he might portray the Crucified before the eyes of men. [34] Francis formed and fashioned himself completely according to the model of the Crucified, and his most important motive for dedicating himself to utter poverty was to follow the Crucified. When he was near the point of death, he summed up his extraordinary spiritual experience in these simple but clear words: "I know Christ who was poor and crucified." [35] Indeed, from the moment of his conversion to God, he lived constantly as one who had the imprint of the stigmata of Christ.

Let us return to the question put at the beginning: "Why does the whole world come to you?" The answer is already quite clear from these words of Jesus Christ: "And I, if I be lifted up from the earth, will draw all men unto myself." [36] All people are attracted to Francis of Assisi, because by following his Divine Master he wanted in some way "to be lifted up from the earth," that is, to be crucified to such an extent that he no longer lived for himself but Christ lived in him, if one is permitted to apply to him the words of the Apostle.[37]

To the people of our times, who try as hard as they can to banish suffering, but can in no way bring this about—nay the more strongly they strive to remove what they consider to be the causes of suffering, the more seriously are they affected by troubles—St. Francis in a few words, but words which are supported by the immense authority of his life, points out to the Christian the way that leads to this. It is a question of removing the ultimate cause of suffering and injustice which is sin, especially the sin of inordinate love of self. If man, as it were, crucifies the love of self, he overcomes that sluggishness which makes him want to love himself alone and avoid associating himself with others. This self-love also makes him use all things insofar as they serve his own interests. But against self-love he breaks, so to speak, the longstanding circle of death and enters a new circle which has God as its center and which includes within its circumference all brothers. In short, he becomes "a new creature in Christ."[38]

Bearing this in mind, the year dedicated to the commemoration of the birth of St. Francis, which is drawing to a close, seems to be a providential period of preparation for the Synod of Bishops which is to take place in 1983 and will have as its theme: "Reconciliation and Penance in the Mission of the Church." May he who experienced a special fulfillment from his resolve "to do penance" obtain for us Christians of these times the grace to understand the truth that we cannot become new men experiencing joy, freedom and peace, unless we humbly acknowledge the sin which is in us, unless we are cleansed in the bath of true repentance and from then on "bring forth fruits worthy of repentance."[39]

IV

We do not want to end this letter in which we are reflecting on the eighth centenary of the birth of St. Francis without mentioning his special attachment to the Church and the ties of filial devotion and friendship which bound him to the Roman Pontiffs of his time.

Being convinced that he who "gathers not" with the Church "scatters,"[40] this man of God from the beginning took care that his work would be confirmed and covered by the approval and protection of the "holy Roman Church." He indicated this in his rule in the following words: "So, always submissive to the same holy Church and as subjects at her feet, steadfast in the Catholic Faith, let us observe the poverty, humility and the holy Gospel of our Lord Jesus Christ as we have solemnly promised to do."[41]

His first biographer had this to say of him: "He considered that the Faith of the holy Roman Church, in which alone consists the salvation of all those needing to be saved, must be preserved, respected and followed in all things and above all things. He respected priests and had a great love for every ecclesiastical order."[42]

But the Church responded to the trust placed in it by the Poverello of Christ to the extent that it not only approved his rule but it also gave him special honor and favor. We spoke of this love of St. Francis for the Church when, at the opening of the year commemorating this remarkable saint, we gave the above-mentioned message in which among other things we said: "The charism and the prophetic mission of Brother Francis were to show in a concrete way that the Gospel has been entrusted to the Church and that one must live it and translate it into one's daily life especially in an exemplary way in the Church with the approval and the support of the Church."[43]

However, the conditions of life which the Church is now experiencing seem to require us to look more closely at how St. Francis in those times really played an active part in the affairs of the Church. Those times were especially striking and conspicuous for the great efforts that were being made to bring about the liturgical and moral renewal of the Church itself. These efforts culminated in the Fourth Lateran Council held in the year 1215. Although it is not known for certain that Francis was present at the sessions of the General Council, there is no doubt that he was perfectly aware of the ideals and the decisions of the Council and that he himself and the order he founded made an important contribution to the accomplishment of that renewal for which the Council had given the guidelines. Certainly the religious controversy about the Eucharist which showed that St. Francis was concerned that the churches, tabernacles and sacred vessels should be more richly adorned so that the love for the sacred body and blood of our Lord Jesus Christ might flourish once again,[44] is clearly related to the Canons of the same General Council and also to the letter of Pope Honorius III.

Furthermore, Francis favored the program of penitential renewal which Pope Innocent III put forward when he addressed those attending the opening of the Lateran Council. In this address this Supreme Pontiff, our illustrious Predecessor, urged all Christians, especially clerics, to undertake a spiritual renewal, conversion to God, and a moral reform. Using the prophetic words to be found in Ezekiel, chapter 9, he stated that the letter Thau (the last in the Hebrew alphabet, having the form of a cross) was the sign of those who "have crucified the flesh with its affections and lusts"[45] and who lament and grieve over the rebellion of man against God. "He who shows the power of the cross in his actions carries this sign on his forehead."[46]

St. Francis took and applied to himself this invitation from the lips of the Roman Pontiff— an invitation to purify and renew the Church. It is said that from that day he gave special reverence to the sign Thau. He wrote this in his own hand in his notes—as in the note addressed to Brother Leo. He also had it written over the cells of the brothers, and he recommended it in his exhortations, "as though," to quote St. Bonaventure, "his complete desire was, in keeping with the prophetic quotation, to put the sign Thau on the foreheads of those who were lamenting and grieving following their genuine conversion to Jesus Christ."[47]

These and other considerations show that Francis wanted to place his work humbly at the service of the Church for the program of spiritual renewal which the hierarchy had begun. He contributed to the achievement of this by his sanctity, that is, by his support, for which there can be no substitute. When he first prepared himself to be entirely at the disposal of the Holy Spirit to such an extent that he made himself like the crucified Christ, he became the instrument which the Holy Spirit Himself used to renew the Church from within, that it might be "holy and without blemish."[48] The man of God accomplished all this moved "by a divine inspiration," as he himself was wont to say, that is, spurred on by the fervor of the Holy Spirit. In everything he sought "Spirit and life."[49] He freely made use of these words of St. John. Whence came the remarkable strength which was able to bring about the renewal and which was present in his person and in his life. So he was a genuine promoter of the renewal of the Church, not by his reproofs or by his austerity but by his sanctity.[50]

The age through which the Church is now passing is in some ways similar to that in which St. Francis lived. The Second Vatican Council has put forward many plans and programs for the renewal of the Christian life. But, as we have said recently in the letter for the 16th centenary of the First Ecumenical Council of Constantinople and for the 1550th anniversary of the Council of Ephesus, "all the work of renewal in the Church, which the Second Vatican Council proposed and initiated providentially, can only be accomplished in the Holy Spirit, that is, with the help of His enlightenment and His power."[51] But this kind of activity of the Holy Spirit, which is of the greatest importance, is normally realized only through human beings to whom the Spirit of Christ has been communicated completely, and who have been made, as it were, His instruments, so that they can pass on the same Spirit in different ways to their brothers.

And so the commemoration of the birth of St. Francis which is being celebrated this year in a solemn way, seems to us, in view of what has been said above, to be a time of special grace given to the Church of God in these days.

Through this gift especially, the movements of the faithful and the new forces which have sprung up in the Church today are reminded that they should adhere to the Church itself by striving zealously—as St. Francis did—to abandon their private programs for renewal and humbly to place the charism given to them at the service of the programs undertaken by the Church in the Second Vatican Council. And so today, as at the time of St. Francis, there is a need for people to attain newness of life by sharing in the sufferings of Christ,[52] people whom the Spirit can use freely for the building up of the kingdom. Unless this comes about, there is a danger that even the best injunctions and directives of this General Council will be rendered ineffective or that, at least, they will not bear those fruits which are expected for the good of the Church.

The Church addresses this invitation to all her children, but especially on this occasion to those who have pledged themselves to follow more closely in the footsteps of the Poverello of Assisi—those in the different orders and institutes founded by him or those who strive to follow his splendid way of life. The Church expects all who are fired by a renewed enthusiasm to contribute by their holiness to her advancement to such an extent that the great gift which was experienced in the world in the past through St. Francis of Assisi may be revived.

Relying on this hope, we willingly impart the apostolic blessing to you, dear sons, to the religious families over which you have been placed and to the cloistered Franciscan nuns and the sisters, as well as to the members of the Third Order of St. Francis, as a pledge of heavenly blessings and a proof of our love.

Given at Rome, in St. Peter's, on the 15th day of August, the Solemnity of the Assumption of the Blessed Virgin Mary, in the year 1982, the fourth of our Pontificate.

FOOTNOTES

1. *The First Life of St. Francis,* no. 37: *Analecta Francescana,* 10, Ad Claras Aquas 1926-1941, p. 29.

2. Cf. *Acts of Blessed Francis and His Companions,* edited by P. Sabatier, Paris 1902, 10, p. 40; cf. also *I Fioretti di San Francesco,* ed. B. Bughetti, Florence 1926, 10, pp. 55f.

3. Cf. Mt. 26:13.

4. The *"Legenda antiqua S. Francisci."* Text of MS. 1046 (M 69) of Perouse, edited by Fr. F. M. Delorme, Paris 1926, no. 97, p. 56; cf. also *Compilatio Assisiensis*, by M. Bigaroni, Portiuncula 1975, no. 120, p. 384; *Scripta Leonis, Rufini et Angeli Sociorum S. Francisci*, edited by R. B. Brooke, Oxford 1970, no. 97, p. 260.

5. Cf. Thomas of Celano, The Second Life of St. Francis, no. 127: *Analecta Franciscana*, p. 205.

6. "And for this subject he proposed in his native tongue: so great is the good that I am waiting for that all pain gives me pleasure": *Acts of Blessed Francis and His Companions*, 9, p. 31; cf. *The likeness of the life of Blessed Francis to the Life of the Lord Jesus*, by Fr. Bartolomeo of Pisa; *Analecta Francescana*, 1, 479; *Reflections on the Stigmata*, I, *Fonti Francescane*, Assisi 1977, no. 1897.

7. *Regula Bullata*, 3, 14: "And according to the holy Gospel it is lawful to eat all foods which are put before us (cf. Lk. 10:8)." Cf. *Opuscula Sancti Patris Francisci Assisiensis* (Bibl. Franc. Ascetica Medii Aevi, 12), ed. K. Esser, Grottaferrata 1978, p. 230.

8. *Salutatio Virtutum*, 14-16: *Opuscula Sancti Patris Francisci Assisiensis*, 303. Cf. *Fonti Francescane*, no. 258; 1 Pt. 2:3.

9. Cf. Gn. 1:28; Wis. 9:2-3.

10. Cf. Thomas of Celano, *The First Life of St. Francis*, no. 58: *Analecta Francescana*, 10, 44f.; *Fonti Francescane*, no. 424.

11. Cf. *The Acts of Blessed Francis and His Companions*, 23, pp. 77-81: The ferocious wolf tamed by St. Francis; *I Fioretti di San Francesco*, 21: *Fonti Francescane*, no. 1852.

12. Thomas of Celano, *The Second Life of St. Francis*, no. 61: *Analecta Francescana*, 10, 74; cf. *ibid.*, no. 166, 227: "...My Brother fire...be propitious in this hour, be courteous."

13. Thomas of Celano, *The First Life of St. Francis*, no. 61: *Analecta Francescana*, 10, 47.

14. 2 Cor. 6:10.

15. *Laudes Dei Altissimi* (Praises of the Most High God), 4: *Opuscula Sancti Patris Francisci Assisiensis*, 90.

16. Eph. 2:14.

17. *Letter addressed to the whole Order,* 13: *Opuscula Sancti Patris Francisci Assisiensis,* 140; cf. Col. 1:20.

18. *Testament,* 23: "The Lord revealed His salvation to me, so that we should say: May the Lord give you peace": *Opuscula Sancti Patris Francisci Assisiensis,* 311f.

19. Mt. 5:9.

20. Thomas of Spalato, *Historia Pontificum Salonitarum et Spalatensium,* ed. Heinemann: Monumenta Germaniae Historica. Scriptores XXIX, p. 580. Cf. *Testimonia minora saeculi XIII de S. Francisco Assisiensi,* ed. H. Boehmer—F. Wiegand —C. Andresen, Tübingen 1961, p. 72; *Fonti Francescane,* no. 2252.

21. Cf. Thomas of Celano, *The Second Life of St. Francis,* no. 108: *Analecta Francescana,* 10, p. 194.

22. *Opuscula Sancti Patris Francisci Assisiensis,* 88. Cf. Mt. 6:12. The canticle of Brother Sun was written in the native tongue; cf. *Legenda antiqua S. Francisci* (Legenda Perusiana), ed. Fr. F. M. Delorme, 44, p. 27; *Scripta Leonis, Rufini et Angeli Sociorum S. Francisci,* ed. R. B. Brooke, p. 168; *Fonti Francescane,* no. 1593.

23. Cf. Thomas of Celano, *The First Life of St. Francis,* nos. 77, 80-81: *Analecta Francescana,* 10, 57-60.

24. Thomas of Celano, *The Second Life of St. Francis,* no. 165: *Analecta Francescana,* 10, 226.

25. Cf. *AAS* 71 (1979), p. 1509.

26. Cf. Rom. 8:21.

27. *Testament,* 1-3: *Opuscula Sancti Patris Francisci Assisiensis,* 307f.

28. Cf. Thomas of Celano, *The Second Life of St. Francis,* no. 15: *Analecta Francescana,* 10, p. 140; Mt. 6:24; Lk. 9:23.

29. Cf. Mt. 10:39.

30. Cf. *True and perfect joy,* 15: *Opuscula Sancti Patris Francisci Assisiensis,* 324-326. Cf. also *The Admonition of St. Francis,* 5, 8; *ibid.,* 67; *I fioretti,* 8: *Fonti Francescane,* no. 1836.

31. Cf. *Legenda trium Sociorum,* no. 14, ed. T. Desbonnet; Archiv. Franc. Hist. 67, 1974, 100.

32. Cf. Rv. 22:2.

33. *L'Osservatore Romano*, March 13, 1982.

34. Cf. Gal. 3:1. Cf. also Thomas of Celano, *The First Life of St. Francis*, no. 112: *Analecta Francescana*, 10, 88: "There appeared on him the marks of the cross and passion of the immaculate Lamb who washed away the sins of the world, while it seemed that recently taken down from the cross his hands and feet bore the imprint of the nails and as if his right side had been pierced with a lance."

35. Thomas of Celano, *The Second Life of St. Francis*, no. 112: *Analecta Francescana*, 10, p. 192.

36. Jn. 12:32.

37. Cf. Gal. 2:20.

38. Cf. 2 Cor. 5:17.

39. Cf. Lk. 3:8.

40. Cf. Lk. 11:23.

41. *Regula Bullata*, 12, 4: *Opuscula Sancti Patris Francisci Assisiensis*, 237.

42. Thomas of Celano, *The First Life of St. Francis*, no. 62: *Analecta Francescana*, 10, 48.

43. Cf. *AAS*, 73 (1981), p. 731 (October 3, 1981).

44. Cf. Canons of the Fourth Lateran Council, 19-20: *Decrees of the Ecumenical Councils*, edited by G. Alberigo and others, Bologna 1973, p. 244; cf. also Apostolic Letter of Pope Honorius III *Sane cum olim*, November 22, 1219: *Bullarum Romanum*, III, Augustae Taurinorum 1858, p. 66 and The Letter of St. Francis to the Clergy *On Reverence for the Body of the Lord: Opuscula Sancti Patris Francisci Assisiensis*, pp. 96f.

45. Gal. 5:24.

46. D. Mansi, *The New and Enlarged Collection of the Sacred Councils*, 22, Venice, 1778, p. 971: cf. *PL* 217, 677.

47. *Legenda minor*, 2, 9: *Analecta Francescana*, 10, p. 662; cf. *Legenda maior* by the same author, Prologue, 2: *ibid.*, p. 558.

48. Eph. 5:27.

49. *Regula Bullata*, 12, 1; *Regula non bullata*, 2, 1: *Opuscula Sancti Patris Francisci Assisiensis*, pp. 237, 243. Cf. also S. Bonaventure, *Legenda maior*, 10, 2: *Analecta Francescana*, 10, p. 602.

50. Cf. *Testament*, 13: *Letter to the Faithful* (former version), 2, 22; *Letter to the Faithful* (later version), 20: *Opuscula Sancti Patris Francisci Assisiensis*, pp. 309f., 112, 118.

51. Letter *A Concilio Constantinopolitano*, March 25, 1981: *AAS* 73 (1981), p. 521.

52. Cf. Phil. 3:10.

Camaldolese Spirituality Is Still a Great Reserve of Grace for Mankind Today

On September 5, 1982, the Holy Father made a brief visit to the Monastery of the Holy Cross in Fonte Avellana to conclude the celebrations of the first millennium of the foundation of the Camaldolese hermitage. During the holy Mass celebrated outside the monastery, the Pope delivered the following homily.

Beloved brothers and sisters,
"Then the eyes of the blind shall be opened,
and the ears of the dead unstopped;
then shall the lame man leap like a hart,
and the tongue of the dumb sing for joy" (Is.
    35:5-6).

1. With the description of these joyful scenes presented to us by the prophet Isaiah to announce the happiness of the messianic era, I address you, beloved brothers and sisters, to show in my turn the deep joy in celebrating the

Eucharist with you today before this ancient church of the Holy Cross in Fonte Avellana which, with its spare, unadorned line, expressed through the solidity of the bare stone, inspires in the heart the sense of eternity and the certainty of heavenly things. The purity of the mystical landscape in which this illustrious hermitage is set is already such as to predispose the mind to meditation and the adoration of God, whose infinite perfection is reflected in the beauties of creation.

I have come to drink at this fountain of spirituality in this atmosphere in which everything recalls the values of the spirit. Here, where silence reigns and peace prevails, God speaks to man's heart.

I greet with sincere affection the Camaldolese community, beginning with their Superior General, Fr. Benedetto Calati. I greet in a special way Cardinal Palazzini and all the bishops present, with particular thought to His Excellency Costanzo Micci, who, as the local bishop, also so much desired this visit. I respectfully greet the political and civil authorities of the Region of the Marches and the Province.

I greet all the faithful and pilgrims who have gathered here to give witness of their Christian faith and to express their affection for the Successor of Peter. To everyone I say: Praised be Jesus Christ!

PERSONAL MEETING
BETWEEN GOD AND MAN

2. At the center of today's Gospel is placed the deaf mute who obtains a cure. "And taking him aside from the multitude privately, he put his fingers into his ears, and he spat and touched his tongue; and he looked up to heaven, sighed, and said to him, 'Ephphatha,' that is, 'Be opened.' And his ears were opened, his tongue was released, and he spoke plainly" (Mk. 7:33-35). In performing this miracle, Jesus, with a meaningful gesture, takes the deaf mute far away from the crowd: there He gives him back his health! The "Ephphatha," that is, the most fruitful way of opening oneself to Christ and of obtaining salvation, always takes place in a strictly personal meeting between man and God. In order to be a true follower of Christ it is necessary to know how to seclude oneself, to let oneself be touched by Him and to open oneself to His Word, to His requests and to His sanctifying grace.

It seems to me that in the Camaldolese vocation, which during the course of the centuries has found in Fonte Avellana one of the clearest and most stable reference points, the "Ephphatha" of Christ takes place in a special way, inasmuch as the monks choose to seclude themselves in silence and solitude in order to better open themselves with their spirits to the invisible realities of God's mysteries. By so doing, they place themselves in direct contact with Christ and occupy an eminent place in the Church, His Mystical Body, because "they offer God a choice sacrifice of praise and with very plentiful fruits of sanctity they honor the People of God and move them by their example, just as they give them increase with mysterious apostolic fruitfulness. Therefore, they are a glory for the Church and a source of heavenly graces" (PC 7).

COMMITMENT TO PRAISE

3. As in every contemplative life, also in the Camaldolese vocation the principal commitment of the monks consists in praising God, that is, in exalting, in glorifying and recognizing His superiority, His love, His fidelity, His justice and His wonderful plan of salvation. It is beautiful to think of the praise that for more than a millennium has risen up to God without interruption from this monastery through the efforts of generations and generations of monks who have made the Psalter their official song on the immortal notes of the Gregorian melodies, that praise which the monks expressed to the Lord a short time ago, manifesting the great works which He never ceases to perform throughout

the centuries when, as we have heard from the responsorial psalm "he sets the prisoners free, opens the eyes of the blind, lifts up those who are bowed down, loves the righteous, watches over the sojourners, upholds the widow and the fatherless, but brings to ruin the way of the wicked" (cf. Ps. 146[145]).

These are the same reasons why perennial praise must be given to God and why the monks withdraw from the world to consecrate their lives to Him. And in this consists the essence of the contemplative life, inasmuch as the efforts of the Church to communicate to the world the salvation accomplished by the divine Redeemer on the cross will above all be made fruitful through the fervent prayers of praise to God. For this reason the institutes of contemplative life also have a significant part in the evangelization of the world.

GREAT RESERVE OF GRACE

4. This mode of life means for the religious an emptying out and denial of himself, following the example of Christ, who "emptied himself, taking the form of a servant" (Phil. 2:7). It means detachment from the material goods of this world which chain us to the earth, preventing us from lifting our gaze to consult with the Lord. It means the choice of evangelical

poverty, which frees the soul from the worldly concerns and disposes it to receive the gifts from on high. For this reason, as St. Paul says, "God chose what is weak in the world to shame the strong" (1 Cor. 1:27). And in the second reading of this liturgy St. James questions us: "Has not God chosen those who are poor in the world to be rich in faith and heirs of the kingdom which he has promised to those who love him?" (Jas. 2:5) James, in affirming this, surely was thinking of the words of Jesus: "Blessed are the poor in spirit for theirs is the kingdom of heaven" (Mt. 5:3). It is in Jesus, in fact, that is revealed, in all its light, the value of the choice which God makes of the poor, having wed their fate and their cause. He Himself was poor and has pointed out the poor as the privileged recipients of His Gospel, having been "sent to preach the good news to the poor" (Lk. 4:18). Jesus loves and favors those who choose evangelical poverty, since that is the "good" ground in which the Word takes root, develops and bears fruit, and since He knows "how hard it is for those who have riches to enter the kingdom of God" (Lk. 18:24).

The monks, living this evangelical beatitude of poverty in its fullness, are the heirs of this kingdom, whose Good News they proclaim not only by preaching, but above all by imitating Christ, poor, chaste and obedient until death.

SOLITUDE AND POVERTY

5. Solitude, openness to God, evangelical poverty: these are the considerations which today come from the sacred pages we proclaimed a short time ago, but they are also the same ideals which, during these thousand years, have inspired the monks of this Abbey of Fonte Avellana, made famous by innumerable religious, because of the depth of their knowledge and for the holiness of their lives, among whom stands out the great figure of St. Peter Damian, hermit, Doctor of the Church. It was precisely he who gave a lasting impression to the Avellana Foundation inspired by St. Romuald and who made concrete the practices of life in written rules and in juridical orders, having at heart the safeguarding of the solitude of the place, its autonomy and the freedom of the hermitage from external interference. With the later foundation of new hermitages and of another three monasteries, he laid the foundation for this congregation, making of the various communities almost one body through the fusion of the essential elements of eastern Anchoritism and of the Benedictine Cenobitism. Great reformer and moralist, he stood beside six Popes, who distinguished themselves above all in the battle for the integrity of the Church and for the dignity of the priesthood. But what St. Peter

Damian desired most of all was the peace of his tranquil monastery of Fonte Avellana where, as soon as it was possible, he returned to being a simple monk, renouncing all the honors which came to him from his dignity as bishop and cardinal, and from where he set out again, in a spirit of obedience, as soon as his efforts as peacemaker were needed in a historical era which was so troubled and divided by rivalries and civil wars.

Following in the steps of his great teacher, Abbot St. Romuald, also from Ravenna as he was, during a period in which the Church was afflicted by grave ills, he foresaw as an antidote the need for a religious life dedicated primarily to contemplation and solitude, affirming the primacy of the search for God over all contingent values.

The history of this abbey is born and develops in the shadow of this great figure, who still today, at a distance of nine centuries from his death, does not cease to instruct and to nurture the life of his monks.

GOD'S LOVE FOR THE POOR

6. In fact, Camaldolese spirituality today, also by virtue of the benevolent encouragement received from the Second Vatican Council, is flourishing more than ever in the Church, con-

stituting a great reserve of grace, of spiritual help for all Christians, rather, for the whole of humanity.

I have come today to Fonte Avellana to honor the witness and the contribution which monastic life gives to the Church and to the world.

Monks have in the Church a place and a function which cannot be ignored, their specific nature being beneficial and edifying for the entire ecclesial community. In fact, they preserve and confirm values which the world cannot do without, since they give life meaning when they are truly lived in fullness.

7. I gratefully recall the benefit which I personally received from contact with the Camaldolese monks in Krakow, and how the faithful remained deeply edified from frequenting their hermitages, from which spread a secret sense of peace, happiness and holiness.

In fact, since the time when St. Adalbert called them for the first time from Italy, they have become wise and exemplary guides to many of the faithful of my homeland.

Beloved Camaldolese monks of this abbey or who, in similar monasteries, generously dedicate yourselves to the Lord: allow me to address to you an exhortation to love your life ever more, a life which is characterized by solitude, by Ephphatha, and by poverty in order to enrich others with heavenly gifts. Well aware that your solitude does not separate you from the Church but, to the contrary, intensifies your communion with her, love the Church your mother always more; support with your prayers her apostolic anxiety, her efforts toward peace and her suffering for the dramatic situations in which so many brothers in the Faith live today. Know how to translate into prayer and penance these great causes of the Church.

Continuing the Eucharistic celebration now, let us especially thank God the Father for the thousand years of monastic life in this Abbey of Fonte Avellana. Let us ask Him for the strength to persevere in this life with courage and consistency, welcoming with a generous spirit the words of the prophet Isaiah heard in the first reading: "Be strong, fear not! Behold, your God.... He will come to save you" (Is. 35:4). Amen!

Our Cross Also Is Needed To Save the World

Before leaving the hermitage in Fonte Avellana, September 5, 1982, the Pope met with the community of Camaldolese monks who look after the Monastery of the Holy Cross. In reply to a welcoming address by the Prior General of the Camaldolese, the Pope made the following address.

Beloved brothers in the Lord!

1. Here we are at the meeting reserved for you! I am grateful to the Abbot Prior for the kind thoughts addressed to me, and I am very happy to renew to each of you the greeting I addressed to you in the homily. I also express my deep appreciation for your life of prayer and study, and especially for the work you carry out for the benefit of the Church.

I extend my greetings to the representatives of the Camaldolese monks, whose presence at this meeting recalls to mind all the cloistered religious spread throughout the world whom, on this occasion, I also wish to reassure of my esteem and appreciation for their life of prayer and sacrifice, and for their daily commitment of joyful and generous offering to the radical demands of the Gospel message.

My visit to Fonte Avellana will remain stamped on my mind and, while I assure you of a remembrance in my prayers, I am certain that I will feel nostalgia for these mystical places where, "happy in contemplative thoughts" (Dante, *Paradiso,* XXI, 117), St. Peter Damian spent many years of his life. And it is my wish that Fonte Avellana regain a renewed and fervent impetus as a center of formation and spirituality, as a beam of faith and certainty, as an austere and hospitable home for who- ever wishes to meet with Christ and to ascend towards the summits of truth and grace.

2. The first reflection which springs to mind is the invitation to utilize silence and contemplation as much as possible. In this place, such an observation is almost obvious; never- theless, it is very useful, if not necessary, especially today when events take place at an ever-accelerated pace, in the whirling imposi- tion of the relentless machinery of commitments and programs. Fonte Avellana confirms the fundamental value of the interior life, of union with God, of reflection on eternal truth, of even exterior silence. The Second Vatican Council rightly brought out that very often "an imbal- ance arises between a concern for practicality and efficiency and the demands of moral con- science; also very often between the conditions of collective existence and the requisites of personal thought and even of contemplation" (GS 8).

It is therefore necessary to create places and oases of "prayer," to set aside a particular

time each day for prayer, so as not to be influenced or overcome by the climate of struggle, of disorder and sin which keeps the world in a state of agitation. Rather, we can confirm that, precisely during our era, the aspiration of the psalmist is making itself felt more strongly: "As a hart longs for flowing streams,
    so longs my soul for you, O God.
My soul thirsts for God, for the living God.
    When shall I come and behold the living
        face of God?" (Ps. 42[41]:2-3)

The Council states further: "God has called man and still calls him so that with his entire being he might be joined to Him in an endless sharing of a divine life beyond all corruption" (GS 18).

Monastic life maintains its value also in the modern world, and is instructive and encouraging to society in general, and in particular to religious and priestly life, which is also exposed to the danger of secularization.

3. The second reflection I entrust to you comes from the message of the cross, typical of Fonte Avellana. The very name of the foundation indicates the mentality of the first hermits; and the ascetic and austere life led by the monks, with penances and flagellations, fasts and prolonged prayer, signifies the propitiatory and satisfactory commitment of their choice. It may be said that the cross was the foundation

and the content of the spirituality of Fonte
Avellana during the first centuries of its foundation; and all the theology and asceticism
of St. Peter Damian are permeated with the
redeeming cross of Christ. *Regnavit a ligno
Deus!* (God reigned from a tree!): the saving
reality of the passion, the death on the cross of
Jesus Christ, the Word made flesh remains for
all time. God wanted to redeem mankind by
means of His cross. "For God so loved the world
that he gave his only Son, that whoever believes
in him should not perish but have eternal life"
(Jn. 3:16).

To save the world and to save ourselves,
our cross is needed. Especially during our era,
characterized by the mentality of prosperity and
pleasure, the message and the example of mor-
tification and sacrifice are necessary, recalling
the statement of the *Imitation of Christ: Tantum
proficies, quantum tibi ipsi vim intuleris* (L.I.,
c. XXV, 11). (You will progress to the degree
that you mortify yourself.)

4. Beloved! You know well the booklet of
St. Peter Damian entitled *Dominus vobiscum*
(PL 145, 225ff.), a small masterpiece of theology
and mysticism in which he explains the doctrine
of the unity of the Church, basing it upon
prayer, the sacrifice of the altar together with
Eucharistic Communion, and the liturgical cycle.
The saint wrote as follows: *"Licet multiplex*

videatur Ecclesia propter numerositatem gentium, una tamen et simplex est, unius fidei et divinae regenerationis confoederata Mysterio" (PL 145, 225). (Although the Church seems to be multiple because of the number of peoples, it is nevertheless one and simple, of one faith and divine regeneration, bound together in mystery.)

Unity within the Catholic Church and among the Christian churches: this too must be your daily incentive! May Mary most holy, who was so loved and revered at Fonte Avellana over the centuries by the monks and especially by Saint Peter Damian, her apostle and her cantor, enlighten you and inspire you too to be witnesses to unity, in truth and in charity!

With these wishes, I impart my heartfelt blessing.

Ecclesiastical and Religious Dress as a Sign and Witness in the World

The Holy Father sent the following letter to Cardinal Ugo Poletti, his Vicar General for the diocese of Rome and district, in which he asks him to study opportune initiatives intended to favor the use of ecclesiastical and religious dress in the diocese.

To the revered Brother
Cardinal Ugo Poletti
Vicar General for the Diocese of Rome

Concern for the beloved diocese of Rome brings to my mind numerous problems among which that concerning the discipline of ecclesiastical dress appears worthy of consideration because of the pastoral consequences deriving from it.

On many occasions in my meetings with priests I expressed my thought in this regard, pointing out the value and significance of this distinctive sign, not only because it contributes to the decorum of the priest in his external comportment or in the exercise of his ministry, but above all because it indicates within the ecclesiastical community the public testimony which every priest is bound to give of his own identity and of his special dedication to God. And since this sign expresses concretely our "not belonging to the world" (cf. Jn. 17:13), I addressed the Lord with this invocation in the prayer composed for Holy Thursday this year, in reference to ecclesiastical dress: "Save us from 'grieving' Your spirit...by whatever shows itself as a desire to hide one's priesthood before men and to avoid all external signs of it" *(AAS 74, 1982, p. 26)*.

Sent by Christ to proclaim the Gospel, we have a message to transmit, which is expressed both by words and also by external signs, especially in today's world which shows itself so sensitive to the language of images. Ecclesiastical dress, as well as religious dress, has a particular significance. For the diocesan priest it has principally the character of a sign which distinguishes him from the secular environment in which he lives; for the religious man or woman it expresses also the character of consecration and makes evident the eschatological end of the religious life. The habit, therefore, helps the ends of evangelization and leads one to reflect on the realities which we represent in the world, and also on the primacy of the spiritual values which we affirm in man's existence. By means of this sign it is easier for others to arrive at the mystery of which we are the bearers—to arrive at Him to whom we belong and whom we wish to proclaim with all our being.

I am not unaware of the historical, environmental, psychological and social reasons which can be adduced to the contrary; however, I could say that reasons of an equal nature exist in its favor. I should however point out above all that contrary reasons or pretexts, when compared objectively and serenely with the religious sense and with the expectations of the greater part of the People of God, and with the positive benefit of the courageous witness also of the habit, appear much more of a purely human character than of an ecclesiological one.

In the modern secular city where the sense of the sacred has been so terribly weakened, the people have need also of these reminders of God which cannot be neglected without a certain impoverishment of our priestly service.

By virtue of these considerations, I feel in duty bound, as Bishop of Rome, to address you, Your Eminence, who more closely share my cares and concerns in the government of my diocese, so that, in agreement with the Sacred Congregations for the Clergy, for Religious and the Secular Institutes, and for Catholic Education, you should study opportune initiatives aimed at fostering the use of ecclesiastical and religious dress, by issuing in this regard the necessary dispositions and by seeing to it that they are put into effect.

In invoking upon you, Your Eminence, and on the whole diocese of Rome, the all-powerful help of the Lord, through the intercession of the most Blessed Virgin *"Salus Populi Romani,"* I cordially impart the apostolic blessing.

From the Vatican, September 8, 1982.

Consecration to God and Service of Man Characterize Today's Apostle

During his pastoral visit to Padua, September 12, 1982, the Holy Father met with the diocesan priests, men and women religious, seminarians and novices in the city's famous cathedral, and addressed the group as follows.

Dearest priests, religious and seminarians,

1. My meeting with you, within the framework of my visit to the Church in Padua, takes on an altogether special value and significance. In you I am happy to see and greet the choicest part of this ecclesial community, those whom the Lord has more intimately called to follow Him and whom by special title He calls His friends, those who bear the daily exertions of work in the Lord's vineyard. I feel the deepest spiritual communion with you.

It is with these sentiments that I address you particularly, dearest priests. With you and for you I offer God fervent praise and heartfelt thanks for the grace of ordination, in virtue of which you have been consecrated and sent to shepherd this community. With you I wish to address a thought full of admiration and gratitude to the forty-five priests of your presbyterate who are exercising their ministry in the missions of Brazil, Kenya and Ecuador. I also greet and express my thanks to the other thirty-two priests whom the diocese of Padua has given to the service of the Apostolic See and other sister Churches. The sensitivity and missionary spirit that characterize your presbyterate are an evident sign of a generosity that certainly has its source in a gift of the Holy Spirit. And today, with you, I pray the Lord to preserve and nourish this charism, which by enriching the other Churches embellishes yours.

My heart is equally open to you, dearest religious, dearest sisters and members of lay institutes. You are excellent witnesses to the absolute of God and the transcendence of the things of the kingdom of God compared to any other value. I exhort you with all my strength to preserve the taste and the aroma of a genuine evangelical radicalism. Your life, which is in itself a marvelous praise of the grace of Christ and a working sign of the dynamic presence of the Holy Spirit, will then become a precious gift offered not only to the Christian community but also to that world which ignores the greatness of your vocation and your eminent service.

I am happy to meet with you also, dearest seminarians, the joy and hope of this Church. I see in you the Lord's chosen, those whom the Holy Spirit sets apart in order to send out tomorrow to proclaim the Gospel as the power of God. Generously cultivate the seed of your divine vocation with gratitude and humility, in recollection, in prayer, in study, in the first experiences of the apostolate under the guidance of your superiors. The mission that awaits you is so sublime and fascinating that it must arouse in you the desire to put all your enthusiasm and your energies at the service of Christ from now on. Remember that your time in the seminary is decisive for your future ministry: know how to live it intensely.

RIGHTLY PROUD
OF SPIRITUAL HERITAGE

2. Beloved, looking at all of you here present, in this moment of intense communion in the Lord, my spirit is raised to contemplate the beauty and the richness of the ecclesial tradition that has been passed on to you and that today is entrusted to your zeal and your responsibility. From St. Prosdocimo, the first father of the

diocese, following a path of centuries, to the gigantic figure of St. Gregory Barbarigo, to more recent times, up to St. Pius X, an alumnus of your seminary, to Cardinal Elia Dalla Costa and Blessed Leopold, right to the pastors that guide you today: what a shining series of apostles! And I am thinking also of the blossoming of so many religious families and innumerable works that have arisen in your diocese in the cultural, educational and welfare fields.

You are justly proud and grateful for what the Spirit has accomplished throughout the centuries in your Church. But you know that the best way to appreciate a heritage is to cultivate and enrich it.

Truly you are called to develop this precious deposit at one of the most decisive turns in history. Today, in fact, we are experiencing the pains of a new cultural synthesis. A new civilization is slowly being formed. On the eve of the third Christian millennium, your mission meets with profound and rapid cultural, social, economic and political changes that have determined new guidelines and have modified mentalities, customs and sensitivities.

It is to this world, to the men of this era, that you are sent to proclaim the Good News. The men of this generation are those whom you must reunite in order to make them the pilgrim People of God in history.

3. This truly is a time in which, in order to preserve the great ecclesial tradition, it is necessary to renew it in fruitful continuity. Yours is an exalting mission, but also a demanding one. It requires a great soul, it requires an ardent spirit, it requires an impassioned heart in order to live at the height of the Church's mission in our era that offers such radical challenges to Christ and His Gospel. If mediocrity, tiredness and surrender could never be tolerated in the life of the Church, always called to renew herself, much less can it be so today.

Allow me in this matter to recall your tradition. In another era, the Council of Trent was put into effect in your diocese in a most exemplary way under the incentive of St. Gregory Barbarigo. From that courageous and far-sighted reform—centered on the seminary, the renewal of the spiritual and cultural life of the clergy, and directed principally to catechesis—there was born an ecclesial community that was distinguished by its commitment to Christian life.

Looking at the present, I am happy to note that, under the wise guidance first of Mons. Bortignon and now of Mons. Franceschi, you have dedicated yourselves and are committing yourselves with apostolic dynamism to the work of evangelization to form communities that will be authentically ecclesial. My wish and my prayer is that you continue with wisdom, fervor and unity of intentions in this effort.

A CONSECRATED PEOPLE

4. In order to fulfill this undertaking, you must have a clear vision of your identity and your mission. The constant and vital reference point is Jesus Christ, He whom the Father consecrated and, anointed by the Holy Spirit, sent into the world.

You are consecrated. Your whole being, down to its deepest fiber, is penetrated by the Holy Spirit who has conformed you to Christ to the glory of the Father. You—I refer particularly to the priests—are men of God, you are configured to Christ the Good Shepherd, not by virtue of a delegation or through the designation of the community, but through sacramental grace, and therefore through a creative intervention of God. Recognize and joyfully give witness to the fact of your consecration to God.

But you are at the same time sent to the world. Your consecration to God is not a separation from the world. The movement that brings you to give yourselves entirely to God brings you at the same time to the world. Authentic consecration, being a participation in that of Christ, is a true commitment to men within history, in the likeness of Christ, who shared man's condition in everything but sin.

From the vital synthesis of these two equally essential elements—consecration to God and service of man—arises the authentic personality of the priest and apostle that the Church desires today. It is the personality of a man who, in the likeness of Christ and the great apostles and prophets, stands alone on the mountain, penetrating with an eagle's eye the very depths of the mystery of God, and then coming down again bright and shining to bring God's message and grace to the furthest frontier of human activities and experiences.

Beloved friends, your vocation and your mission are truly exalting. But you also well understand how arduous it is and what ascetical route is required to maintain this balance. Truly, you must be in the world, but without being of the world (cf. Jn. 17:11, 14, 16). You must be incarnate in the life of today's men and share their environment, but at the same time you must be witnesses and dispensers of a life different from the earthly one (cf. PO 13).

In seminaries, in houses of formation, in your personal and communal meditations, in prayer meetings and in pastoral meetings, study this biblical and conciliar view of your identity and your mission.

In concluding this discussion, for which I give thanks to God, I entrust all of you—priests, religious, souls consecrated to the Lord, seminarians—to the motherly protection of Mary, Mother of the Church, that she may support and comfort you, while I bless all of you with sincere affection.

Witness Faith in Charity To Build a Society of Love

The meeting of the Holy Father with the women religious of the diocese of Albano on September 19, 1982, took place in the ancient cathedral. The Pope gave the following address to the sisters.

1. I am very happy—in the framework of my visit to the diocese of Albano—to meet with you, dear sisters, and I greet each and every one of you with affection.

Seeing you here in such great numbers, representing various religious institutes which carry out so many different activities, ranging from charitable and public assistance works to those of education, formation or general direction, my heart is filled with joy for the witness which you bear, not only within the framework of this local Church, but in the broader range to which your activity extends, especially with regard to the nearby diocese of Rome, to which Albano as a suburbicarian diocese is already linked with a bond of collaboration which dates back many centuries. I thank you therefore also for the work which you carry out with generous dedication for the benefit of the Roman diocese.

Addressing you, I would like to exhort you to live ever more fully—following the example of Mary, Mother of Jesus and of the Church—your vocation of being called to a service which the world and the ecclesial community need today more than ever.

CONTINUE THE WORK OF JESUS

2. When, after the annunciation of the angel, Mary set out toward the hill country and entered Zechariah's house, she was welcomed by Elizabeth with this greeting: "And blessed is she who trusted that the Lord's words to her would be fulfilled."

Whoever believes in the words of the Lord to the point of fulfillment thereby himself becomes a sign, a witness to Him who so loved men as to sacrifice His only-begotten Son for their salvation. God, who by His nature transcends the values of the visible world, sent His Son as man into the midst of the mass of other men, that His humanity might be the "image" of the invisible Father.

Dear sisters, it is the duty of the entire Church to continue the work of Jesus over the course of the centuries, to bring to each human being the gift of salvation. Still, how many, like you, have given themselves to bring to each human being the gift of salvation. Still, how many, like you, have given themselves to bring to each human being an irreversible consecration, how many have assumed the specific task of being "images" of God, to reveal through the manifestations of their lives Him who cannot be seen, but is, who loves men and, if they believe in Him, saves them.

This is the mission-witness of whoever, like Mary, believes in the fulfillment of the words of the Lord, meriting in addition, beginning here on earth, the divine promise of blessedness.

All persons consecrated to the Lord enter the category of living witnesses to the existence of this "Other," of a Reality so "different" from the reality verifiable by the senses; and their whole lives, individual and community, are committed to the final aim of recalling mankind— distracted by the temptations of material goods— to the reality of the supreme Good, to the attraction of values which are not visible, but are true and much higher.

Therefore, when the documents of the Council and the subsequent directives of the Church insist upon the need for the renewal of religious life, they intend above all to emphasize the need for a renewal of an "interior" nature to be realized in such a way that by eliminating the shadows of useless things or superstructures it may more easily become the transparency of God before the eyes of today's men.

The relevance of religious life in today's world, so violently shaken by raging currents of secularism and agnosticism, arises from the need for the "Transcendent," the "Other," from the imperative to witness in a more concretely credible manner the existence of values which are not ephemeral, from the urgency to render more authentic a life organized and lived in the personal possession of an ineffable Good, to make easier the invitation to raise one's eyes and heart beyond the closed confines of human horizons.

WITNESS LINKED TO A LIFE OF CHARITY

3. But if this type of witness is characteristic of all religious in general and forms the basis of their charism, to you sisters, as women, there falls, in a completely special way, the duty of a witness to God more linked to the practice of a life of charity. A duty that is both witness and sign of an evangelical faith which refers to a Love in whom you believe and which is fulfilled

in you and for which you have given up everything with joy and generosity, willing to expect
only meaning and fruitfulness for your lives
from the total donation to the Lord. God's love
which has chosen you, which has won you over,
one by one—this love you live as the greatest
value, having become your very life. And it is so
superabundant that you in turn are able to give
it to everyone: to children, to the aged, to the
sick, to the needy, to the healthy, to the great.
May the words of the decree *Perfectae caritatis*
be your guide and your program, dear religious:
"Those who profess the evangelical counsels
love and seek before all else that God who took
the initiative in loving us (cf. 1 Jn. 4:10); in
every circumstance they aim to develop a life
hidden with Christ in God (cf. Col. 3:3). Such
dedication gives rise and urgency to the love of
one's neighbor for the world's salvation and the
upbuilding of the Church" (no. 6).

The new society of love cannot be built in
the future if the quality of love does not change.
You are the privileged sign of this new love
destined to change the world. Your love, "different" from other loves, is the image of God's
love. And so your life, evangelically lived and
donated, becomes, through your sincere and
pure love for mankind, a convincing witness of
the love of the Father who is in heaven.

RETURN TO ORIGINAL SPIRIT

4. Here is your role in the Church, dear sisters, your most authentic vocation. And it is in this way that you, like Mary who believed in the word and the love of the Lord, contribute to the mission of Jesus to create the new world.

And that you may live and give Christ's charity more fully, the Church exhorts you to return to the authentic spirit of the founders, to their intentions and to wholesome traditions. Indeed, all of that constitutes the heritage of each community (PC 2).

Study, investigate, take advantage of the whole of your heritage which is also the heritage of the Church. Do not abandon it. Do not underestimate it. Do not waste it. Do not let yourselves be deceived by gusts of wind which pass or overturn.

May the divine Spirit, who chose your founders, enlightened them and constantly guided them through the increasing span of their lives to the point of their human and spiritual maturity, give you also the light to gather the wealth of this spirituality; and may He lead you to the achievement of the perfection of love. May Mary, intensely loved and invoked, help you to live your vocation day by day.

With these sentiments and these wishes I impart to you my heartfelt special apostolic blessing.

Bring the World the Consolation of God's Love and Mercy

On September 26, 1982, about seven hundred priests and four thousand sisters crowded the new cathedral in Brescia to hear the following message delivered by Pope John Paul II.

1. The meeting with you, dearest priests and religious of the Church in Brescia, renews in my mind the feeling of joy that I always experience when in the See of Peter or on pastoral journeys I speak with priests and consecrated souls and pray with them.

I thank the Lord who has guided my steps to you. I thank all of you and your revered bishop for such an affectionate welcome, but also for all you have done to make my visit to the Church and the people of Paul VI an occasion of grace for everyone. Know that you are very dear to me, that I follow you in your generous pastoral work, that I have looked forward to praying this moment that is so important for you and for me.

First of all, let us turn all our adoring thought and praise to our Lord Jesus Christ. We are gathered in His name. We have been called together by His love. We have been called by Him, one by one, personally, to follow Him. May our meeting be a hymn to Him, a hymn of our faith, our hope and our charity. For this present meeting let us recall what Paul VI said on September 29, 1963, when he opened the second session of the Council. He prayed over that extraordinary Catholic assembly: "May no other light be shed on this assembly except Christ, the light of the world; no other truth occupy our minds except the words of the Lord, our only Teacher; no other hope guide us but the desire to be absolutely faithful to Him; no other confidence sustain us except that which gives strength, through His word, to our desolate weakness."

"MY TRUE FATHER"

2. I experience a special feeling, a deep emotion, standing in the cathedral church where on May 29, 1920, "my true father," as I liked to call him in my first encyclical letter, received the imposition of hands from his most reverend bishop, Most Reverend Giacinto Gaggia, and became a priest forever. This is one of the places that I greatly desired to come to visit on my pilgrimage to the Church and the land of Paul VI.

Here, in this holy place, the young Giovanni Battista Montini gave himself completely to God. Here he sealed his mystical marriage to Christ, to whom he would remain faithful till death. Here he abandoned himself to the action of the Holy Spirit to receive from Him the grace that transforms and the gifts that would shine with wonderful splendor during his life. Here, under the glance of Mary most holy, to whom this cathedral is dedicated, he declared to her his filial devotion and his most tender love.

Dear, great, venerated Paul VI! May your memory be blessed. May the memory of your life and your holy death be preserved as a precious good. May your testimony not be lost.

I have come to this place of grace as a pilgrim. Here I stop, thoughtful and in prayer, adoring the will of God who chose Paul VI to guide the Church of Christ, and chose me to be his Successor and continue that "service of Peter," that is, the service of the merciful and salvific love of Christ for all mankind. In the communion of saints, in this place I unite my adoration with Paul VI's, renewing, in memory of him, my total obedience to Christ. Christ alone! Christ always!

OUR FUTURE PRIESTS

3. In this cathedral church, almost all of you, beloved priests of Brescia, also received Holy Orders. You also, therefore, along with me, are led to think at this moment of the mystery of grace that was accomplished in each one of you with the imposition of the bishop's hands, and of the providential plan to which, with your total giving to the Lord, on a day more or less distant, you were associated forever. For you also the

memory of Giovanni Battista Montini's ordination is reason to adore the divine will that has called you, as it did him, to the priesthood for service to the Church and to mankind. In you also the wonders wrought by grace, which in this church have been and are being realized, leave the heart full of wonder and in need of prayer.

Let us never forget the blessed day of our ordination! The memory of it is an inexhaustible fountain of spiritual energy. On that day we were called, and on that day our response was quick and joyous. Then we pronounced an irrevocable "yes." And that "yes" to God and to the Church we must repeat every day of our life, as though to renew that mystical experience of total giving. The life of Paul VI, a priest who came from your presbyterate, its boast and crown, can well be said to have been completely a "yes," after the example of the Son of God, who, as St. Paul writes, "was not alternately 'yes' and 'no'; he was never anything but 'yes'" (2 Cor. 1:19). In that "yes" to God, after the example of Christ, in memory of Paul VI, we must renew each day the grace of ordination and the generosity of our first giving.

PROVIDENTIAL PLAN

4. I cannot but think at this moment of the endless line of Brescian priests who have preceded you and your generation and who now

enjoy in paradise the reward prepared for good and faithful servants. You are the heirs and continuers of a marvelous tradition of priests who in fidelity to Christ and the Church were able to give life to the typical figure of priest: hard-working, genial, ready to sacrifice; obedient to the bishop; always near his people to share with them their life, their sorrows, their joys, their happy and sad experiences; always concerned that religion be yeast also for civil and social life.

Do not abandon this tradition. It continues to bear abundant fruit. Your seminary has not known the devastating crisis that unfortunately is evidenced elsewhere. The number of ordained each year is still good. I am deeply happy about this, and I thank you for all you do with a vocations apostolate that is well established and renewed at proper times. But do not forget that all this is due in decisive measure to a tradition that is a "precious treasure," as the same Paul VI said to you, which "brings us such good experience, example, wisdom, the peculiar character of a people, a custom, left in heritage from generation to generation" (Insegnamenti, vol. VIII, June 1970, p. 603).

Paul VI always remembered the priests who had educated him, and those whom he had known and admired in the exercise of an apostolate that had deeply rooted the Faith in your

people. How can those he often called on remain
silent? Mons. Mosè Tovini, Mons. Defendente
Salvetti, Mons. Giorgio Bazzani, Fr. Peppino
Tedeschi, Fr. Paolo Caresana, Fr. Ottorino
Mascolini, Mons. Pietro Raggi, Mons. Giovanni
Marcoli, Mons. Angelo Zammarchi, Fr. Battista
Zuaboni, and first among all of them, his friend
and teacher, Fr. Giulio Bevilacqua, the future
cardinal. They are names well known to you.
They are priests who like a constellation illumi-
nate your closest tradition, whose beneficent
influence you still feel. Paul VI was certainly
thinking of them when in his message to priests
at the end of the Year of Faith he wrote, "The
priest is *per se* the sign of Christ's love for
mankind and the witness of the total measure
with which the Church seeks to realize that love,
which reaches even to the cross" (*Insegnamenti*,
vol. VI, 1968, p. 315).

VOCATION TO SANCTITY

5. Dearest priests, and also you beloved
religious, how many times have we meditated on
our vocation or call, and each time we have had
reason to thank God and adore His immense
goodness. Allow me today to recall with you two
aspects of our vocation.

We are called above all to sanctity. The
Council has taught that all men are called to
sanctity, and that the universal vocation to

sanctity is constitutive of the Church. A marvelous doctrine that opens up the horizons of a Christianity that for everyone is a vocation to the fullness of life known in Christ. The priestly and religious vocations are therefore essentially a call to sanctity in the form that arises from the Sacrament of Orders or from the charism connected with the profession of the evangelical counsels.

Sanctity is intimacy with God; imitation of the poor, chaste and humble Christ; unreserved love for souls and giving for their true good; love for the Church which is holy and wants us to be holy, because such is the nature and mission that Christ has entrusted to her. The sanctity of a priest, of a man or woman religious, is nourished by prayer, a simple life, poverty, chastity preserved with all discretion, and above all by praise in reciting the Liturgy of the Hours and in the Eucharist.

Each one of you, however, must be holy also in order to help your brothers and sisters to follow their vocation to sanctity. In this sense as well, ours is a sacred ministry, that is, a gift that God has given us that we might place ourselves at the service of others. While it is true that all forms of sanctity refer to one another and mutually help one another, we must never forget that it falls upon priests to offer "to everyone a living witness of God" (LG 41).

TO BRING GOD'S MESSAGE

6. The other aspect of vocation that I wish to emphasize is our call to bring into the world, to all men and women, in every environment, the consolation of God's love and mercy. Today this consolation is more than ever necessary. Man has lost the ultimate and unifying meaning of life: for this reason he is insecure and is almost afraid of himself.

Even in an environment like yours, where work has produced a well-being that was unimaginable up to a generation ago, there unfortunately have blossomed, no less than elsewhere, the signs of loss and dissatisfaction: drugs, dissolute living, loneliness, violence. We must understand the man of today. We must love him and communicate to him, above all by our witness, the certainty that God loves him. We must be convinced that our vocation brings us to an irreplaceable service to man, who cannot live without knowing the reasons for life.

It is not easy when the environment seems to have become indifferent, polemic, perhaps hostile. But do not be afraid. Christ is with you, and you can have a daily renewed experience of this presence of His by intensely living the bonds of ecclesial communion. You have recently celebrated the Synod, and in its results and directions you can find wise directives for deepening the communion among you and for improving your pastoral collaboration.

Live your vocation generously, with that heart which has brought the Church in Brescia to assist, with generosity and by the assignment of many of you, the Churches that are suffering a lack of people totally consecrated to the cause of the kingdom.

With these wishes that come to my lips from the depths of my heart, I extend over you my hand of blessing, invoking for each and every one abundant gifts of grace that will fill your soul with spiritual consolations and constantly enrich your ministry with new fruits.

Experience of God Cannot Be Had Without Prayer

More than six thousand pilgrims, representing the great family of the Teresian Carmel of Italy, assembled on October 2, 1982, in the Paul VI Hall to meet John Paul II and to present to him the proposal to witness with their own lives to the great heritage of love and of fidelity of St. Teresa of Avila for the Church.

After an address of tribute by Cardinal Ballestrero, the Pope gave the following talk.

Dear brothers and sisters!

1. I greet you with special affection and tell you of my joy at meeting today with you, who

constitute the pilgrimage to Rome of the entire Teresian Carmel of Italy. I know that those of you here represent the male and female religious of the various Teresian Carmelite Congregations, the members of the Carmelite Third Order, the confraternities and the communities which gain inspiration from Carmel. Your presence in Italy is certainly significant and is distinguished among the many religious families for its typical evangelical witness to communal life, to prayer and to the spread of a solid spirituality, centered on contemplation. For all of this I thank the Lord, who always stimulates new energies in His holy Church, providing them with fruitful and stimulating vital forces. At the same time, you immediately have my assurance that I commend you all to the Lord and to the power of His grace so that the deepening of and the fidelity to your original vocation may remain alive and, indeed, grow in the Italian Carmel.

ROLE OF CONTEMPLATION

2. Our meeting today acquires its full meaning from the fact that it takes place not only close to the feast day of St. Teresa of Avila, but also, and above all, during the fourth centenary of her death. Therefore, this circumstance imposes upon our careful reflection the figure of

this woman, who was and remains a giant in the Church's history. Indeed, it is always important to discover again and to appreciate adequately, and above all to translate into our own lives, her special charism. And it is not difficult to recognize it in her works. This is what I wrote on October 2 of last year to the Superior General of the Order of Discalced Carmelites: "Teresa understood that her vocation and her task were to pray in the Church and with the Church, which is a community of prayer and which the Holy Spirit stimulates with Jesus and in Jesus to adore the Father in spirit and truth.... Therefore, when someone prays and lives for prayer and thus experiences the living God by giving himself over to Him, then it also happens that he more deeply perceives the reality of the Church, in which Christ continues His hidden presence through the work of grace; in addition, he feels the need for total fidelity toward the Bride of Christ." On the other hand, the experience of God cannot be had without prayer, and therefore St. Teresa in her *De via perfectionis* urgently invites us to dedicate ourselves to contemplation (cf. 18, 3). And what was the foundation of the various monasteries achieved by her if not the institution of many and fervid communities of prayer? (cf. *ibid.*, 21, 10)

3. Here, then, is a fundamental commitment which is asked today of Christians, and in

particular of you who are inspired by the Teresian doctrine: to give the witness of prayer. And here it is not a case of repeating to you today how much that is needed by mankind and the modern world, which risk losing the sense of transcendence because of their dizzying material and technological progress. It is necessary to make known that there always exists in every man a window open to the blue sky of supreme spiritual values, even though many keep it closed. It is necessary to invite the men of our time to open, rather to throw wide open, this window so that an abundance of fresh and uncontaminated air can blow in, giving new breath and therefore greater energy to the carrying out of their activities. In substance, this is precisely contemplation: to expose oneself and to let oneself be blown by the wind of the Spirit of God, as the Apostles were touched and transformed by it on the day of the first Pentecost: welcome its proddings in oneself and let oneself be conditioned by them. In this way it is felt that contemplation cannot, does not, isolate one from the social and cultural contexts of which one is a part; on the contrary, it gives the possibility of introducing into them new seeds of life, rich in renovative potential. On the other hand, as I recalled in my letter of last May 31 to the Discalced Sisters of the Carmelite Order, it was St. Teresa herself who expressed herself in this way: "It would truly be a tragedy if we could pray only during bits of solitude" *(Fondazioni* 5, 16).

CONFORMITY TO GOD'S WILL

4. Together with this fundamental dimension, there is another just as indispensable in Teresian spirituality. In fact, the saint makes the conformity to the will of God not only the basic motivation, but also a criterion for spiritual progress. And she even says that true perfection is not found in action or in contemplation, but in the conformity of our will to that of God. Here are her words: "The highest perfection is not found in interior sweetness, in great rapture, in visions, nor in the spirit of prophecy, but in the perfect conformity of our will to that of God" *(Fondazioni* 5, 10). But where the will of God is made flesh and is manifested is in Jesus Christ; therefore, whoever truly wants to achieve this perfection must follow Jesus and allow himself to be led by Him. It is in this way that religious life becomes a special form of *sequela Christi:* not only in the sense of a mere exterior imitation, but even more as an immersion in His mystery and almost as a personal fusion with Him; so that Teresa from being a disciple becomes a bride, in a full mystical union.

SPIRITUAL FRUITS

5. Dear brothers and sisters! At the conclusion of this Teresian centenary I hope that everyone will have gained from it many flavorful spiritual fruits. But that of a reconfirmed life of prayer should be common to all. In fact, from this spring others, like that of a greater commitment to the life of the Church, of a more intense study of the Word of God in order to comply always better with His will, of a more generous dedication to the coming and the spread of the kingdom of God, and also of a more enlightened and balanced perspective of the dignity of woman and her legitimate place in the Church and in society. Know, therefore, how to derive ever more profit from the intense spirituality of the great saint, whose inspiration you recall. And live your religious state with joy. For my part know that, as I have already assured you, I remember you to the Lord. The Church needs you and your witness. May all of you be most worthy of the hopes which rest in you.

And may you have my special apostolic blessing, which I impart from my heart, extending it to all the members of your Carmelite families, in pledge of abundant and fruitful heavenly graces.

Spread the Message of Jesus' Love Throughout the World

More than three thousand persons representing the Institute of the Sisters of Charity of Sts. Bartolomea Capitanio and Vincenza Gerosa assembled on October 23, 1982, in the Paul VI Hall to celebrate with the Pope the one hundred fiftieth anniversary of the foundation of the religious institute better known as the "Sisters of the Child Mary." With the religious, led by their Superior General, Mother Angela Maria Campanile, and their general council, there were also many of the laity present, among whom were students of the schools run by the institute in Italy.

After listening to the Superior General's greeting, the Holy Father delivered the following address.

Dear brothers and sisters!

1. It was with great joy that I granted the request made by you, dear religious of the Child Mary, to have a moment of communion on the occasion of your recent general chapter and the one hundred fiftieth anniversary of the foundation of your institute.

First of all, I wish to express my appreciation for the commitment and the vitality of your spiritual family. These realities arouse in my heart feelings of comfort and pleasure. They are confirmed by the large number of young people who ask to share your life; by the Catholic and universal spirit which permits you to carry out a fruitful apostolate in the most diverse environments of Europe, Asia, Africa and America, bringing to everyone, according to the individual needs of each one, the unique message of the love of our Lord Jesus Christ; by the praiseworthy expansion toward the south of the beloved country of your congregation's origin; by the sensitivity to the most pressing and urgent educational problems of our youth.

And I myself—as you well know—have experienced your generous dedication at the Gemelli Polyclinic. At that time you had desired an audience on the occasion of the last general chapter, but the Lord disposed that I should unexpectedly meet with your congregation— even though represented in your fellow sisters who assisted me—in a different way, perhaps more beautiful and more profound—in the charity of Christ lived and suffered.

KEEP ALIVE YOUR ENTHUSIASM

2. Now that the Lord has permitted all of us to meet, together with the laity and young people assisted by you, I most willingly wish to pause with you over some thoughts which may be for you support and encouragement to render your calling even stronger and more fruitful.

Following the work of your general chapter last year, you have just come from regaining the original spirit even in the changed conditions of our time. You realized that, despite such

changes, the intuition of your saintly foundresses is today more valid than ever and enjoys
the full approval of the Church. Keep alive the
enthusiasm which you have acquired during this
blessed event in your history. A "return to the
origins" in the Christian and religious life has
nothing of a conservative, quite impossible re-
vival of a past which is not over, but on the
contrary it has the capacity to rediscover in the
past those lively and gushing sources, those
strong and nourishing roots which are the ultimate motive for our deepest choices, our lives,
our present and future histories. It is the capacity to draw again upon that Eternal in our lives
which allows us to give meaning and life to all
the moments of our time, and to find in them the
"signs" of this Eternal. And who is this "Eternal"
if not Christ, "yesterday, today and always"
(Heb. 13:8)?

FOLLOW THE EXAMPLE
OF YOUR SAINTLY FOUNDRESSES

3. Therefore, nourish yourselves constantly
with the example of your saintly foundresses,
women like you, who knew how to achieve,
through the teaching of the Virgin Mary and
guided by that divine grace of which she is full,
the most beautiful ideals of the female religious
vocation. Nourish yourselves with their tenacity,
their faith, their courage, their humility, their

charity, always seeking to understand what they would do if they were alive today. Make your own the breadth and universality of their intentions which have permitted and are still permitting the congregation founded by them to give proof of evangelical and missionary openness toward various peoples and races. Do not tire of seeking, as you already do, with the mercy of Christ, the situations in greatest need of your care and your concern, especially in the area of young people who are lost and in search of love and ideals.

4. These are serious tasks, superhuman tasks. But the Lord is with you, have no fear. Always maintain the nobility of the original nature of your task. God has called you to this. He who considered you capable has the power to confirm you, to support you, to make you able to fulfill the mission that He has entrusted to you.

Always know how to gather and preserve the first roots of your being, which are the will of the Father, the grace of Christ, the power of the Spirit—the three Most Holy Persons, welcomed and working in the most pure heart of the Mother of God from the very first moment of her conception. May you also be, like the Child Mary, the blessed place, the temple of welcome of this infinite Mystery, so that shattered and disheartened humanity might find consolation, light and rest in this "place."

LIVE THE CHRISTIAN LIFE INTENSELY

5. And now my warm greeting to you, young people and children, students and parish groups, who have accompanied these dear religious who dedicate themselves to you with tireless care.

You, too, in circumstances proper to the laity, share in the faith and the spiritual enthusiasm of Sts. Bartolomea and Vincenza; you share it by receiving the spiritual service of your sisters and by seeking to imitate what was of inspiration in the two foundresses for the particular duties of your state in life. It would also be well for you to contemplate as models for your lives the shining and still relevant examples of those two young saint-friends who found the meaning and the flavor of their existence in love for Christ and for their brethren.

Know, therefore, how to look deeply into the reality that these sisters of yours and their great international family can represent for you: try to understand the deep significance of their dedication and the prime source from which they derive or can derive the strength and the greatness of this dedication. You also go to draw from this fount! Root yourselves too in these roots! Your hearts will expand, your strength will increase, your days will become more intensely filled with true and interior joy.

Live the Christian life intensely and may my blessing and the protection of the Child Mary accompany you.

A Life Hidden with Christ in God

November 1, 1982, the second day of the Holy Father's visit to Spain, began in Avila with a discourse to a large representation of Spanish cloistered nuns. It was held at the monastery of the Incarnation before the celebration of the Mass commemorating the conclusion of the fourth centenary of the death of St. Teresa of Avila. Following a brief address by the superior of the convent of the Incarnation, the Pope spoke as follows.

My dear sisters, cloistered religious of Spain,

1. While making this pilgrimage in the footsteps of St. Teresa of Jesus, I come with great satisfaction and joy to Avila. There are many "Teresian" places in this city, such as the monastery of San José, the first of the *palomarcicos* ("dove cotes") which she founded; and this monastery of the Incarnation, where St. Teresa took the habit of Carmel, made her religious profession, had her definitive "conversion," and lived her experience of total consecration to Christ. It can well be said that this is the sanctuary of the contemplative life, a place of

great mystical experiences, and the center from which radiate other monastic foundations.

I am pleased to meet here with you, cloistered Spanish nuns, who represent the various contemplative families which enrich the Church: Benedictines, Cistercians, Dominicans, Poor Clares, Capuchins, Religious of the Immaculate Conception, besides the Carmelites.

This occasion demonstrates how diverse paths and charisms of the Spirit are complementary in the Church. This is a unique experience for the cloistered convents and monasteries which have opened their doors so that these religious might come in pilgrimage to Avila, to give due honor, in company with the Pope, to St. Teresa, that exceptional woman, Doctor of the Church, yet nevertheless "totally enveloped in humility, penance and simplicity," as my Predecessor, Paul VI, said (Homily, October 4, 1970).

I thank God for such a sign of ecclesial union, and for my being able to fulfill this visit with you who are spread out before my eyes like one great Spanish cloister.

"YOUR LIFE IS HIDDEN WITH CHRIST IN GOD"

2. The contemplative life has occupied and will continue to occupy a place of honor in the Church. From the cloister, "your life is hidden

with Christ in God" (Col. 3:3); it is dedicated to prayer and to silence, to adoration and penance. Your consecrated life has its foundation in the gift received in Baptism and it continues to unfold. By the Sacrament of Baptism, God, who has chosen us in Christ, "before the foundation of the world so that we might be holy and immaculate before him in charity" (Eph. 1:4), has saved us from sin and has incorporated us in Christ and in His Church so that we might "live a new life" (Rom. 6:41).

That new life bears fruit in you through the radical following of Jesus Christ in virginity, obedience and poverty, and is the foundation of the contemplative life. Christ is the center of your life, the reason for your existence: "Good of all goods and my Jesus," as St. Teresa would sum it up (Libro de la Vida, 21, 5).

The experience of the cloister makes still more absolute this following of Christ until you are identified in your religious life with Christ: "Your life is Christ" (Moradas Quintas, 2, 4), said St. Teresa, making her own the exhortation of St. Paul (cf. Col. 3:3). For the religious this becoming one with Jesus constitutes the focal point of the consecrated life and the seal which identifies it as contemplative.

In silence, in the framework of a humble and obedient life, your vigilant waiting for the

Bridegroom is changed into a friendship which is pure and true: "I can relate to Him as a friend even though He is the Lord" *(Libro de la Vida,* 37, 5). This relationship, cultivated day and night, is prayer, the fundamental duty of the religious and an indispensable path for her identification with the Lord: "they begin to be servants of love...those who go by this path of prayer to Him who has loved us so" (cf. *Libro de la Vida,* 11, 1).

SACRIFICE OF PRAISE

3. The Church knows well that your silent and separate life in the exterior solitude of the cloister is a leaven for renewal and for the presence of the Spirit of Christ in the world. That is why the Council said that contemplative religious "occupy an eminent place in the Mystical Body of Christ.... In effect, they offer to God an outstanding sacrifice of praise, they illumine the People of God with the richest fruits of holiness, they animate it with their example, and they extend it by the mystery of their apostolic fecundity. Therefore, they are the honor of the Church and fountainhead of heavenly graces" (PC 7).

That apostolic fecundity of your life proceeds from the grace of Christ which absorbs and integrates the total oblation of your life in the cloister. The Lord has chosen you; and as He identifies you with His Paschal Mystery, He joins you with Him in the work that sanctifies the world. As branches grafted onto Christ, you can give much fruit (cf. Jn. 15:5) through the wonderful and mysterious reality of the communion of saints.

This should be your perspective of faith and ecclesial joy for every day and every action of yours: your prayer and meditation, your praise in the Divine Office; your life in your cell or at work; your mortifications, whether in your rules or voluntary; your sickness or suffering—all should be joined to the sacrifice of Christ. For Him, with Him and in Him, you will be an offering of praise and of sanctification for the world.

"So that you will not have any doubt in this respect," as I said to your sisters in the Carmel of Lisieux, "the Church, in the name of the same Christ, took possession one day of all of your capacity to live and to love. It was the day of your monastic profession. Renew it often! And, following the example of the saints, consecrate yourselves, immolate yourselves each time more, without pretending to know how God will use your cooperation" (Allocution to the Cloistered Religious, Lisieux, July 2, 1980).

Your life in the cloister, lived in full fidelity, does not separate you from the Church nor does it impede an effective apostolate. Recall the daughter of Teresa of Jesus, Therese of Lisieux, from her cloister so near to the missions and missionaries of the world. Like her, *may you be the love in the heart of the Church.*

COMMUNITIES OF PRAYER

4. Your virginal fecundity ought to be the life in the bosom of the universal Church and of your particular Churches. Your monasteries are communities of prayer in the midst of Christian communities, to which you offer support, encouragement and hope. They are sacred places and can be also centers of Christian encounter for those persons, especially the young, who are often searching for a simple and transparent life, in contrast to that offered to them by the consumer society.

The world needs, more than it even believes at times, your presence and your witness. It is necessary, therefore, effectively to demonstrate the authentic and absolute values of the Gospel to a world which often exalts the relative values of living, and which, choked off by an excessive estimation of what is material, of what is passing, of what does not know the joy of the Spirit, runs the risk of missing the meaning of what is divine.

You will do so by showing to the world the evangelizing message which sums up your life and which finds an echo in those words of Teresa of Jesus: "Disappear, then, worldly goods...even though I lose all things, God alone is enough" (*Poesias,* 30).

MONASTIC TRADITION

5. Today, as I look on so many cloistered religious, I cannot do less than think of the great Spanish monastic tradition, its influence on Spanish culture, customs and life. Is it not here that we find the basis of continual references to the moral strength and spirit of Spain?

Today the Pope invites you to continue cultivating your consecrated lives through a liturgical, biblical and spiritual renewal, following the norms of the Council. All of this requires a continuing spiritual formation, having a solid doctrinal, theological and cultural foundation. In this way you will be able to give the evangelizing response which so many young persons of our time seek, who today also approach your monasteries, attracted by a life of generous commitment to the Lord.

In this regard I call on the Christian communities and their pastors, reminding them of the irreplaceable importance which the contemplative life has in the Church. We all ought to value profoundly and appreciate the commitment of the contemplative souls to prayer, to praise, and to sacrifice.

You are very necessary for the Church. You are the prophets and living teachers of all: you are the *front line of the Church moving toward the kingdom.* Your attitudes before the realities of the world, which you contemplate in the light of the wisdom of the Spirit, enlighten us about the meaning of ultimate goods and make us feel the gratuity of the saving love of God. I exhort everyone, then, to strive to develop vocations among youth for the monastic life, with the certainty that these vocations enrich the whole life of the Church.

MAINTAIN FIDELITY

6. I must bring this visit to a close, even though it is so delightful for the Pope to be with you, faithful daughters of the Church. I conclude with a word of encouragement: Maintain your fidelity! Fidelity to Christ, to your contemplative vocation, to your founding charism.

Daughters of Carmel: may you be living images of your mother Teresa, of her spirituality and humanism. May you truly be, as she was and wanted to be called, and as I want her to be called, Teresa *of Jesus.*

All contemplative religious: may your founders and foundresses also be seen through you.

Live your ecclesial vocation with joy and pride; pray for one another and help one another; pray for religious vocations, for priests and for priestly vocations. And pray also for the fruitfulness of the ministry of the Successor of Peter who speaks to you. I know that you do, and I thank you sincerely.

I present you and your intentions to the Lord. I entrust you to the most holy Mother, model of contemplative souls, so that she will make you, from the cross and glory of her Son, a joyous gift to the Church.

Carry my cordial greetings to your sisters who have not been able to come to Avila. And to all of you I give my blessing with love in the name of Christ.

The Church Needs Your Witness and Apostolic Initiatives

The Holy Father brought his third day in Spain, November 2, 1982, to a close with a Liturgy of the Word service. It was held in the Church of Guadalupe where the Holy Father addressed male religious and members of male secular institutes.

Dear brothers,

1. This prayerful meeting on this afternoon in Madrid, nearly at the beginning of my apostolic pilgrimage through Spain, is a great joy for me. I am meeting with persons who are very

dear, whose existence, consecrated by the three evangelical vows, "belongs in an unquestionable way to the life and holiness of the Church" (LG 44).

You belong to that great living spring which has flowed with such generosity in the land of Spain, and which has made the evangelical seed abundantly fruitful among a multitude of peoples in all parts of the world. As religious belonging to families of long traditions, or of more recent origin, you have served all men of all races and of all languages with a magnanimous heart; and, now as then, you give strength to the living tree of the Church already two thousand years old.

I speak to you with the words of St. Paul: "I give thanks to God always for you because of the grace of God which was given you in Christ Jesus, that in every way you were enriched in him with all speech and all knowledge—even as the testimony to Christ was confirmed among you" (1 Cor. 1:4-6). The Pope also appreciates having the opportunity of this meeting which St. Teresa of Jesus has made possible for me because she has provided the desired occasion to speak to your heart.

You are a great treasure of spirituality and of apostolic initiatives in the bosom of the Church. On you depends in great measure the destiny of the Church.

This places a grave responsibility on your shoulders and requires that you have a profound awareness of the greatness of the vocation which you have received and of the necessity of continually making yourself equal to it. It means, in effect, to follow Christ and, with an affirmative response to the call which you have received, to serve the Church joyfully in holiness of life.

A GIFT TO THE CHURCH

2. Your vocation is a divine initiative; it is a gift given to you and at the same time a gift given to the Church. With confidence in the fidelity of the One who called you and in the strength given by the Spirit, you have placed yourselves at God's disposition by the vows of poverty, consecrated chastity, and obedience; and this not for a limited time, but for your entire life through an "irrevocable commitment." In faith you have pronounced a "yes" for everything and for always. Thus, in a society which frequently lacks the courage to make commitments, and in which many prefer in vain to live a life without bonds, you give testimony to a life of definitive commitments through a decision for God which embraces the whole of life.

You know how to love. The quality of a person can be measured by the class of his commitments. Therefore, it can joyfully be said that your liberty *has been freely bound to God* in a voluntary service, in a loving servitude. And in so doing, your humanity becomes mature. "Mature humanity means full use of the gift of freedom received from the Creator when He called to existence the man made 'in his image, after his likeness.' This gift finds its full realization in the unreserved giving of the whole of one's human person, in a spirit of the love of a spouse, to Christ and, with Christ, to all those to whom He sends men and women totally consecrated to Him in accordance with the evangelical counsels. This is the ideal of the religious life, which has been undertaken by the orders and congregations both ancient and recent, and by the secular institutes" (RH 21).

Always give thanks to God for the mysterious call which one day sounded in the depths of your hearts: "Follow me" (cf. Mt. 9:9; Jn. 1:45). "Sell what you possess and give to the poor, and you will have treasure in heaven; and come, follow me" (Mt. 19:21). This call and your response—which God Himself with His grace has placed in your will and on your lips—are found at the foundation of your personal journey; it is, never forget, the reason for your every action.

Revive now and again in prayer this personal encounter with the Lord who throughout your life continues to insist: "Follow me." I say to you with St. Paul: "The gifts and the call of God are irrevocable" (Rom. 11:29). God is faithful and He will never regret having chosen you.

And when in the daily ascetical struggle contrition and conversion are necessary, remember the parable of the prodigal son and the happiness of the father. "This joy indicates a good that has remained intact: even if he is a prodigal, a son does not cease to be truly his father's son; it also indicates a good that has been found again, which in the case of the prodigal son was his return to the truth about himself" (DM 6). Frequent the Sacrament of Penance, with the regularity counseled and indicated by your rules and constitutions.

Your vocation is an essential part of the deepest truth about yourselves and your destiny. "You did not choose me," says the Lord in words which are applicable to you, "but I chose you and appointed you that you should go and bear fruit and that your fruit should abide" (Jn. 15:16). God has chosen you!

ATTENTIVE LISTENING
TO THE MYSTERY OF GOD

3. Your commitment, perhaps made a long time ago, or even recently, ought to be strengthened always in the Lord. I ask you for a

renewed fidelity, one which will make love for Christ blaze in your hearts, make your self-giving more sacrificial and joyful, your service more humble, knowing—I quote to you the words of St. Teresa of Jesus—that "whoever truly begins to serve the Lord cannot give less than his own life" *(Way of Perfection,* 11, 2).

For this there is required attentive listening to the mystery of God, the daily entering into the love of Christ crucified, a committed cultivation of prayer under the sure guidance of the pure sources of Christian spirituality. Read assiduously the works of the great masters of the spirit. How many treasures of love and faith you have at hand in your beautiful language! And, especially, savor with faith and humility the Sacred Scriptures in order to reach the "sublime knowledge of Christ" (Phil. 3:8). Only in Him, through His Spirit, will you find the necessary strength to overcome the weakness now and again experienced.

Keep alive the certainty that yours is a divine vocation through a profound vision of faith nourished by prayer and the sacraments, especially by the holy mystery of the Eucharist, the source and apex of all authentic Christian living. Thus you will easily overcome all incertitude about your identity, and you will progress in fidelity, identifying yourselves with the Christ

of the beatitudes and witnessing, at the same
time, to the kingdom of God in the present
world.

This fidelity implies before all else, and as a
foundation of all else, a growing desire for
friendship with God, for a loving union with
Him. God wants the consecrated person—I say
this with St. John of the Cross—"to be such a
religious that he will have finished with everything and that all will be regarded as worthless
by him, because He Himself wants to be his
riches, his consolation and his delightful glory"
(Letter 9). Those desires for union with God will
make you experience the truth of the words of
the Lord: "My yoke is easy and my burden is
light" (Mt. 11:30). His yoke is love and His
burden is a burden of love. And that same love
will make sweet its weight.

FIDELITY TO LOVE

4. This dimension of total self-giving and of
permanent fidelity to love constitutes the basis
of your *witness before the world*. In fact, the
world seeks from you a sincere lifestyle and a
kind of work in keeping with what you really
are. The witness is not simply a teacher who
teaches what he has learned, but he is one who
lives and acts in conformity with a profound
experience of what he believes in.

As consecrated persons you are, above all, consecrated precisely by the profession and practice of the evangelical counsels; therefore, your life should offer an essentially evangelical witness. You must continually turn to Christ, the living Gospel, and reproduce Him in your life, in your way of thinking and of working.

One must recover confidence in the value and current importance of the evangelical counsels which have their origin in the words and example of Jesus Christ (cf. PC 1). You must be poor as Christ was poor; obedient, accepting this attitude of the heart of Christ, who came to redeem the world not by doing His own will but that of the Father who sent Him; living a perfect continence for the kingdom of heaven with all its consequences, as a sign and stimulus of charity and as a source of apostolic fruitfulness in the world. Today the world needs to see the living examples of those who, in leaving all, have embraced as an ideal the life of the evangelical counsels. It is the real sincerity in the radical following of Christ which will attract vocations to your institutes because youth is searching exactly for that evangelical radicalness.

The Gospel is definitive and does not pass away. Its criteria are for ever. You cannot "reread" the Gospel according to the times, conforming yourselves to whatever the world asks. On the contrary, you must read the signs of the times and the problems of the world today in the indefectible light of the Gospel (cf. Inaugural Discourse to the Assembly at Puebla, I, 4, 5).

WITNESS TO THE CHURCH

5. A decisive factor in every age in which the Church has had to undertake great changes and reforms has been the fidelity of the religious to her doctrine and norms. Today we live in one of those epochs in which it is necessary to offer the world the witness of your *fidelity to the Church*.

Christians have a right to expect the consecrated person to love the Church, to defend her, to strengthen her, and to enrich her with his support and obedience. That fidelity should not be merely external, but principally internal, deep, joyful and self-sacrificing. You have to avoid anything that might lead the faithful to believe that there exists in the Church a double Magisterium, the authentic one of the hierarchy and another of the theologians and thinkers; or that the norms of the Church have lost their force today.

Not a few of you are dedicated to the theological formation of the faithful, to the management of educational or relief centers, and some of you direct information and formation publications. Through all of these means seek to give an integral education, inculcating a profound respect and love for the Church and encouraging a true adherence to her Magisterium. Do not be bearers of doubts or of "ideologies," but rather of the "certainties" of faith. The true apostle and evangelizer, declared my Predecessor Paul VI, "will be a person who even at the price of personal renunciation and suffering always seeks the truth that he must transmit to others. He never betrays or hides truth out of a desire to please men, in order to astonish or to shock, nor for the sake of originality or a desire to make an impression. He does not refuse truth" (EN 78).

All of this must be kept especially in mind when you address religious women who attend your courses and listen to your conferences. Above all, you must faithfully transmit *the doctrine of the Church,* that doctrine which has been expressed in such rich documents as those of the Second Vatican Council. In the renewal of the consecrated life, which these new times call for, fidelity to the thought and to the norms of the Church must be safeguarded; more specifically, in the sphere of doctrine and in liturgical matters, avoid certain critical postures which are full of bitterness, which obscure the truth, and which disconcert the faithful and even consecrated persons themselves. Fidelity to the

Magisterium is not a brake put on proper investigation, but a necessary condition for the authentic progress of true doctrine.

ELEMENTS
OF TRUE COMMUNITY LIFE

6. *Community life* is an essential element, not of the consecrated life as such, but certainly of the religious form of that consecration. God has called religious to sanctify themselves and to work in community. Community life has its foundation not in human friendship, but in the vocation from God who has freely chosen you to form a new family, one whose finality is the fullness of charity and whose expression is the observance of the evangelical counsels.

Some of the elements of a true community life are: the superior who possesses authority (cf. OT 14), which he ought to exercise in an attitude of service; the rules and traditions which shape each religious family; and, finally, the Eucharist, which is the principle of every Christian community. In effect, when we partake of the Eucharist, we all eat the same body, we drink the same blood, and we receive the same Spirit. For this reason the center of community life cannot be other than Jesus in the Eucharist.

The community dimension ought to be present in your apostolic activity. The religious is not called to work as an isolated person or on his own account. Today, more than ever, it is necessary to live and work in unity; first, within each religious family, and then by collaborating with other consecrated persons and members of the Church. Union makes for strength. Furthermore, community life offers an extraordinary sphere for the sacrifice of oneself, for forgetting self and thinking of one's brother, embracing all in the love of Christ.

7. The consecrated person is one who, by renouncing the world and himself, completely devoted to God, and filled with God, returns to the world to work for the kingdom of God and for the Church.

The consecrated person is profoundly marked by this exclusive belonging to God, while having as the object of his service both mankind and the world. The life and activity of the consecrated person cannot be reduced to an earthly horizontalism, forgetful of his consecration to God and of his obligation to impregnate the world with God. In all of his activities this theological purpose must be present.

There exist within the Church diverse charisms, and consequently, diverse services, which are mutually complementary. It would not be just that religious should enter the sphere proper to seculars: the consecration of the world from within it (cf. LG 31; GS 43).

This does not mean that your religious consecration and your eminently religious ministries should not have a profound repercussion in the world and in the changing of its structures. If the hearts of men do not change, the structures of the world will not be able to change in any effective way (cf. EN 18). The ministry of religious is ordered principally to achieve the conversion of hearts to God, the creation of new men, and to point out those areas in which seculars, consecrated or simple Christians, can and ought to act to change the structures of the world.

To this end I wish to express my most profound esteem, accompanied with my cordial greeting to all members of secular institutes for men in Spain and to those who are present here. You have your own special form of consecration and your proper place within the Church. Nourished with a solid spirituality, be faithful to the call of Christ and of the Church, so that you may be effective instruments of transformation of the world from within.

Reflecting on the theme of the coming synod, I would like to invite you who are religious priests to value as one of your primary ministries the sacrament of confession. In the hearing of confessions and the forgiving of sins, you are effectively building up the Church, spreading over it the balm which heals the wounds of sin. If there is to be achieved in the Church a renewal of the Sacrament of Penance, it will be necessary that the religious priest dedicate himself with joy to this ministry.

MISSIONARY GENEROSITY

8. Before concluding, I want to remind you of a characteristic of Spanish religious which is perhaps undergoing a temporary eclipse and which it is necessary to restore in all its ancient splendor: I refer to the missionary generosity with which thousands of consecrated Spaniards have given their lives for the apostolic work of establishing the Church in lands not yet evangelized. Do not allow the ties of flesh and blood, nor the affection which you justly nourish for your homeland where you were born and learned to love Christ, to become bonds which curtail your liberty (cf. EN 69) and jeopardize the fullness of your surrender to the Lord and His Church. Always remember that the missionary spirit of a determinate portion of the Church is the exact measure of its vitality and authenticity.

DEVOTION TO MARY

9. Finally, always maintain a tender devotion to the holy Mother of God. Your piety for her should retain the simplicity of its first moments. May the Mother of Jesus, who is also our Mother, model of surrender to the Lord and

to His mission, accompany you, make sweet the cross for you, and bestow on you, in whatever circumstances of your life, that joy and unalterable peace which only the Lord can give. In pledge of this, I affectionately impart to you my cordial blessing.

The Missions Are Focused on the Family: Privileged Place for Proclaiming the Gospel

During the period from November 13 to 28, 1982, six hundred male missionaries and five hundred female missionaries visited the families of thirty-four Roman parishes, renewing the ancient tradition of "Missions to the People" in the Diocese of Rome. The initiative was that of the Franciscan congregations, directed by Fr. Francesco Gioia, but representatives of other orders and congregations dedicated to "Missions to the People" took part as well.

On November 15, 1982, the one thousand one hundred missionaries assembled in the Hall of Blessings in the Vatican for a meeting with the Holy Father.

After a short greeting by a representative of the Franciscans and of all the missionaries present, the Pope delivered the following speech.

Beloved brothers and sisters,

1. You are welcome in the house of the Pope, the Bishop of Rome!

With a heart full of joy I address my cordial greeting to you during this meeting which, because of the occasion on which it is taking place, is of very special importance. You have begun the city's "Mission to the People."

The Franciscan families in Italy could not have made a more pleasing gift to this diocese and to me personally on the occasion of the eighth centenary of the birth of St. Francis of Assisi. You are undertaking a pastoral work which, because of its broad extension and the methodology with which it is conducted, attracts the admiring attention of those who have at heart the Christian life of Rome. Useful directives for the evangelization of our local Church will surely result from your generous and brilliant initiatives.

FRANCISCAN FLAVOR

2. Your "gift" is a "prophetic gesture" of exquisite Franciscan flavor. A wonderful page in the history of your order and in the history of the Church comes to mind. When, in 1210, Saint Francis went to Innocent III for approval of his "way of life," the Pope remembered a dream he had had a few days earlier and, enlightened by the Holy Spirit, declared that it would be fulfilled precisely in St. Francis. In fact, he had dreamed that the Lateran Basilica was about to collapse and that a religious, small and abject, was propping it up with his shoulders so that it wouldn't fall. "Here," he thought, "is the one

who by deed and word will sustain the Church of Christ" (Tommaso da Celano, *Vita Seconda,* no. 17).

GIFT TO EVANGELIZATION

3. Your "gift" is part of the constant commitment to evangelization, which in recent years the Church, "sent by God to the people to be the 'universal sacrament of salvation'" (AG 1), has been carrying out with greater incisiveness and enthusiasm. Living and eloquent witnesses of this are, among other things, the third General Assembly of the Synod of Bishops (September 27—October 26, 1974), called to study the question of evangelization in the modern world; the fourth General Assembly of the same Synod of Bishops (October 1977), which dealt with the theme of catechesis directed above all to children and young people; the Apostolic Exhortation *Evangelii nuntiandi* of my venerated Predecessor Paul VI; and *Catechesi tradendae,* arising from the same pastoral concern.

Your initiative is a concrete witness of this missionary journey of the Church!

TRADITIONAL MISSIONS

4. The missions to the people, as you know, have beautifully glowing pages in the history of the Church, written by such gifted figures as St. Charles Borromeo, St. Ignatius Loyola, Saint

Vincent de Paul, St. Leonard of Port Maurice, St. Paul of the Cross, St. Gaspare of Buffalo, St. Alphonsus Liguori, Blessed Eugene De Mazenod and many other tireless apostles. The Church owes much to the orders and congregations which promote this type of evangelization.

The traditional missions, "often too quickly abandoned," as I observed in *Catechesi tradendae,* are in reality "irreplaceable for a periodic and vigorous renewal of Christian life; therefore, it is necessary to resume them and renew them" (no. 47), and "to repropose them with updated and adapted methods and criteria in the dioceses and parishes, in agreement with the local Churches" (Talk to the participants in the "Missions to the People for the 80's," *L'Osservatore Romano,* English Edition, March 16, 1981).

Nevertheless, one thing must be made clear: in the catechetical commitment it is not a question of adapting the Gospel to "the wisdom of this age" (cf. 1 Cor. 2:6). That is, it is not the analyses of reality, or the use of the social sciences, or the use of statistics, or the perfection of methods and organizational techniques— although useful means—which determine the contents of the Gospel received and professed. You must announce Jesus Christ, and "him crucified"! Your words are not based on "the persuasive force of 'wise' argumentation, but on the convincing power of the Spirit" (cf. 1 Cor. 2:2, 4). "The method and language used must truly be means for communicating the whole and not just a part of 'the words of eternal life' (Jn. 6:68) and the 'ways of life' (Acts 2:28)" (CT 31).

DOMESTIC CHURCH

5. A clear indication for an incisive pastoral action of the missions in our times comes above all from the choice of the family, the "domestic Church" (LG 11; AA 11), as a privileged place for proclaiming the Gospel. Paul VI noted in *Evangelii nuntiandi:* "the family, like the Church, ought to be a place where the Gospel is transmitted and from which the Gospel radiates. In a family which is conscious of this mission, all the members evangelize and are evangelized. The parents not only communicate the Gospel to their children, but from their children they can themselves receive the same Gospel as deeply lived by them. And such a family becomes the evangelizer of many other families, and of the neighborhood of which it forms part" (no. 71).

My beloved Diocese of Rome, the part of the Church to which you proclaim the Good News, is also making every effort for the family apostolate, as is attested by the "Unitary Diocesan Convention" held last October 18-20 on the theme "The Family, Sign and Instrument of Communion for the Community." In the face of the situation of many Christians today, tempted by agnosticism, by rationalism, by hedonism, by consumerism, by a sociological Christianity without dogmas and without objective morality, "the family's catechetical activity has a special character, which is in a sense irreplaceable" (CT 68).

The "sacred place" most suited to the psychology of modern man seems to be the home, as in apostolic times, when the Apostles "day after day, both in the temple and at home, never stopped teaching and proclaiming the good news of Jesus the Messiah" (Acts 5:42; cf. 12:12; 20:20). The roots of the "domestic Church" are to be sought precisely in the missionary activity of Jesus, who did not have His own home (cf. Mt. 8:20), but who often found Himself in homes in order to speak to His listeners about the Word of God (cf. Lk. 5:19; 7:36; 10:38-39; 19:9-10).

As the home remains the ideal place for safeguarding on the human level the dignity of the person from the intrusive and often sorrowful invasion of a consumeristic society, so the "domestic walls" can become a suitable place to revive the Faith. Within these walls the parents, aware of their common priesthood, must be for their children, by word and by example, "the first preachers of the Faith" (LG 11). "Family catechesis therefore precedes, accompanies and enriches all other forms of catechesis" (CT 68).

"On entering any house, first say, 'Peace be to this house.' If there is a peaceable man there, your peace will rest on him; if not, it will come back to you" (Lk. 10:5-6).

In the family atmosphere, a spontaneous "dialogue" may be begun which may start from a distant point and take unforeseen paths, but in the end always succeeds in establishing a confrontation with the Word of God, and is often transformed into fervent prayer when those present rediscover that they are the People of God, ready to again take part, renewed, in the parish community which "must remain the prime mover of catechesis...(and) a major point of reference for the Christian people, even for the nonpracticing" (CT 67). In the parish the synthesis, indispensable to salvation, takes place between evangelization and the sacraments: "Sacramental life is impoverished and very soon turns into hollow ritualism if it is not based on serious knowledge of the meaning of the sacraments, and catechesis becomes intellectualized if it fails to come alive in the sacramental practice" (CT 23).

SPREAD YOUR APOSTOLATE UNIVERSALLY

6. Beloved sons and daughters, do not stop only in homes, but spread your apostolate to

universal places, as the Lord wills: "Go into the whole world and proclaim the good news to all creation" (Mk. 16:15). Be aware that "the efforts to proclaim the Gospel to the people of today, who are buoyed up by hope but at the same time often oppressed by fear and distress, is a service rendered to the Christian community and also to the whole of humanity" (EN 1). Go to the "innumerable people who have been baptized but who live quite outside Christian life" *(ibid., no. 52)*! Go "to reveal Jesus Christ and His Gospel to those who do not know them" *(ibid., no. 51)*! Go, you who are "the brothers of the people," into the heart of the masses, toward that crowd, lost and exhausted "like sheep without a shepherd," for whom Jesus felt compassion (Mt. 9:36). Your Seraphic Father preached before the Pope, the Cardinals (I Celano, 73), the Saracens *(ibid., no. 55)*, and even to the birds *(ibid., nos. 58, 59)* and to the expanses of fields and flowers *(ibid., no. 81)* and invited all creatures to praise God.

Therefore, you too go to meet the men and women of our times! Do not wait for them to come to you! Strive to reach them yourselves! Love impels us to do this. Love must strive! *"Caritas Christi urget nos"* (2 Cor. 5:14). "The love of Christ impels us." The entire Church will be grateful to you!

LET FRANCISCAN JOY
ACCOMPANY YOUR MISSION

7. The words of Jesus: "Go into the whole world and proclaim the good news to all creation" (Mk. 16:15), which confer upon evangelization a limitless universality, find a wonderful response also in your spirituality, characterized by its itinerant nature.

St. Francis, impassioned imitator of Jesus, preferred evangelical wandering to the traditional structure of the religious life of his times, based upon the principle of *stabilitas loci* (stability). "Having obtained the investiture from the Pope, Francis, traveling to cities and villages, began to preach everywhere" *(Leggenda dei tre compagni,* 54; cf. I Celano, 62 and II Celano, 17) and sent out his brothers into the world as "pilgrims and strangers" *(Regola,* chapter IV; *Specchio di perfezione,* 10).

May your itinerant evangelization be distinguished by unmistakable "Franciscan joy." Remember how your Seraphic Father "always strove with burning passion to feel, outside prayer and the Divine Office, a continual interior and also exterior spiritual joy. He loved and appreciated the same thing also in his brothers, and indeed was always prompt to reproach them when he saw that they were sad or in a bad mood, since it does not suit a servant of God to show melancholy or a troubled countenance before his brother or others" *(Specchio di perfezione, 85-95).*

REJOICE IN THE LORD

In your preaching repeat the words of the Apostle: "Rejoice in the Lord always! I say it again: Rejoice! Everyone should see how unselfish you are" (Phil. 4:4, 5). Be witnesses to this with your behavior. May your lives be the "witness of your joy, a joy that can be read in your eyes and in your attitude as well as in your words; a joy which clearly manifests, to those who look at you, the awareness of possessing that 'hidden treasure,' that 'pearl of great value,' the purchase of which takes away all regret at having renounced everything in accordance with the evangelical counsel (cf. Mt. 13:44-45)" (Discourse of John Paul II to the religious of Rome, November 10, 1978).

"The society of technology has succeeded in multiplying pleasurable occasions, but it is not likely that it is able to provide joy, since joy is to be found elsewhere. It is spiritual. Money, comfort, health, material security, often are not lacking; nevertheless, boredom, melancholy and sadness unfortunately remain the portion of many," noted Paul VI in the Apostolic Exhortation *Gaudete in Domino,* I.

May the Virgin Mary, Mother of the Word, who saw Jesus "progress steadily in wisdom and age and grace before God and men" (Lk. 2:52), help you to "form Christ" (Gal. 4:19) in the souls of those whom you approach.

May my affectionate and intercessory blessing accompany you.

As Religious Educators You Participate in the Church's Mission To Preach and Teach

On November 16, 1982, the Holy Father celebrated Mass in the Matilde Chapel of the Apostolic Palace for about 150 School Sisters of Notre Dame who were then holding a general chapter in Rome. The congregation was founded in the diocese of Regensburg exactly 150 years ago and at the present time numbers some 8,000 sisters working in 31 countries.

Concelebrating with the Holy Father were Mons. Erwin Ender, Generalate Chaplain, and Fr. Martin, CMM, Procurator General of the Marianhill Missionaries. Before the Mass the Pope addressed the group in German, a translation of which follows.

Cordial greetings to you, dear sisters, on the occasion of today's Eucharistic celebration which takes place during your 17th General

Chapter. I am happy to join in your prayer of thanksgiving to God, the Giver of all good gifts, for the one hundred fifty years of existence of your congregation, the "Poor School Sisters of Notre Dame."

In the name of the Church, I also thank you and the many thousands of sisters throughout the world for your successful work in the service of Christian education among the young. As you face the growing insecurity of young people, may the great model and legacy of your foundress, Mother Theresa of Jesus Gerhardinger, be your challenge and your encouragement to work even more resolutely for the training of responsible Christians who are strong in their faith.

As religious women and Christian educators, you are also messengers of the Faith and participate in a special way in the Church's mission to preach and to teach. In this shared Eucharistic celebration, we ask God's special support and blessing for the work of the General Chapter as well as for your entire congregation, that you as school sisters may ever more effectively carry out your high calling.

Priest, Be What You Are and Have the Courage of Fidelity!

The last meeting of the Pope's first day in Sicily was with the clergy, male religious and seminarians in the Cathedral of Palermo on November 20, 1982.

Pope John Paul II delivered the following address to the secular and religious clergy of the archdiocese of Palermo and the dioceses of Sicily.

"My love to all of you!" (1 Cor. 16:24)
Beloved!

1. Entering this marvelous cathedral on the vigil of the Solemnity of our Lord Jesus Christ, King of the Universe, I address my affectionate greeting to the entire Holy Church of God that is in Palermo: to its zealous and courageous pastor, the revered Cardinal Salvatore Pappalardo, the successor of St. Mamilian, bishop and martyr; to the auxiliary bishops; to the priests; to the religious; to the seminarians; to the members of the diocesan pastoral council and to the representatives of the parish pastoral councils of the whole diocesan community. I address all the parts of the local Church, all directed toward working tirelessly to correspond, in the various pastoral and ecclesial activities, to the plan of God, who—as the liturgy of tomorrow's solemnity says—wants to renew all things in Christ

His Son, King of the Universe, so that every creature, freed from slavery to sin, may eternally serve and praise the Lord God (cf. Opening Prayer).

Yes, dear brothers, "My love to all of you." The Pope loves you, and has come among you borne by the deep impulse of the love "poured out in our hearts through the Holy Spirit who has been given to us" (Rom. 5:5).

In the days that have preceded this pilgrimage, I have reserved a special place in my prayers for you, priests of Palermo and Sicily. On the altar of the Lord and at the feet of the most holy Virgin I have placed the zeal that is woven through your daily work, the apostolic aspirations that animate you, the problems and difficulties that you encounter. Trying to identify myself in the situations in which you have been called to work for the sake of the kingdom of God, I have implored for you an abundance of light and strength.

Now I am sure that in receiving my embrace "in a holy kiss" (1 Pt. 5:14) your thoughts, excited and emotional, return to the dawn of your priesthood, to the kiss of peace that you received at that time from the ordaining bishop. Today I would like to make the perennial value and the personal and ecclesial significance of that gesture come alive for you again.

A DIVINE BEAUTY

2. The divine beauty of the priestly character!

The walls of this famous church celebrate it in eloquent language. And not so much through their relics of history and art as through the care and witness of the religious heritage that has permeated life and culture, and has survived the swift course of centuries.

Mother-Church, the cathedral: nest, cradle, fountain of the grace of the priesthood. The see of the episcopal office, that office to which falls the duty of externally ratifying the definitive utterance in the personal dialogue with God in response to His mysterious call. The sacred place of priestly firstfruits, center of their emanation, pole toward which thoughts and hearts incessantly flow, and where Gospel workers are assembled from the various areas of their work, protected by the bond of a pleasant and binding unity.

"The ministerial priest," states the Second Vatican Council, "by the sacred power he enjoys, molds and rules the priestly people. Acting in the Person of Christ, he brings about the Eucharistic Sacrifice, and offers it to God in the name of all the people" (LG 10).

In this statement we grasp the nucleus of the sacredness of the *essence,* of the intimate nature, of the priesthood, and at the same time its triple protection: God, Christ, the People of God. *God,* the Creator and Father, Supreme Beginning and End, He who by His spontaneous and prevenient initiative has loved us, has chosen and called us; *Christ,* the divine Mediator, the Eternal High Priest, who comes to be identified, in a certain sense, with our lowly persons, and entrusts to our poor lips the divine power of His Word; the *people,* also holy by virtue of the common priesthood, for which, however, they are indebted to the qualified and essentially different priestly service, which therefore takes on an ontological and irreplaceable necessity.

The conciliar texts and subsequent pontifical and synodal documents broaden the view of this priestly reality, emphasizing its essential union with the bishop and the expressions of its actual exercises, always stressing the mystical identification "in the person of Christ," which is our primary *raison d'être.*

Today I wish to confirm you, strengthen you, root you ever more deeply in that sacred reality which constitutes the essence of the priest. Like Jesus, I knock at the door of your hearts, beloved confreres, and with all the power of persuasion at my command I say to each one: priest, be what you are—without restrictions, without allusions, without compromise in the face of God and your conscience—first of all.

What you are by a free gift in the order of grace, be that in the stature of your personality, in your way of thinking and loving. Have always and clearly the courage of the truth of your priesthood. Let no shadow obscure the light that is within you. Let no detour distance you from the structure of your sacred character. Let no hint of death stop the circulation of life, of which you are the trustee.

How I wish that the entire priestly community would make its own the attestation of the Apostle: We are and we truly consider ourselves men of God and His co-workers! (cf. 1 Cor. 3:9)

SANCTITY OF LIVING

3. The courage of the sanctity of essence carries with it the courage of the sanctity of living.

It is a question of elementary consistency which, if it may encounter refusals and misunderstandings in the sectors of society, which still place total trust in conceptions inspired by materialism, is for us something entirely natural.

All of us in the Church are called to sanctity. The Council has accurately illustrated this in the splendid fifth chapter of *Lumen gentium,* dedicated to the "universal vocation to sanctity in the Church" (nos. 39-42).

Priests are obliged to it in a special way, "since they have been consecrated to God in a new way by the reception of Orders. They have become living instruments of Christ the Eternal Priest" (PO 12).

In the frailty of human nature the duty to clothe oneself with Christ, with the never-ending effort to realize His potentials in us, acquires a decisive value: "Put on the Lord Jesus Christ" (Rom. 13:14).

It is an arduous and painstaking work, which can have nothing but pale comparisons in earthly life, because Christ is *perfect God* and *perfect man.* The same Apostle Paul does not offer himself as an example except in how much he strives to imitate Christ: "Be imitators of me, as I am of Christ" (1 Cor. 4:16). The impressive band of fellow priests, whose heroic degree of virtue the Church has recognized, repeats the same appeal. And they offer spotless examples of ways and means, with which the tension of imitating the divine Model can be satisfied. The ways and means are very diverse, as diverse as the individuals and the eras. As though to confirm, as if there were need to, that no priest, under any circumstance, can consider himself even only partially excused from the heights of such a sublime call.

It implies the readiness not only to deny themselves and take up the cross, but also to immolate themselves, to make a continued Mass of their lives.

To shorten the distance on a difficult road, to smooth its roughness and overcome its obstacles, may Mary, Mother of the Eternal Priest and of all priests, watch over you with the sensitivity of her heart and the power of her intercession. Never tire of having recourse to her, revered and dear confreres. Pray with humble persistence and complete trust. The all-holy Virgin will hear your prayers. She will be the Morning Star which at every reawakening will cast an ever new light before your steps.

THE COURAGE OF FIDELITY

4. And so, finally, the courage of fidelity to the mission of salvation to which you have been called. It is an aspect of fidelity to God, to Christ, to the Church.

Many circumstances, certainly, are not favorable to the priestly mission in our times. My venerated Predecessor, Paul VI, in his homily for the final session of the Second Vatican Council on December 7, 1965, lamented with sorrowful clarity that our time "is turned to the kingdom of earth rather than to the kingdom of heaven," so that "the forgetfulness of God is made habitual and seems, wrongly, suggested by scientific progress," and "expressions of the spirit reach the heights of irradiation and desolation" (cf. *AAS,* 58, 1966, pp. 52ff.). A realistic diagnosis! The acute increase of violence and terrorism, the multiple underground net of delinquency, which widens in crimes and murders, are the alarming signs of the decadence of the religious sense and, with it, the level of civilization.

In this tragic reality, the Gospel must be proclaimed loudly and clearly. Therefore, the priestly minister is called to a work that does not know fatigue, to an apostolate harmonious in its ends and methods, to a total unity around his pastor, who discharges the primary responsibility in guiding the local Church. This unity will be expressed in the daily and capillary work in the diocesan and parochial see, in the branches of the specialized apostolate, and will have clear application in the fundamental commitment to promoting spiritual and moral values, which coincide with the authentic values of man. I very warmly recommend to you the catechesis of children and youth, a catechesis adapted to their potential and need, which will solidly direct them to truth, honesty, goodness. Be educators and formers of sure consciences, correct and illuminated, that the faithful may be well guided in their conscious choices in the moral realm.

The principal and incomparable support is the grace of God.

God follows with love the workers in His kingdom and makes the seed that they have sown germinate. He asks trust in His assistance and the courage of fidelity. In exchange, He will

make the talents entrusted to each one of us
bear fruit, "if"—as St. Gregory the Great, widely
read by the people of Sicily, recalled—"with our
life and our word we win the souls of our
brothers; if we strengthen weaknesses in supernatural love by preaching the joys of the kingdom of heaven; if by echoing the terrible threat
of the pains of hell we convert the evil and the
proud; if with no one we use an indulgence
incompatible with truth; if we maintain friendship with God and do not fear the hostility of
men" *(Epistolarum lib. II, Ep. 47; ad Domi-
nicum Episcopum: PL 77, 587).*

I would not want to fail to stress the
particular title with which I offer these reflections also to the beloved religious priests, a
predominant part of the presbyterate, involved
in the apostolate of guiding numerous parishes
in the archdiocese of Palermo and in the various
dioceses of Sicily, and represented in all the
organisms of ecclesial life at various levels. I am
also addressing the seminarians, who are preparing for the priesthood in prayer and study. I
address also to the laity committed to the apostolate a pressing invitation to give generously,
on the parochial and diocesan level, the precious
and irreplaceable contribution of their activity,
their time, their energies, their gifts of intelligence and culture, in order to share in spreading
the kingdom of Christ!

Beloved, I conclude by entrusting my best wishes to the words of the Apostle: "May the Lord increase you and make you overflow with love for one another and for all, even as our love does for you. May he strengthen your hearts, making them blameless and holy before God our Father" (1 Thes. 3:12-13).

With my affectionate apostolic blessing.

Let Your Works Attest to the Eminence of Religious Life

During his pastoral visit to Sicily, the Holy Father met with a group of sisters representing the women religious of Sicily on November 21, 1982, in the cathedral in Palermo. After introductory addresses by Cardinal Salvatore Pappalardo and one of the sisters, the Pope delivered the following message.

Beloved sisters,

1. Let us together thank the Lord for having allowed us this meeting in the place which more than any other represents the heart of the Sicilian Church, the cathedral of Palermo, and all the more on the Solemnity of Christ, the King of the Universe, the Alpha and the Omega (Rv. 1:8), He who from the height of the cross draws all things to Himself.

We are all called to work with perseverance and with the power of the Holy Spirit, that His kingship may be asserted and extend evermore into the hearts of men.

I have assembled here before my eyes, as a sole heart and a sole mind, the female religious soul of Sicily, present certainly in only small representation, but which brings to my thought and affection all the women religious of the island.

I cordially greet all of you: I would like to do this individually and have a word with each one, but this is clearly not possible. At least accept this sincere desire of mine. I am thinking of, and sending my greeting to, particularly those of you who are tried by suffering or by difficulties. I greet with deferential respect those sisters who have been spending themselves for a long time in the Lord's vineyard. I greet with admiration and satisfaction those who, in the vigor of their strength, generously give themselves in the service of God and their brethren. My greeting is meant to be hope and encouragement for the young who are probing and inspecting their path and their choice. I thank all of you, in the name of the universal Church whose shepherd I am, for your response to God's call, and for your will to continue to work and to suffer for the sake of the *kingdom of Christ*, to whom you want to be exclusively consecrated, for the purpose of offering to men, even here below, through your fraternal communion and the practice of works of charity, the "firstfruits" (cf. Rom. 8:23) of that kingdom of "justice, peace and joy in the Holy Spirit" (Rom. 12:17).

ILLUSTRIOUS VIRGINS AND MARTYRS

2. It is cause for great emotion for me to know you as the heiresses of a very ancient and glorious Christian tradition, such as the Sicilian Church's, rich right from the far-off beginnings in illustrious virgins and martyrs, mentioned in the Roman Canon of holy Mass itself, such as Agatha and Lucy. I mention also St. Rosalia, patroness of this beautiful city.

Your presence in this land, dear sisters, is worthy of the examples of the past. I know that you generously commit yourselves to the spiritual life and to the various forms of apostolate proper to you: in educational institutions, in socio-health services, in social services, in the apostolate, in fraternal and active collaboration with the pastors and priests, in the permanent search for a cultural deepening.

I am here among you to congratulate you for what you are already doing, to assure you of my total support in the initiatives of charity that you undertake or carry on, and to express to you my sincere participation in your sufferings and your difficulties. I am here above all to give you a word of encouragement and hope, to give new strength to your enthusiasm, to open new ways to you, to help you remove obstacles.

UNIQUE VALUE
OF A RELIGIOUS VOCATION

3. Most of all, the recommendation I would want to give you is this: preserve and foster a correct and lofty concept of religious life and consecration, according to what the Master always taught and still teaches. The Church today certainly encourages secular and "lay" forms of religious life which, if properly understood, are a great blessing for the People of God and for the world. The council made clear the dignity of the earthly values and the spirituality of the laity. Nevertheless, the same council, stressing the unique value of the religious vocation, takes care not to depreciate it with the distortion of a misunderstood secularism which forgets that the religious life achieves a perfection beyond baptismal consecration.

It certainly is not a matter of feeling, with vain presumption, that one is on a level higher than the simple laity, since, as St. Thomas already taught (Summa Theologica, II-II, 184, 4), not everyone who is in the "state of perfection" is necessarily "perfect." On the contrary, more is required of the religious, precisely because she has received more: greater humility, greater gratitude to God, greater awareness of her Christian duties, a greater commitment to charity, since "when much has been given a man, much will be required of him. Much more will be asked of a man to whom more has been entrusted" (Lk. 12:48).

The superiority of the religious state certainly does not depend on the Christian's relationship with the final end, which is the same for everyone: blessedness in God, attained in the sanctity and the perfection, which as such are superior to those deriving from baptismal consecration, sufficient to characterize the secular or married state. The religious, however, if she wants to attain that greater intimacy with Christ that characterizes her vocation, must make wise and persevering use of those special means that are at her disposal.

WORDS AND WORKS

4. This eminence of the religious life is attested to in words and above all in works: it is proven in deeds, that the world may see and believe.

For this reason, the concept and practice of religious life that one has are immediately and consequentially reflected in the activity that is carried out for the promotion of vocations, which I know you have discussed in your fifth regional convention.

The human heart instinctively seeks the best, that which is most elevated and is the loftiest: and if you do not give that "witness of the Transcendent," about which your cardinal archbishop spoke in a recent letter, that is, if you are not a "sign" of that which goes beyond this world and its perishability, and of that which is most greatly elevated—the divine and eschatological realities—you will not be able to exercise a true attraction to the religious life on young girls who today are searching for the Absolute.

Therefore, do not be afraid to propose to the world the ideal of a life that transcends the present. Remember that the profound meaning of your consecration is that of being, together with your confreres, the prefiguring signs of future mankind, of the "new man" and the "new woman" of the resurrection. Through your very behavior be living and concrete "proof" of the existence of God, of His goodness, of the kingdom of peace that He has promised us with His cross!

WOMEN IN THE CHURCH

5. In the second place, do not forget your specific role as women, within the Church and in the service of mankind. Help yourselves and help the Church, with the assistance of the Holy

Spirit and with your considered reflection, to put this role always in better light. As Mary most holy is an integral part of the divine plan of salvation, so the woman, especially if she is a religious, is the image of Mary, the Ideal of woman, and therefore she too has her own essential part in the salvation of mankind. Reproducing in herself, then, the Marian mystery, the woman religious is also an image of the Church, of which Mary, as the council says (cf. LG 63), is "figure" and "type."

If you are always convinced that this role you fulfill cannot be substituted, you will feel a wholesome and humble pride in it, without being tempted to desire other roles or functions that would pervert your features in the bosom of the Church.

AN ACTIVE CHARITY

6. But the choice of consecration according to the model of femininity cannot be an end in itself: it must be rooted on what is the truly fundamental value, that of active and generous charity, which made St. Paul say, "The love of Christ impels us" (2 Cor. 5:14).

I have had other opportunities to say that the profound essence of religious consecration is an act of love for Christ. Religious, male and female, are called to reproduce more closely to

Christ His same love. They are a "sign," as I have said, of resurrection. But they can be this only insofar as their love shines through their oblation and their spirit of sacrifice, like Christ's, "who gave himself for us as an offering to God, a gift of pleasing fragrance" (Eph. 5:2). They must be "dead to the world" (cf. Col. 2:20) in order to be "raised up in company with Christ" (Col. 3:1).

YOU ARE LIGHT AND SALT

You too, dear sisters, like the Apostles, are "the light of the world and the salt of the earth" (Mt. 9:50). You are the hope of the world. Your very existence disproves the bitter and some-times hypocritical fatalism of one who, believing injustices to be insuperable, is tempted to follow the examples of the violent and evildoers. It is not asked of you to overcome these injustices with severity and the force of interventions, which do not form part of your mission. Never-theless, you have weapons which, while they may be less conspicuous, are no less effective: the weapons of prayer, of persevering dedica-tion, of responsible obedience, of an educative and charitable mission, of purity of life, of the honest and sincere word, of Christian patience, full of a hope of immortality. These are the very weapons of Christ, "King of ages" (1 Tm. 1:17); Christ, the Lamb who is "King of kings" (cf.

Rv. 17:14). They are the weapons of His most holy Mother. They are the weapons that have conquered the world.

May my blessing accompany and sustain you.

Awareness of the Specific Nature of the Catholic School

On November 27, 1982, in the Paul VI Hall, John Paul II received in audience the scholastic communities of the Roman institutes of the Sisters of Nevers and "Maria Adelaide." In meeting with the Holy Father, the teaching staff, students and parents wished to celebrate important occasions for the two institutes. The first institution celebrates the third centenary of the founding of the religious congregation of the Sisters of Charity and Christian Instruction of Nevers, who have maintained a school in Rome since 1906. The second, "Maria Adelaide," run by the Society of the Daughters of the Heart of Mary, is celebrating the second centenary of its foundation.

Following the welcoming addresses by a student and by one of the parents, John Paul II delivered the following discourse.

Beloved brothers and sisters,

1. With this simple but very cordial greeting I address all of you, present here in such a large number. You form a group both diversified and homogeneous at the same time. You are a diversified group since you are made up of the religious of two different families, the

Sisters of Nevers and those of the "Maria Adelaide" Institute, then by the students who have the good fortune to attend the schools directed by you, and in addition, by their relatives, their teachers, as well as former students. But you also form a homogeneous unit since all of you in various measure gravitate around the complex and fascinating world of the school, with its problems and its promises, which brings you together in the same responsibilities and the same commitments. I therefore repeat to all of you my affectionate greeting while I openly express my joy in welcoming you into this house and addressing a word to you.

2. Above all I would like to address the well-deserving religious of the two institutes. I know that the Sisters of Charity and Christian Instruction of Nevers, whose institute has been present in Rome since 1906, are celebrating the third centenary of their foundation, and the occasion offers to our meeting a particular reason for being joyful. The Society of the Daughters of the Heart of Mary, who direct the "Maria Adelaide" Institute, operating in this city since 1882, is also close to the celebration of the second centenary of its foundation, and I also share your joy for this. Above all, together with you I thank the Lord, who has raised up for the Church from the generous land of France two important religious families who take care of the

human formation of children in its entirety, with self-denial and with competence, as is demonstrated by the very large school population which has confidence in the efforts and guarantees of seriousness offered by you.

In addition, I assure you of my special remembrance to the Lord, that as He has assisted you until now with munificent providence, He will continue in the future to ceaselessly shower His grace upon you. The very diocese of Rome also owes much to your activity, which is both educational and apostolic, and I wish to recognize this and express to you my gratitude as encouragement for you to continue in the future with ever greater dedication and effectiveness.

3. I wish to confirm my confidence in the parents, and I especially want to address all of you beloved students, who are receiving your basic formation in the two institutes mentioned, the formation which is so important to the rest of your lives. The range of the schools you attend is very great, from nursery school to high school, and this means from age three to eighteen— your best years! Each of your respective age groups deserves a separate comment. I would like to say to the students of the nursery schools that the Pope loves you very much, to those in the elementary schools that you must have great confidence in your teachers, to those in the middle schools that your dedication to your

studies can never be too much, and to those in the high schools that by studying hard you must seriously prepare yourselves for the duties of life in civil society and in the Church. But my great hope for a better future for the world rests equally in all of you. All of you, therefore, have a special place in my heart. And my exhortation applies to all of you: make yourselves worthy of the expectations of the adults who surround you. Human coexistence in the future will or will not be better, depending on what you yourselves will be. Therefore, all that you do today for your formation not only serves you as individuals, but certainly has or will have repercussions in society and therefore in the very way you make yourselves part of it and live in it. From this comes that sense of responsibility which you are called to cultivate even in these years with love and with determination. And on this is based that broad and profound concept of education which is characteristic of Christian orientation, inasmuch as it deals with the whole person, in his diverse and correlated parts, both physical and spiritual.

4. In this regard, I believe that it is necessary to reflect briefly with you on the nature and aims of the Catholic school. The Second Vatican Council has already wisely made a pronouncement on the subject: "It is...the distinctive purpose of the Catholic school to create for the

school community an atmosphere enlivened by the Gospel spirit of freedom and charity.... To help the adolescent in such a way that the development of his own personality will be matched by the growth of that new creation which he became in Baptism.... To relate all human culture eventually to the news of salvation, so that the light of faith will illumine the knowledge which students gradually gain of the world, of life, and of mankind" (GE 8). This implies a clear responsibility on the part of all the members of the school itself: first of all the teachers, but then necessarily also the students, and not last their parents. The Catholic school must distinguish itself from state schools not only on an organizational and methodological level, that is, by greater didactic seriousness, but also by a totally specific overall form which places both the subject matter and the person of the student in the wider framework of the divine plan of man, realized and proposed in Jesus Christ. Only in this way will it "contribute so substantially to fulfilling the mission of God's people, and further the dialogue between the Church and the family of man, to their mutual benefit" *(ibid.)* All this must come about without controversial opposition, but with the firm awareness of serving only the truth and with the clear prospect of offering the witness of a harmonious concept of man and of his promotion.

5. Beloved, in conclusion I want very much to give all of you my best wishes for the school year which began a short time ago. Be proud, each one respectively, of belonging to your institutes. Both enjoy much prestige, but their level depends upon each one of you, on your own collaboration, according to the place you occupy.

In any case, know that the Pope follows you, encourages you, and above all remembers you to the Lord. I am happy to commend you to Him since it is He who makes your toils fruitful and who crowns your successes. Always place in Him your confidence, your strength, your joy. Strive to aim for and achieve that higher wisdom which is the reward only of whoever lives in union with the Lord and sees things with His eyes. The Bible calls "blessed" that man (Prv. 1:13) who can truly say, "All good things together come to me in her company" (Wis. 7:11).

With this wish, which comes from my heart, I am happy to impart my intercessory apostolic blessing to all of you, which I also am happy to extend to the fellow religious of the sisters here present, to the teachers and to their colleagues, to the dear students and to their friends, to their parents and to all their relatives.

Humanize Hospital Work!

On December 17, 1982, John Paul II received in audience in the Consistory Hall the participants in the sixty-first general chapter of the Hospitaller Order of St. John of God (Fatebenefratelli). Sixty-eight religious representing the twenty-three provinces of the Fatebenefratelli spread throughout the world took part in the meeting.

At the beginning of the audience, the Prior General, Fr. Pierluigi Marchesi, delivered a devout welcoming address to the Holy Father expressing the affectionate greeting of the entire religious community, the sixty thousand sick assisted by them and their thirty thousand lay collaborators.

In response to the greeting, John Paul II delivered the following discourse.

Beloved brothers in Christ!

1. As the crowning point of your general chapter you desired a special meeting with the Pope to express concretely your fidelity and your devotion to the Church, and to have a word of encouragement for your religious life. I am very happy to welcome you, and while I extend my respectful greeting to those of you present and to all your confreres scattered throughout the world, I also express to you my gratitude for the work that your order carries out in the Church.

In the history of every order and every congregation the general chapter is always an event of great importance, since it not only permits casting a glance at the comprehensive progress of religious life according to its own constitutional charism, but above all it is an incentive to new spiritual fervor and to a more decisive consecration to its proper ideal: the past is meditated upon, the present is considered, and proposals are made for the future.

CARING FOR THE SICK
WITH LOVE AND COURAGE

Every general chapter must be considered a true grace of God, and consequently also a responsibility not only of the superiors, who must decide for the best, but also of the individual members. This is my heartfelt wish for you, religious of the Hospitaller Order of the *Fatebenefratelli,* which for more than four centuries has cared for the sick with supernatural love and total dedication. When on March 8, 1550, St. John of God's earthly life came to an end in the city of Granada, the small following of disciples who had joined him did not let die the work he had begun (so necessary during that age that unfortunately was insensitive to the lowly and the poor), and made the humble seed sown by the founder bear much fruit. After many historical events and many troubles of the times and of men, through difficulties and consolations, your order now numbers 191 houses,

1,721 religious, among whom are 116 priests. Thanks to the Lord for all the good that you have been able to do, and may you also be thanked and blessed, that you may continue caring for the sick with courage and with love.

A GREAT MISSION

2. Together with the deep satisfaction for the work carried out, I next address to you the exhortation to persevere in your ideal and always to improve in making hospital work and the medical profession more human and sensitive. You doubtlessly have a great mission to carry out which presupposes a "vocation" and is shown to be evermore valid and necessary.

It is a relevant mission, as it was relevant during the time of Renaissance humanism and, subsequently, during the era of illuminism. In fact, despite scientific progress and social development, pain remains, and disease, physical and moral suffering, misfortune remain; the race for well-being does not eliminate illness. The thirst for pleasure crashes into the unrelenting wall of pain! From this tragic and permanent contradiction is born the danger of putting aside those who suffer because illness becomes a burden, an irritation, an annoyance. Sometimes the sick are not considered as persons. And their care can become a "job." Therefore, you are called to

"humanize" sickness, to treat the sick as creatures of God, as brothers in Christ. You recall
the dramatic and moving scene of the passion, when Pilate, pointing to Jesus—wounded,
scourged, crowned with thorns—says to the
crowd: *"Ecce Homo!"* ("Look at the man!")
(Jn. 19:5) You, when you are in the hospitals, in
the infirmaries, in the pharmacies, see the
person who is suffering, bewildered and in pain,
in the light of faith, and say: *"Ecce Christus!"*
("Look at Christ!") It is without a doubt a
difficult and demanding mission which takes up
your whole life and each one of your days, spent
beside those who are suffering in the mystery of
sickness and misfortune. But it is also a consoling mission, because always, but especially during our age, men ask the "why" of pain and of
life itself, and many sometimes reach the abyss
of despair, finding neither comfort nor meaning.
You, by your presence and by your patient and
loving charity, make faith in Christ and in the
fatherhood of God credible; you open new
horizons and new perspectives; you are of spiritual help not only to the ill but also to the doctors
and hospital personnel. May you always be
where there is suffering man, following the
example of St. John of God! And, therefore,
given the present needs of society, I wish from
my heart for numerous vocations in your Hospitaller Order! May the Lord inspire many

young university students to give their lives and their abilities to the service of suffering mankind among the ranks of your consecrated ones.

MAINTAIN AN INTENSE UNION WITH CHRIST

3. In order to be in this way a true help and example to the sick and to the doctors, you essentially need to maintain an intense conversation with Christ, through personal and liturgical prayer, meditation, community life in understanding and mutual affection. May the General Chapter make itself the apostle and guarantor everywhere of a profound interior life—sole foundation and sole basis of every authentic apostolate.

I would like to conclude by offering for your consideration the significant person of Blessed Riccardo Pampuri, whom I personally had the honor and consolation to elevate to the glory of the altars in October of last year. An affable, sensitive, refined, sympathetic person, heroic in carrying out his duty as a doctor, he stated in a letter to his sister: "The greater I feel my inadequacy, the more deeply and completely I place my confidence in God"; and a short time before his death in Milan on May 1, 1930, at only thirty-three, he confided to his relatives: "I am content and happy to have always done the will of the Lord."

I want to wish such joy to you and to all the religious of Fatebenefratelli: may the joy of Christmas accompany you always, with the special protection of Mary most holy and with my apostolic blessing.

Love Is the Only Ideal of Your Total Consecration

In the new church of the Sanctuary of Greccio, the Holy Father met with the cloistered nuns of five monasteries of the diocese of Rieti during his pilgrimage there on January 2, 1983. The Pope addressed the following words to the more than one hundred religious.

Dearest sisters in the Lord!

1. On the joyous occasion of my visit to Greccio and in the mystic and gentle atmosphere of this locality, so intimately Franciscan and therefore Christian, I am very pleased to be able to address a particularly cordial greeting to you, cloistered religious, assembled here to meet me, remembering and imitating well the love and the veneration toward the Roman Pontiff that St. Francis always felt and taught.

I thank you, moved by your presence, so affectionate and expressive, and I also wish to renew for you the sentiments I feel for your total consecration to the contemplative life. This gift of yours to the Absolute, which requires a vocation and which uniquely has love as its ideal, is a typical way of being the Church, of living in the Church, of accomplishing the illuminating and saving mission of the Church. I intend to emphasize strongly the essential value of your presence in the providential plan of Redemption and to confirm you in the validity of your proposals of prayer and penance for the salvation of mankind.

SEEKING THE KINGDOM

2. Your ideal is first of all a "sign" for modern man who is troubled by thousands of problems and tormented by so many social and political events. Cloistered nuns, with their life of prayer and austerity, propose to the world the words of Jesus: "Seek out instead his kingship over you, and the rest will follow in turn" (Lk. 12:31); and the words of the letter to the Hebrews: "For here we have no lasting city; we are seeking the one which is to come" (13:14). Your real and concrete example therefore becomes an exhortation and an invitation to man to reenter himself, to leave superficiality, dissipation, the hunger for efficiency, to feel that in effect our heart—as St. Augustine said—is made for the Infinite, and it finds peace and rest only in Him. For you the words that St. Teresa of Jesus wrote in her auto-

biography are also of value: "After having seen the great vision of the Lord, there was no longer anyone who in comparison would seem so pleasing to me as to occupy my mind any longer..." *(Life,* 37, 4). It is the continual challenge which, with your choice, you throw down to the world.

3. Your total consecration to Love is also a warning for all Christians, for priests, religious, theologians, and leaders of the Church. Certainly, for the proclamation of the Gospel and for the salvation of souls, the various means of the apostolate are necessary: the search for new methods, creativity, novelty, active dynamism, updating ideas and proposals.... But personal prayer, the entreaty for light and strength for oneself and for the entire world, remains essential, just as the fundamental concern must always be the maintenance and the defense of the "deposit" of truth which Jesus, by being born in Bethlehem, revealed and then entrusted to the Church.

JUBILEE YEAR AT HAND

4. Being a few months away from the beginning of the commemorative Jubilee of Christ's Redemption, I entrust to you, dearest cloistered sisters, the successful outcome of this initiative, which I feel so necessary for reflection and conversion. I entrust to your prayers and to your spiritual fervor the entire Jubilee Year, and

in a particular way, two events which are near to my heart: the Italian National Eucharistic Congress and the Synod of Bishops on the theme "Reconciliation and Penance."

May the divine Savior always fill you with the holy joy which St. Francis of Assisi felt here at Greccio! May the holy Virgin and St. Joseph accompany you with their heavenly protection! And may my apostolic blessing, which I heartily impart to you, help you.

The Gospel Points Out the Way to Joy, Liberty, Peace, Love

On January 2, 1983, after spending the morning visiting Rieti, Pope John Paul II made a pilgrimage to Greccio for the conclusion of the celebrations of the eighth centenary of the birth of St. Francis of Assisi. The Holy Father met with the superiors of the four male Franciscan families. After greetings by Father John Vaughn, Minister General of the Friars Minor, and the Honorable Clelio Darida, Minister of Grace and Justice, the Pope delivered the following message.

Dear brothers and sisters,

1. My pilgrimage today to the Rieti Valley reaches its climax in this hermitage of Greccio,

located among the rough rocks and lonely woods, built with sacred stones and worn down by the prayerful presence of uninterrupted generations of pilgrims, in search of Franciscan peace and joy. Here I intend to conclude the solemn celebration of the eighth centenary of the birth of St. Francis of Assisi, which during the last year has aroused on all sides a very vast blossoming of timely initiatives, imparting new impulses to the life of the whole Church and especially to that of the most direct followers of the saint.

2. I thank, first of all, Minister Darida for his presence and for the words he addressed to me in the name of the Italian government, and I offer my thanks to the superior general of the order, who has expressed the sentiments of the Franciscan families.

I then direct my greetings to Cardinal Antonelli and to the Bishop of Rieti; moreover, I cordially greet all of you, inhabitants of Greccio, with special thought to the authorities and in particular to your mayor and your council, addressing to everyone the wish for *pace e bene*, repeated many times in this Holy Valley, "resonant with silence and serenity," from the very lips of the Assisian, who left on this earth an extraordinary imprint of his soul as a saint, as an apostle, and also as a legislator. Many centuries have passed, history has written many pages, but in the ancient convents of the Rieti Valley, the memories of the *Poverello,* who preached, prayed, did penance, and worked wonders here, remain alive.

The name of Greccio has passed into history since the Christmas of 1223, that is, since the time St. Francis built the first crib scene here, a mystical and popular insight that spread throughout the world, raising up leaven of Christian life. Greccio, the "Franciscan Bethlehem," addresses also to the man of today, who is adventurously projected into space, but also surrounded by an alarming emptiness of values and certainties, a message of salvation and of peace: The incarnate Word, the divine Child wants to reach and to convert the hearts of this generation also, inviting them to have the experience of an infinite Love, who came to put on our mortal flesh in order to be the fountain of pardon and new life.

St. Francis, moreover, loved the inhabitants of Greccio best for their poverty and simplicity, and had to say: "In no large city have I seen so many conversions as in this little town of Greccio." This is a valid testimonial to render even to the present and it concerns the practice of the virtues of frugality and of detachment, for the purpose of rediscovering a genuine dominion over things, and even more, to be near—in an opulent and thus often unjust society—those who suffer the greatest poverty. Thus they relive that brotherhood and that sense of universal solidarity, immanent to Franciscan spirituality and so necessary for mankind to rediscover, in genuine freedom, the capacity to raise, together with the entire created world, a song of praise and thanks to God.

With this I will end my greeting to you, the people of Greccio, with the words of the saint: "May every creature which is in the sky and on earth and in the sea...give God praise, glory, honor, and benediction, because He alone is omnipotent and admirable and glorious and holy and worthy of praise for ever and ever" (*Lett. ai Fedeli,* 10, FF 202).

3. And now, from this sanctuary which, in some way, symbolizes the double dimension—contemplative and apostolic—of the Franciscan vocation, I intend to address myself particularly to the most immediate followers of the saint of Assisi, to the friars of his four families, addressing to them a message at the conclusion of the centennial observance.

Jesus Christ, who was made flesh and died for man, is the center of the spirituality of Francis. The mysteries of the Incarnation and Redemption are everything for him who seeks to adhere to the Master with such exact imitation as to be opposed in this even by his own.

Omitting every symbolic language, the dominant note of medieval culture, his relationship with Christ is direct, prescinding from too many doctrinal mediations. For him, God is truly "He who is"; and Jesus, only-begotten Son of the Father and Son of Mary, is the Master and companion in the human adventure, which derives certainty and joy from His Redemption. Francis is in constant dialogue with Jesus Christ: he has Him intervene in the disputes on the Rule; he asks His advice, comfort, and help. One can say that he lives in His continuous presence. In this Franciscan style must be recognized a fountain of perennial evangelical authenticity, a school always turned towards the origin, the essence, the truth of Christian life.

Here come to mind the sober but incisive words of Thomas of Celano regarding the saint: "His highest aspiration, his dominant wish, his firmest will was to perfectly and always observe the holy Gospel and with complete vigilance, with total commitment, with all the impulse of his heart and soul, to imitate faithfully the doctrine and the examples of our Lord Jesus Christ" *(Vita Prima* 83; FF 466). This earned St. Francis the title of "the New Evangelist"; in fact, he placed the Gospel as the foundation of his legislation and of his spiritual life, and in its light he resolved all the problems which faced him along the way.

4. Dear brothers of the four great Franciscan families, you belong to distinct orders whose particular aims and special formative directions you share, but all together you form the great family of the sons of St. Francis, of those who intend to profess his charisma and his evangelical ideal. Always be more aware of living in a time similar in many respects to that of the saint and which urgently requires a witness of pure authenticity, of Christian radicalism, to be able to emerge from the suffocating spirals of a "horizontal humanism" which, because it is emptied of transcendental values from within, risks leading all society to self-destruction. It is time to bear witness to the Gospel with renewed, clear vigor and to preach it *sine glossa* (without any gloss).

The only way to attain joy, liberty, brotherly love and peace—goals yearned for even in the present generation—is the one pointed out by the Gospel. For all men it constitutes the way toward God, whose fatherhood it lets us rediscover; towards themselves, to rediscover their own dignity; towards their neighbor, to realize true brotherhood.

Joy, liberty, peace, and love, eminently Franciscan values, were not found combined in the saint through an exceptional or fortunate event, but as a result of a dramatic process which he implied in the expression "to do penance," the most frequent expression on his lips, and to which he compares that utterance of Jesus at the beginning of His preaching: "Reform your lives and believe in the gospel" (Mk. 1:15). He achieved joy through suffering, liberty through obedience, love for all creatures by his victory over his own selfishness. Everything in him was modeled on Christ crucified; even his radical poverty has the following of the Crucified as its ultimate motive. Thus Francis becomes the authentic sublime follower of Christ and shares with Him the power of universal attraction.

5. To a society like ours, reaching out to overcome suffering, slavery, violence and war, and at the same time thrown into anguish before the fearful futility of its efforts, it is necessary— after giving witness to the Gospel—to preach it with all meekness (cf. II *Reg.* 3; FF 85), but also with saintly courage in order to convince Christians that we do not become new men who taste joy, liberty and peace, without recognizing first of all the sin which is in us, in order to pass then through a true repentance, to achieve "fruits worthy of penance" (cf. Lk. 3:8).

The rejection of God, in fact, the atheism erected to a theoretical or practical system or simply lived in a consumer society, is at the root of every present evil, from the destruction of life yet incipient to all the social injustices, through the loss of the sense of all morality. The theme of penance, as a condition of a living experience of the Lord's merciful love, on all levels of the human condition, is a theme of extreme relevance in this anticipation of the Jubilee Year of the Redemption.

6. From this hermitage of Greccio, I repeat to you, who are called to be men of the Gospel like your father Francis, that it is necessary to approach the men of today, to embrace their vicissitudes, problems and sufferings, but first of all to convince them that in the Gospel is the sure way to salvation, and that every other way becomes inaccessible, unsure, insufficient, and often unproductive. Bring to this age of ours the Good News which is the announcement of hope, of reconciliation, of peace; make Christ live again in the hearts of anguished and oppressed men; be bearers and witnesses for everyone of the hope which does not disappoint. Like Francis, be the "heralds of the great King" (1 *Cel.* 16; FF 346).

A suitable opportunity to renew your mission as evangelizers and to intensify your valuable service to the Church is offered to you by the Jubilee Year, which we are about to celebrate in this final stage of the millennium, in order to rekindle in hearts the joyous and sure meaning of eternal Redemption, from which every good for mankind comes (1 Cor. 8:6).

Sons of St. Francis, confident in your docility as men of the Gospel, of whom the Spirit can freely make use for the building up of the kingdom; sure of your fidelity to the Successors of Innocent III and Honorius III, to whom your Seraphic Father had promised obedience even for all the future generations of the Friars Minor, I invoke for each one of you abundant graces of Franciscan and perfect joy and of a fruitful evangelical apostolate, while I impart to you my apostolic blessing.

Fidelity to Your Charism and to the People of God

On March 3, 1983, the Pope met with the Costa Rican priests, religious and seminarians in the metropolitan cathedral of San José. Although meeting with all these categories of collaborators of the Costa Rican bishops, the Holy Father intended to address the sisters in particular. After the introductory address by Sr. Marina Urena, the Holy Father gave the following talk.

Dear brothers and sisters,

1. I respond with deep gratitude to the affectionate welcome which you have given me in this metropolitan cathedral of San José, where I know that members of the clergy, men and women religious, and seminarians are united. You are the elect part of the Church in Costa

Rica, its most precious and necessary vital force. I express to you my most profound appreciation for your position and your activity. I encourage you to continue in your fidelity to the Lord without hesitation, with joy and optimism. I want to tell you that I pray for your needs and intentions, and I bless you with all my heart. In particular, I pray for the perseverance and the good training of the seminarians, who are the future ministers of the Church.

Since I will be speaking specifically to the priests in El Salvador and to the male religious in Guatemala, today I wish to address the sisters in particular.

Dear sisters consecrated to Jesus Christ and to His kingdom, I see you in the variety of the apostolic commitments of your various institutes and in their presence in the individual countries. Some of you are from the peoples of Central America, Belize or Haiti, where I am carrying out my apostolic visit; others come from the remaining nations of the American continent or have come from other continents. However, I know that all of you feel that you fit in well in these lands which are your spiritual homeland, and thus you give a dimension of universality to the holy Church.

I have the joy of perceiving that you are enthusiastic about the ideals of the Church which lives in these lands, because one of the characteristics of your presence must be the deep penetration into the particular Churches, where you provide a precious help to evangelization, enlivening the parish communities and ecclesial groups; you are authentic collaborators of your pastors, who appreciate your work, and of the faithful, who with their love and respect help you keep strong both your identity as consecrated people and your commitment to those in greatest need.

YOUR BOND WITH JESUS CHRIST, YOUR SPOUSE

2. During this meeting of faith, prayer, and spiritual communion with Peter's Successor, to whom your consecration binds you in affection, obedience and apostolic collaboration, my words are intended to bring you a message of joy and hope to confirm your identity and open up new ways to your ecclesial commitment, now strengthened by my presence among you.

As the Church has always done with regard to Christian virgins since the earliest days of Christianity, I would like to remind you of *your bond with Jesus Christ, your Lord and Spouse,* whose love and whose cause you have embraced at the same time.

You are disciples, because you have followed Him with the evangelical counsels of chastity, poverty and obedience. Along with

St. Paul, you can say: "For to me, 'life' means Christ" (Phil. 1:21), because you have personally consecrated yourselves to Him and you have been called to feel this communion of love fully, so as to be able to say that it is He who lives in you and who communicates true life to you. You have identified yourselves with His cause and for this reason, leaving everything behind, as the Apostles did, you have chosen to be witnesses of the values and obligations of the kingdom.

Your contribution is very precious to the Church. I know that you enthusiastically bear a good part of the burden of many parochial activities, of evangelization, of teaching, of works of mercy, of community inspiration, of ecclesial presence and witness among the poorest, the alienated, the needy; with the ability to make the Church present with an authentically maternal appearance, with sensitivity and affection, with wisdom and balance. In this dimension you feel the joy of the consecration through which you can say, paraphrasing the words of St. Paul: For me, "life" is being the Church.

YOU ARE THE VERY PRESENCE OF CHRIST'S LOVE

3. At a moment in history when woman is acquiring in society a place which belongs to her, with an advance which gives her dignity, I see

with satisfaction your qualified presence as messengers and witnesses of the Gospel. This movement which is now acquiring a greater form of expression in the pastoral community has its foundation and roots in the very attitude of the Teacher towards the women who followed Him (cf. Lk. 23:55); who enjoyed His friendship, like Martha and Mary of Bethany (cf. Jn. 12:1-8); and who were messengers of His resurrection, like Mary Magdalene (cf. Jn. 20:18); or who were invited to recognize Him as the Messiah, like the Samaritan woman (cf. Jn. 4:39).

The Church also entrusts to you the service of the Word and catechesis, education in the Faith, cultural and human advancement; she requires of you an adequate preparation, more intense every time, therefore, in biblical and dogmatic theology, liturgy, spirituality and science; and at the same time she recognizes with what enthusiasm and generosity you bring the Gospel among the poor, the most simple, the restless youth of this geographical area.

However, the Gospel is life, and in your heart, consecrated to Christ, you carry the instinct for life, for charity—which is the very life of God—which takes on flesh in the works of welfare and advancement. The Christians of these lands rightly claim your irreplaceable presence near the sickbed, in the school, in the various manifestations of the evangelical mercy proper to religious creativity. In these places, in these environments, you are the *very presence of the love of Christ,* you are the *face of the Church,* which shines before men through His love, translated into goodness, help, consolation, liberation and hope.

EVANGELICAL MISSION

4. Looking concretely at the situation of your peoples, the restlessness which agitates society, the fragile balance of peace, the commitments to promote justice—which is yet to be realized—I can do no less than reaffirm my confidence in your mission.

At this time, I would like to reecho the words of the Second Vatican Council in its message to women: "You, consecrated virgins, in a world where egoism and the search for pleasure would become law, be the guardians of purity, unselfishness, and piety...you to whom life is entrusted at this grave moment in history, it is for you to save the peace of the world" (Message to Women, nos. 8, 11).

Your mission could seem to be too exacting for you, too great for your abilities. In many cases, since you are near the people, you hold in your hands the education of children, young people and adults; by nature and evangelical mission, you must be sowers of peace and concord, of unity and fraternity; you can disengage the mechanisms of violence through an integral education and a promotion of man's authentic values; your consecrated life must be a challenge to egoism and oppression, a call to conversion, a factor of reconciliation among men.

ECCLESIAL AWARENESS

5. To be able duly to fulfill this mission, remain firm in the radical nature of your faith, in the love of Christ and in ecclesial awareness. Thus in the necessary preferential, but not exclusive, option in favor of the poor, you will avoid possible deviations and using the Gospel as a tool.

Do not let yourselves be deceived by party ideologies; do not succumb to the temptations of choices which one day could cost you the price of your freedom. Have confidence in your pastors and always be in communion with them. In this communion with the Church, in the identification with its guiding principles, you will find the norm for sure action. You, too, collaborate in being able to discern the reality upon which the light of the Gospel must fall. Almost through supernatural instinct, always direct the authenticity of your apostolic choices with the compass of the direction of the Church, composed of *sincere communion with its Magisterium,* in unity with its pastors.

With this guarantee, embrace the cause of the poor; be present where Christ suffers in His needy brothers; arrive with your generosity in places where only the love of Christ knows how to perceive the lack of a friendly presence. Be patient and generous in the hope of a better society, sowing the seed of a new humanity which builds rather than destroys, which transforms the negative into the positive, as an announcement of resurrection.

The Holy Spirit, who has stirred up the charism of religious life in the Church and has also stirred up the charism of each one of your institutes, will give you light and creativity so you will know how to incarnate it into new values and new situations, with the charge of evangelical newness which possesses every charism inspired by the Spirit, when it remains in ecclesial communion.

FIDELITY TO CHRIST

6. As points of this meeting for you to reflect on, I want to leave you some reasons for fidelity which will broaden your heart and give you the full joy of an authentic disciple of Jesus, even in the midst of persecution, lack of understanding, the apparent ineffectiveness of your apostolic efforts.

First of all, *fidelity to Christ,* through loving communion with Him through prayer, for which you must reserve long and frequent periods in your life, however much apostolic necessities may press upon you. Your prayer must seek the experience of Christ—followed, loved and served.

Fidelity also *to the Church*. Your consecration unites you to the Church in a special way (cf. LG 44); and in the perfect communion with her, with her mission, with her pastors and her faithful, you will find the full meaning of your religious life. As consecrated women, continue to be the honor of Mother Church.

Carry her sorrows and pains in your heart and in your life; be capable of reflecting at every moment the evangelical countenance of the Spouse of Christ.

Remain *united to the fidelity of your charism*. In this way the Church shows the beauty of the various evangelical expressions assumed by your founders and foundresses. In communion with your institutes, contribute a universal dimension in the particular Churches, a dimension which your religious families have. By living in communion with your sisters, you realize this first communion which assures the presence of Jesus in your midst and guarantees a community's apostolic fruitfulness (cf. PC 15).

Also live the communion between the various institutes, in order to offer the People of God the example of an evangelical unity which reflects the union of the Mystical Body, where all the charisms are united by the same Spirit.

Finally, be *faithful to your people, to your particular Churches,* to their efforts and to their hopes for justice and advancement, so that the Church may appear with you completely incarnate in the various nations, in their characteristics, in their values and traditions, in the ambiance of the one, holy and catholic Church.

CONTEMPLATIVE AND SECULAR INSTITUTES

7. All that I have wanted to entrust to you has its suitable application, respecting the kind of life proper to them, *to the religious of the contemplative life.* They live silently and give witness to the value of union with God, in penance and in total sacrifice. With their prayer they embrace the needs of the poor, they assume the concerns of the universal Church and of the particular communities. They are the tangible manifestation of the fact that your peoples have an authentic contemplative capacity.

The consecrated persons who in the midst of society live their commitment of animation, *according to the characteristics of the secular institutes,* also will be able to make their own the points I wanted to give, accenting their presence in society, particularly in the specific environments of their apostolate.

DEVOTION TO THE VIRGIN MARY

8. Dear sisters, I cannot leave you without showing you the perfect model of this fidelity which I have just asked of you: the Virgin Mary. In her you will find the first disciple and the first word of presence in the midst of her people. She is the expression of all the charisms and the Mother of all the consecrated.

Your peoples are devoted to our Lady and perceive in the preaching of the Gospel the mark of catholicity *when she is spoken of,* or its absence *if she is not spoken of.* By loving the Virgin, by speaking of her, you will enter into the heart of your people. Above all, however, if you know how to reflect her in your life, you will be these qualified messengers of the Gospel which the Church in Central America needs.

May she keep you faithful to the Gospel. I entrust you to her, so that with your word and your life you may be able to say to everyone, only and always: Jesus Christ is the Lord. Amen.

Continue Generously in Your Work

On March 6, 1983, in San Salvador's "Marcelino Champagnat" Gymnasium, the Pope met with the priests, religious and seminarians of El Salvador to celebrate the Liturgy of the Word, during which John Paul II gave the assembly the following homily.

Dear brothers and sisters,

1. At this meeting dedicated to the priests of El Salvador and all the Central American area—a meeting which takes place in the frame of the "Beato Marcelino Champagnat Educational Center," there are also El Salvadoran brothers, sisters and seminarians present who wanted to come to see the Pope.

Although I have already addressed the sectors of consecrated life of other nearby nations—or will do so within the next few days—I greet all of you very cordially and I express my deep esteem and my thanks for your most important ecclesial work. I ask the Lord to give you strength, encouragement and hope to continue generously in your work. I bless you all with great affection....

At this point, the Holy Father addressed the priests. In concluding, he said:

As Peter's Successor, I want to assure you of the love and support of the universal Church, which looks to you with the hope of seeing peace confirmed in your nations, reconciled in justice with all the children of the Salvadoran and Central American people. I entrust you to our Lady, Queen of Peace, the title by which you invoke her in this land. She is the Mother of all, the example of a commitment to God's will and to the history of her people. I ask her to help you in your ministry of reconciliation, in your mission of evangelization, to be, with your commitment, authentic disciples of Christ. Amen.

Complete Fidelity to the Gospel and the Spirit of the Founders

On March 7, 1983, in the National Expiatory Sanctuary of the Sacred Heart, annexed to St. John Bosco College in the city of Guatemala, the Pope met with the priests and religious of Guatemala. Addressing the male religious in particular, the Holy Father gave the following discourse.

Dear brothers and sisters,

1. Today this National Expiatory Sanctuary of the Sacred Heart is the meeting place of the Pope with the religious of the whole geo-

graphical area which I am visiting these days. However, there are also priests, sisters and seminarians here from Guatemala. These are the central sectors of Church life in this nation. I therefore address to everyone my thought full of esteem, my most affectionate and grateful greeting, my word of encouragement for your dedication to Christ and for your ecclesial vocation, along with my special blessing.

Dear brothers, I have saved a special meeting to be able to be with you. First of all I wish to express my gratitude to you for your ecclesial presence in this land, where you are at the service of particular Churches.

Many of you are sons of this land. Others have come from near and far. But all of you are urged on by the same love for these peoples from whom you have also received much, through their simple faith, their sincere life of piety, their generous affection.

The special situations which these people are living and their very closeness favor an intense communion between you and them. For my part, I would like to encourage the efforts for ecclesial communion, for collaboration with your bishops, for the search for your better insertion into the ecclesial life in these sister nations, in order to be, as religious, a sign of communion and reconciliation.

ALL IN PERFECT CHARITY

2. You are committed to making the supreme rule of your life the following of Christ according to the Gospel (cf. PC 2, a). Allow me to remind you of this: you must be the *specialists of Jesus' Gospel,* vitally identified with His words and with His example.

The distinctive mark of religious life in the Church must consist in maintaining the purity of the Gospel not only in the vows which are characteristic of your consecration, but above all in perfect charity towards God and your neighbor, which is the essence of the Gospel; in the beatitudes which affirm their originality with respect to the mentality of the world, and in these specific manifestations of the Gospel which are the charisms of your founders.

Fidelity to the Gospel assures the vitality of religious life, of which my Predecessor, Paul VI, opportunely spoke: "Thanks to their consecration they are eminently willing and free to leave everything and to go and proclaim the Gospel even to the ends of the earth. They are enterprising, and their apostolate is often marked by an originality, by a genius that demands admiration. They are generous: often they are found at the outposts of the mission, and they take the greatest risks for their health and their very lives" (EN 69).

Thus, be faithful to the perennial youthfulness of the Gospel which Christ has entrusted to the life-giving action of the Holy Spirit and His charisms (cf. LG 4).

THE GOSPEL IS JESUS CHRIST

3. The awareness of your consecration to Christ in the Church is a guarantee of fidelity. Yes, one does not embrace the Gospel merely as a just cause or as a utopia. *The Gospel is a Person:* it is Jesus Christ, the Lord. He who "was handed over to death for our sins and raised up for our justification" (Rom. 4:25). He has called you to follow Him to the cross; and one cannot follow Him with fidelity, if one does not first of all love Him deeply. For this, religious consecration vitally unites you to Jesus Christ and becomes a bond of love which requires friendship, communion with Him, nourished by the sacraments—especially the Eucharist and Penance—by the meditation of His Word, by prayer, by identification with His very sentiments.

Embracing the counsels for the kingdom of heaven means serving the kingdom of Christ, which is the Church. Thus, religious life directly signifies a bond "with the Church and her mystery" and is developed for her benefit (cf. LG 44).

However, always remember that in Christ's plan one cannot conceive of religious life as being independent of the bishops, or as indifferent to the hierarchy; because there cannot be charisms except in the service of communion and the unity of the body of Christ (cf. 1 Cor. 12:4-11). Consequently, not only must any type of apostolate or magisterium parallel to that of the bishops be excluded, but it must also be emphasized that it is the very nature of religious life by all means to increase communion, to promote it in the faithful, to solidify it where it loses vigor. This has been the characteristic which all the founders have evidenced.

"FAMILY SPIRIT"

4. Yes, dear religious, I know that by mentioning the founders of your institutes you feel within yourselves this type of "family spirit" which identifies you with them and with your brothers. It is the feeling that the charism is something alive, vital, animated by the Spirit, made flesh and blood in your experience of formation and of religious life.

You are the trustees and the ones responsible for this "experience of the Spirit" which is the charism of the founders. You are the sons of these "men of the Spirit," their living presence in the Church of today, in this land.

The faithful recognize you by your union with these saints. And these same faithful expect you to be and act as true sons of these saints—united with God, and through Him committed to promoting justice, to elevating man culturally and humanly, in the cause of the poor. Remember, however, that in working first of all on their behalf, you must not exclude anyone.

5. One cannot think of the founders' work without seeing in them the incarnation of the Gospel, as extending through the geography and the history of the Church.

From this clear evangelical perspective, they offer you the example of a presence alongside the people and their suffering. Without allowing themselves to be carried away by temptations or currents of a political nature, they are a valid example for you even today; because, as I said to the priests and religious of Mexico, "you are not social directors, political leaders or officials of a temporal power." Your founders were able to embody Christ's charity effectively, not only with words, but with generous gestures, with services and institutions. In this way they have left a trace in history, they have made culture, they have sown truth and life, from which we continue to gather the fruits.

This remembrance, my dear brothers, allows me to ask you for *complete fidelity to the Gospel and to the spirit of your founders,* so that, today as yesterday, religious might live in perfect charity with a profound sense of faith, with generous dedication to the task of evangelization, which is the first task entrusted to you, without ever permitting manipulating ideological motivations to replace your evangelical identity or inspire your action, which *must always be that of men of the Church.* Starting from this clear conviction, also work with enthusiasm for man's dignity.

6. With this evangelical charity which, as your founders demonstrated, *is the most concrete and complete of any human ideology,* and which concerns itself with man in his spiritual, material and social dimension, I exhort you to renew the fervor of your life and your works. The children of the Church who live in this land ask this of you. They want to feel that you are near, *first of all as spiritual guides,* as specialists in Christ's charity, which urges one to love others and to commit himself with all his strength for man's justice and dignity.

Before your eyes, there are the tasks of evangelization and of the formation of the Christian communities. With your generosity, make up for the lack of vocations or for distances between ecclesial groups, so much more in need of your presence the farther away they are from the great urban or rural centers. Also educate popular piety so that it might bear the fruits of this simple and generous faith which animates it.

Continue to train a mature laity that will responsibly assume its place in the Church and give itself with clear-sightedness to the mission which belongs to it: to transform civil society from within. And give to the poor first of all—as I indicated to you before—the bread of the Word, the defense of their rights when they are oppressed, promotion, integral education and every possible assistance which will help them live with dignity. In this, follow the indications of the Church's social teaching just as she proposes it and have confidence in this social teaching of the Church. The times in which we live give us historic proof of its validity.

7. I ask you to give particular attention to the youth. Your young people are generous; they expect the sympathy and the help of those who have received from their founders a special mission of Christian, cultural, working, human education. Therefore, may your presence not be missing from education centers of all levels, where the values which inform those who one day will rule the destinies of your peoples are determined.

In this important field, as in all your apostolic activity—as an individual, as a religious community or institute or as associates in the widest sense—faithfully follow the directions of your bishops and demonstrate your love for the Church with the respect, communion and collaboration which they deserve as the pastors of the particular Churches. Through them you will be united with the visible head of the Church, to whom Christ entrusted the charism of His brothers in the Faith. Also be generous in helping and collaborating with the diocesan clergy.

With these requests the Pope renews his confidence in you; he encourages you toward a fruitful growth in your charisms and towards an enthusiastic dedication which must be the distinctive sign of your radical option for Christ, for the Church, and for man—our brother.

EVANGELICAL BROTHERHOOD

8. Do you want a key to apostolic fruitfulness? Live unity, the source of a great apostolic strength (cf. PC 15). In fraternal communion there is, in fact, the guarantee of the presence of Christ and of His Spirit, to put your responsibilities into practice, following the rules of your institutes.

The Church needs the example and the witness of religious who live *evangelical brotherhood*. The groups and communities await encouragement based on your experience of the communion of goods, of common prayer, of reciprocal help.

The young people who knock on your doors want to find an ecclesial life that is characterized by the *fervor of prayer,* by the *family spirit,* by *apostolic commitment.* These young people are sensitive to community values and expect to find them in religious life. Be capable of welcoming them and guiding them, carefully cultivating new vocations, the search for whom must be one of your principal concerns.

9. My dear brothers: all of your institutes profess a special love for the Virgin Mary; under various titles and with various emphases, the Virgin appears as the reflection of a living Gospel, and therefore as the Mother of all religious. In her name I ask that you be able to maintain mutual appreciation for your charisms and collaboration in your work of the apostolate.

I entrust you to her, to preserve and increase your fidelity to Christ and to the Church. I ask her for the flowering and perseverance of abundant vocations for your religious families. The Church of this geographical area needs your presence, to live this fullness of the Gospel which belongs to religious life. May Mary, the Virgin who is faithful and solicitous about man's needs, grant you this grace. Amen.

The Charity of the Revealed Truth Is the Vital Sap of Your Mission

On the occasion of the beginning of the centenary year of the birth of Don Giacomo Alberione, founder of the Society of St. Paul, on March 21, 1983, in the Clementine Hall, the Holy Father received in audience numerous male and female religious members of the various parts of the great Pauline Family led by the Superior General of the Society of St. Paul, Don Renato Perino. The Holy Father delivered the following discourse.

1. To welcome the Pauline Family by receiving you, beloved brothers and sisters, is a cause of great joy for me. And not only because of the present circumstances, although so significant, which have inspired this meeting— namely, to commemorate the beginning of the centenary of the birth of your founder, Don Giacomo Alberione, and to celebrate the twenty-fifth or the fiftieth anniversaries of the ordinations or the religious professions of many of his sons and daughters—but also because of a general reason: a more direct contact and a more intense communion *in fide et caritate* between each one of you and the Successor of Peter.

The Paulines are now present throughout the world with their multiple works, with their apostolic initiatives, with the creativity of their achievements in the vast sector of the social communications media. You are a living part of the Church, and it is therefore natural that you not only be recognized, but followed and encouraged in your fruitful ministry by the one in the Church who has the gravest responsibility in regard to fulfilling the supreme mandate of Christ: "Go into all the world and preach the gospel to the whole creation" (Mk. 16:15); "Go therefore and make disciples of all nations..." (Mt. 28:19).

2. *A tree with many branches*.... Glancing through the list of the various congregations, institutes and associations into which the Pauline Family is divided and to which the ardent soul of the founder gave rise with inexhaustible fruitfulness, I believe that this can be its most appropriate and comprehensive definition. It is a tree with many branches since, from the first congregation of Pauline priests and disciples which sprang up in long ago August 1914 to the most recent congregation of the Apostoline Sisters, founded towards the end of the 1950's, it has nine branches to which can also be added the numerous and flourishing associations of alumni. And I am pleased to recall here that one of these branches, the Pious Disciples of the Divine Master, has a community at the service of the Holy See in the Vatican.

It is a tree, because in this multiplicity of offshoots the original trunk was and remains one and—what is more important—the vital sap which nourishes it and makes it develop is one. In fact, unvaried and constant was the idea that gradually inspired Don Alberione to study and put into effect the possible ways of penetration and the new modes of presence in the folds of modern society in order to make room in it for the Gospel. It was precisely this search, lasting the entire span of his long life, which made him very dear to the Supreme Pontiffs and in a special way—as is known—to my Predecessor Paul VI.

3. In naming his foundations after St. Paul, your father evidently did not limit himself to an onomastic or verbal choice, but intended to go back to the unmistakable spirit and style of the Apostle of the Gentiles. In fact, Don Alberione wanted to take from St. Paul not merely his name or patronage, but also and above all ideal, inspiration and spiritual nourishment. He proposed to himself and to those who already followed him in his earliest initiatives, just as to you who follow him in the present, *the outline of an open, up-to-date, modern apostolate*, according to the teachings and the examples of the Apostle himself. As Paul was always in search of new forms and courageous methods for proclaiming Christ and His mystery to the Gentiles (cf. Eph. 3:1-2), and in this context are placed his missionary journeys, his letters, his tireless dedication, it is thus worthwhile for you to look

to him willingly to confirm yourselves in your specific vocation and to persevere in your commitment to original, generous action, with no sparing of effort or sacrifices.

It is therefore obvious what the interior sap is which must nourish your ministry in the Church and in society: it is the charity of the truth revealed by Christ and entrusted by Him to the Apostles and their successors, and that is to the Church, which is its guarantor, and transmits it and defends it with its authentic and permanent Magisterium.

4. But there is a sector to which the Paulines are dedicated with particular commitment: that of the press, for the preparation and distribution of editions of books and periodicals with a Christian orientation and therefore corresponding to a pedagogical-formative purpose. This sector is extremely vast and important since on the one hand it extends to and is linked with the audiovisual sector, and on the other hand it very closely touches—also in relation to so many things produced which are morally equivocal and damaging—the problem of the Christian education of youth.

Your mission in the specific field of publishing is of extreme relevance and necessity. May your ideal and your concern always be predominantly that of human, Christian and Catholic formation. Yours is a true evangelical-ecclesial mission: it is for this that you have been called, following the footsteps of Don Alberione.

May his high example serve to inspire and sustain you in a vigilant and active, disinterested and generous commitment, always inspired by an authentic evangelical spirit.

In the sector of social communications—as in all others—may you always be animated by an authentic apostolic spirit so that your constant guide may be not the criteria of profit or of other advantages of a temporal nature that a particular initiative may produce, but solely that of the good which it may sow in society.

At the beginning I defined your family as *a tree of many branches:* this is no more than a recognition of what you are and represent. But I want to conclude with a wish: in the strengthened fidelity to the spirit and to the directives of your founder I hope that, through the multiplicity of initiatives and the wealth of good results, it may be also and above all a *tree bearing much fruit!*

With my apostolic blessing.

Foster Vocations in the Light of Conciliatory Redemption

On April 23, 1983, the large religious family of the Rogationists and the Daughters of Divine Zeal met with the Holy Father in the Paul VI Hall to celebrate the centenary of the beginning of their educative and charitable activity. Besides the male religious and the sisters, many seminarians, students and former students, representatives of vocational groups and parish groups were present. In all, there were over 10,000 people.

After an introductory address by Fr. Ciranni, the Holy Father gave the following discourse.

Dearest brothers and sisters,

1. I sincerely thank you for your visit, which is so meaningful and affectionate, and I express my gratitude to Fr. Gaetano Ciranni, Superior General of the Congregation of Rogationist Fathers, for his courteous words, with which in fact he has been the spokesman for the common sentiments in this meeting, which signals an important stage in your Congregations of Rogationist Fathers and the Sisters Daughters of Divine Zeal. In fact, this year is the first centenary of the institution of the "Works of Charity," desired by your venerated founder, the Servant of God, Fr. Annibale Maria Di Francia. He dedicated himself to the service of the Church in two specific fields: that of prayer to obtain from the Lord holy priestly and religious

vocations, according to the Master's exhortation: *Rogate ergo*, (Pray, therefore), and that of the education and welfare of children and young people particularly in need of help.

With sincere joy in my heart and with gratitude to the Lord for what you represent and do in the Church, I greet all of you who are assembled here in such great numbers: the priests, religious, sisters, young people and students of the educational institutions, seminarians, former students, those enrolled in the Rogationist Priestly Alliance and in the vocational groups, members of the secular institute, the members of the missionary stations and of the parishes entrusted to your institutes, and finally the friends and admirers who support your work.

I open my heart to all, wishing you with the words of the Apostle Paul: "Grace and peace from God our Father and the Lord Jesus Christ" (1 Cor. 1:3).

SIGNIFICANT DAY

2. This meeting of ours occurs on the eve of the Twentieth World Day of Prayer for Vocations. One could not have chosen a more significant day for you who belong to the great Rogationist family and who thus make the promotion of vocations the distinctive sign of

your specific initiatives, born from the charism of your founder, who dedicated his whole self to this noble cause, which he called the "propagation of the holy Evangelical Rogation." I am certain that tomorrow, Good Shepherd Sunday, inspired by the exemplary witness of your founder, you will not fail to encourage your communities and to make them sensitive to the great and serious problem of vocations, which is at the center of the Church's attention and worries, and to unite yourselves in a special way to my prayer: "that the Lord will send out laborers to gather his harvest" (Mt. 9:38). As you well know, today the harvest is large; the Church is continuously expanding. It grows and expands under every sky, but the workers are few: few not only in the face of the growing needs for pastoral care, urgently claimed by the ever growing phenomenon of urbanization, but also (and I would say above all) few in the face of the profound requirements of the modern world. Contrary to what might appear on the surface, the world is desirous and thirsty for the Word of God which saves, enlightens and gives security.

The problem of a sufficient number of priests touches the Church closely, because the religious future of Christian society depends on it. This, then, is an eloquent index of the vitality of faith and of love working in the individual religious, parochial and diocesan communities.

JUBILEE YEAR PILGRIMAGE

3. But the purpose of your coming to Rome is also to gain the Jubilee indulgence during the observance of the 1950th anniversary of the Redemption, which, as I have already said on another occasion, "must bring all Christians to the rediscovery of the mystery of love...to a probing of the riches hidden for centuries in Christ in the 'burning furnace' of the Paschal Mystery" (cf. Address to the Sacred College, December 23, 1982).

Beloved, take advantage of this pilgrimage to welcome with sincerity of spirit and with humble disposition those graces necessary to make an examination of your personal situation and, if need be, to correct it. Look into the depth of your heart to give God the place which belongs to Him in your life and to see if there are not offenses to forget, or peaceful relationships to revive through a charitable conversation. Be able to "overcome evil with good" (Rom. 12:21) by creating around you an atmosphere of goodness, generosity and trust, and by seeing in others, not strangers, but brothers to understand, to respect and to love.

This is the message and the appeal which come to you from the centenary of your foundation, in this Jubilee Year of the Redemption. Live them in this way: and you will experience in your soul the joy of being authentic Christians, redeemed and reconciled in the blood of the immaculate Lamb, and you will find that peace which He alone knows how to, and can, give.

Be bearers of the vocational announcement, of this "holy ideal," as your founder called it, in the light of the conciliatory Redemption, and the Lord will not fail to hear your petitions.

With my heart I invoke upon you and upon your resolutions the comfort of our Lord the Good Shepherd, and I gladly impart to you my apostolic blessing.

Africa Has Great Need of You for Progress in the Work of Evangelization

On May 5, 1983, the Holy Father received in audience the participants in the General Assembly of the African Missions Society.

After hearing the address of homage by the new Superior General, Fr. Patrick Harrington, the Holy Father addressed them as follows in French.

Dear Father Superior,
Dear brothers in the priesthood,

The Society of African Missions (of Lyons) has a long and rich history: just over 125 years.

If Mons. Marion de Bresillac, your founder, were to speak to you in my place, I think he would begin by thanking Fr. Joseph Hardy for having so generously borne the burdens of the generalate for ten years, and that he would strongly encourage his successor, Fr. Patrick Harrington, son of Ireland, to continue the missionary epic begun in 1856. I think that through all of you delegates at this general assembly he would communicate a breath of Pentecost to the 1350 members you represent.

I have read with great interest that Mons. de Bresillac made it his aim to found and build in Africa, at the time set by Providence, ecclesial communities capable of taking their future in their own hands, under the pastoral care of shepherds arising from their own land—communities whose own culture would flourish from its contact with the Gospel of Christ, the only Redeemer; communities which would be recognized by the founding Churches and nationalities as worthy of respect and admiration, capable of creativity and of sharing their rich uniqueness. On the whole, your founder's dream has become a reality.

At the same time, I can easily understand that this very fact poses a question for you, you who are neither religious nor diocesan priests, but solely missionaries living in a society of apostolic life. Your question would seem to me to be this: in these local Churches, becoming more and more African in their structures, their personnel, their legitimate searching for their own liturgical and theological expression, their pastoral initiatives and the creation and setting up of indigenous religious institutes, yes, in these Churches, do you still have a role? In your assembly you will have profoundly investigated this topic, in a climate of brotherhood, loyalty, prayer and hope.

For my part, in the name of the Lord and of the Church, while being well aware of the changes happening nearly everywhere, and of the complications arising from them, I want to give you a strong message of encouragement: discover again, as deeply as possible, the inspiration of your founder. All united together, turn yourselves towards the future, with realism and optimism, with faith and serenity. As a consequence, in one way or another, and in all your provinces, renew your missionary consecration, which essentially consists in being witnesses, especially among the Africans, to the Gospel of Jesus Christ, the only true liberator and unifier of mankind. The continent of Africa is at this very moment an extremely important stake in the future of the world and of the Church. Continue to imbue your missionary witness with an ever greater respect for what the African is, without in any way losing your own identity.

It is by constant dialogue with the men and women and the young people of the various countries in Africa that you must be missionary. I insist especially on the importance of doing everything to have yourselves recognized explicitly and accepted fraternally as men dedicated to proclaiming the Gospel among those who have never heard about it—they are legion! —and especially among the poorest. It is truly this way that has made you—and will make you—witnesses to the catholicity of the Church, both in the dioceses that receive you and in your dioceses of origin. In both, you will promote openness to the missions, awaken new missionary vocations, create concrete links between the older and the younger Churches. You will contribute to making the rich nations hear the voice of the Third World, too long left disregarded and even lamentably exploited. Dear fathers and brothers of the African Missions, your missionary work is far from over! Mons. de Bresillac, along with your most ardent forerunners, is begging you to be new servants of the Gospel, transparent signs of communion and of sharing between the Churches, apostles constantly and humbly attentive to the cultural values of peoples, to the riches of other Churches, of other religions, while remaining loyal and faithful to your own identity, and clearly responsible for total witness to the Good News of the Lord Jesus.

In conclusion, allow me to share another conviction with you. You are, and you will be, good workers for the missions, for its future, on the condition that you sincerely and practically accept the day-to-day demands of individual and communal conversion. Does not your missionary formation always need to be reexamined and completed? Does not Christ Himself expect a complete opening of the doors of our hearts?

Sons of Mons. de Bresillac, go forward! Africa has great need of you "so that it may grow greater because you made yourselves lesser," to echo in some way the words of John the Baptist. I am happy to convey to you the confidence and the support of the Church. Persevere in your dialogue with the Congregation for the Evangelization of Peoples. Like all the Roman Congregations, its vocation is to be at your service. I believe that an updating of your constitutions is under way. May it be well concluded and without too much delay! It is with fervor that I invoke on your new superior general and his council, on the delegates of the assembly, and on all the members of the African Missions, the most abundant blessings of evangelical peace and joy, of judicious and persevering apostolic adaptation, of ardent love for Jesus Christ and His Church.

Secular Institutes, Faithful Expression of the Council's Ecclesiology

On May 6, 1983, the work of the plenary assembly of the Sacred Congregation for Religious and for Secular Institutes, begun on May 3, concluded with an audience with the Holy Father. "The Secular Institutes: Their Identity and Their Mission" was the central theme of the meeting, which examined consecrated life in the light of the new Code of Canon Law.

The numerous cardinals, prelates and superiors general who took part in the assembly were led at the audience, held in the Throne Room, by the Prefect of the Sacred Congregation, Cardinal Eduardo Pironio, along with the Secretary, Archbishop Augustin Mayer, and the Undersecretary for the Secular Institutes, Reverend Mario Albertini.

Responding to Cardinal Pironio's greeting, the Holy Father addressed the following discourse to the group.

Revered brothers and beloved sons and daughters!

1. I thank you for your presence and I express to you my joy for this meeting, and my gratitude for the work that you do to inspire and foster consecrated life. The evangelical counsels, in fact, are a "divine gift which the Church has received from her Lord and which she ever preserves with the help of His grace" (LG 43),

and therefore what is done in the Congregation on behalf of their profession is extremely sound and valuable.

The plenary assembly which you are concluding today was held along this line of inspiring and fostering consecrated life. You have taken into particular consideration the identity and the mission of those institutes which, because of their distinctive mission *in saeculo et ex saeculo* (Can. 713, par. 2—New Code), are called "secular institutes."

It is the first time that one of your plenary assemblies has dealt with them directly: therefore it was a timely choice, which the promulgation of the new Code has inspired. The secular institutes—which in 1947 received ecclesial recognition with the apostolic constitution *Provida Mater* issued by my Predecessor, Pius XII—now find in the Code their rightful place on the basis of the doctrine of the Second Vatican Council. In fact, these institutes are intended to be faithful expressions of that ecclesiology which the Council reconfirms when it emphasizes the universal vocation to holiness (cf. LG chap. 5), the inherent tasks of the baptized (cf. LG chap. 4; AA), the Church's presence in the world in which she must act as leaven and be the "universal sacrament of salvation" (LG 48; cf. GS), the variety and the dignity of the various vocations, and the "particular honor" which the Church pays toward "total continence embraced on behalf of the kingdom of heaven" (LG 42) and towards the witness of evangelical poverty and obedience *(ibid.)*.

OUTPOURING OF GRACE

2. Quite rightly your reflection dwelled on the constitutive, theological and juridical elements of the secular institutes, keeping in mind the formulation of the canons dedicated to them in the recently promulgated Code, and examining them in the light of the teaching which Pope Paul VI, and I myself with the discourse of August 28, 1980, have confirmed in audiences granted them.

We must express profound gratitude to the Father of infinite mercy, who has taken to heart the needs of mankind and, with the life-giving power of the Spirit, has undertaken in this century new initiatives for mankind's redemption. Honor and glory be to the triune God for this outpouring of grace which the secular institutes are, and with which He manifests His inexhaustible benevolence, with which the Church herself loves the world in the name of her God and Lord.

The newness of the gift which the Spirit has made to the Church's everlasting fruitfulness in response to the needs of our times is grasped only if its constituent elements in their inseparability are well understood: the religious and the secular; the consequent apostolate of witness, of Christian commitment in social life and of evangelization; the fraternity which, without being determined by a community of life, is truly communion; the external lifestyle itself, which is not separate from the environment in which it may appear.

EVANGELICAL RADICALISM

3. Now it is necessary to know and make known this vocation that is so relevant and, I should say, so urgent—the vocation of persons who consecrate themselves to God by practicing the evangelical counsels and strive to immerse their whole lives and all their activities in that special consecration, creating in themselves a total availability to the Father's will and working to change the world from within (cf. Discourse of August 28, 1980).

The promulgation of the new Code will surely allow this better knowledge, but it must also urge pastors to foster among the faithful an understanding which is not approximate or yielding, but exact and respectful of the qualifying characteristics.

In this way, generous responses to this difficult but beautiful vocation of "full consecration to God and to souls" (cf. PC 5) are aroused: a demanding vocation, because one responds to it by carrying the baptismal commitments to the most perfect consequences of evangelical radicalism, and also because this evangelical life must be embodied in the most diverse situations.

In fact, the variety of the gift entrusted to the secular institutes expresses the various apostolic aims which embrace all areas of human and Christian life. This pluralistic wealth is also shown in the numerous spiritualities which animate the secular institutes, with the diversity of the holy bonds which characterize various modes of practicing the evangelical counsels and the great possibilities of their incorporation in all areas of social life. My Predecessor, Pope Paul VI, who showed so much affection for the secular institutes, rightly said that if they "remain faithful to their vocation, they will be like an experimental laboratory in which the Church tests the concrete modes of its relations with the world" (Paul VI, Discourse to the International Congress of Secular Institutes, August 25, 1976). Therefore, lend your support to these institutes that they may be faithful to the original charisms of their foundation recognized by the hierarchy, and be alert to discover in their fruits the teaching which God wants to give us for the life and action of the entire Church.

SECULAR INSTITUTES
AND THE LOCAL CHURCHES

4. If there is a development and strengthening of the secular institutes, the local Churches also will derive benefit from this.

This aspect has been kept in mind during your plenary assembly, also because various episcopates, with the suggestions given with regard to your meeting, have pointed out that the relationship between secular institutes and local Churches is worthy of being deepened.

Even while respecting their characteristics, the secular institutes must understand and adopt the pastoral urgencies of the particular Churches, and encourage their members to live the hopes and toils, the projects and concerns, the spiritual riches and limitations with diligent participation; in a word, the communion of their concrete Church. This must be a point for greater reflection for the secular institutes, just as it must be a concern of the pastors to recognize and request their contribution according to their proper nature.

In particular, another responsibility rests on the pastors: that of offering the secular institutes all the doctrinal wealth they need. They want to be part of the world and ennoble temporal realities, setting them in order and elevating them, that all things may be brought into one

under Christ's headship (cf. Eph. 1:1). Therefore, may all the wealth of Catholic doctrine on
creation, incarnation and redemption be given
to these institutes that they may make their own
God's wise and mysterious plans for man, for
history and for the world.

TRUE ESTEEM
AND DEEP ENCOURAGEMENT

5. Beloved brothers and sons and daughters! It is with a sentiment of true esteem and
also of deep encouragement for the secular
institutes that today I have taken the opportunity offered me by this meeting to emphasize
some aspects treated by you during the past few
days.

I hope that your plenary assembly may
fully achieve the goal of offering to the Church
better information on the secular institutes and
helping them live their vocation in awareness and
fidelity.

May this Jubilee Year of the Redemption,
which calls everyone to "a renewed discovery of
the love of God who gives Himself" (*Aperite
portas Redemptori*, no. 8) and a renewed encounter with the merciful goodness of God, be particularly for consecrated persons also a renewed
and pressing invitation to follow "with greater
freedom" and "more closely" (PC 1) the Master
who calls them for the pathways of the Gospel.

May the Virgin Mary be a constant and sublime model to them, and may she always guide them with her motherly protection.

With these sentiments, I gladly impart my intercessory apostolic blessing to you here present and to those enrolled in the secular institutes throughout the world.

The Community Nature of the Religious Apostolate

On May 13, 1983, in the Hall of the Blessing, the Holy Father received in audience seven hundred seventy superiors general belonging to the International Union of Superiors General.

The Holy Father addressed the following discourse to the religious.

Beloved sisters in Christ!

1. Accept my most heartfelt greeting! It is always a reason for joy for me to meet with female religious and to express openly the Church's deep esteem for their lives of total consecration to the Lord, the keen interest and the faith which the Holy See nourishes for them and for their mission.

But today's meeting assumes an altogether special importance because of its so universal nature: in fact, in the persons of the superiors general of the various religious institutes spread throughout the world, in a certain way there is expressed the presence in Rome of all female religious and their desire to attest to their devotion to the Church and to the Pope, and to accept personally his teachings and directives.

Therefore, through you, I send a heartfelt special blessing to all the female religious in the world: to the contemplatives; to those who in humble generosity are dedicated to the service of the brethren; to those tried by age, by sickness of body or mind. The sacrifices of all of them have an incomparable value in the eyes of the Lord.

To you, gathered in Rome to examine the "Apostolic Spirituality of Religious," I want above all to offer a word of encouragement and comfort, which is required by such an important, such a delicate, but at the same time such a pastoral mission, conferred on you by your very election: that of building up in Christ a fraternal community where, above all, God may be sought and loved (cf. Can. 619).

GIVE WITNESS
TO YOUR CONSECRATED LIVES

2. The theme of your works, in preparation for some years, is rich in teachings and offers you the opportunity not only to treat of your apostolic

activities, but even more to draw from the sources which must nourish them.

Moreover, I strongly advise you to meditate on the teachings of the new Code of Canon Law bearing on this subject. It will offer you valuable insights into a fundamental part of your lives.

In fact, the Code recalls in the first place (cf. Can. 673) that the apostolate of religious consists above all in giving witness to their consecrated lives, nourished by prayer and penance. This basic affirmation is of particular importance since it places the apostolic role of religious in its true place. Precisely through their innermost beings they join the dynamism of the Church, thirsty for the absolute of God, called to sanctity. Above all, they are called to witness this sanctity (cf. EN 69).

Before being translated into proclamation or action, the apostolate is the revelation of God present in the apostle. And this revelation postulates that the religious be in intimate and constant contact with the Lord. In this way, it matters little whether she be in the fullness of her strength or infirm, young or of advanced age, active or without any direct activity: evangelization is real and deep to the degree that Christ's life is reflected through her personal life. The great evangelizers were primarily prayerful souls, interior souls: they always knew how to find the time for prolonged contemplation.

At this historical moment when you all have reason to suffer from the lack of apostolic workers, it is especially well to pause and meditate on this truth, in the faith that "being" has more value than "doing," which is always limited and imperfect. Moreover, be certain that your courageous and joyful fidelity to the fundamental demands of consecrated life will offer a pressing invitation to young women, always ready to be generous, to follow the Lord along the path marked out by you.

APOSTOLIC ROLE
OF CLOISTERED NUNS

3. In this perspective, although they are not present among you, I want to reaffirm strongly the eminently apostolic role of cloistered nuns. To leave the world to devote oneself in solitude to deeper and constant prayer is none other than a special way of living and expressing Christ's Paschal Mystery, of revealing it to the world and, therefore, of being an apostle.

It would be an error to consider cloistered nuns as creatures separated from their contemporaries, isolated and as if cut off from the world and the Church. Rather, they are present to them, and in a deeper way, with the same tenderness of Christ, as *Lumen gentium* (no. 46) affirms. It is therefore not surprising that the bishops of the new Churches solicit, as an eminent grace, the possibility of receiving a monastery of contemplative religious, even if workers for the active apostolate are still in such insufficient number.

Sisters of the contemplative life! May your vocation be dear to you; it is more precious than ever in today's world, which seems unable to find peace. The Pope and the Church need you; Christians count on your fidelity.

IN UNION WITH THE CHURCH'S MAGISTERIUM AND HIERARCHY

4. May you who are consecrated to the works of the active apostolate always be more greatly convinced of the Council's teachings, so appropriately recalled in the Code. Live them! That is, may your lives be steeped in the apostolic spirit and may your every apostolic action be inspired by an evangelical spirit.

In this way your activities will constitute an authentic "service," humbly respectful of persons, concerned with avoiding undue pressures and every intolerable, overbearing characteristic.

I exhort you again never to forget that the religious apostolate is, by its nature, communitarian: the witness given by a religious cannot be purely individual; it is communitarian in nature, and all religious are called to exercise the apostolate along the line of the charism recognized by the Church and through the mandate of their lawful superiors.

It is not a matter of a simple disciplinary dependence, but of a reality of faith. We must ceaselessly remind ourselves that we are in the Church, intimately incorporated in it, ordained to its mission, inseparable from its life and from its sanctity, as *Lumen gentium* teaches.

This conception must stimulate in religious the will to work in strict and profound union with the Church's Magisterium and its hierarchy. Certainly, in carrying out the multiple, traditional forms of your apostolate you must not fail to listen to your contemporaries in order to understand well their problems and their difficulties and be better able to help them.

Never forget, however, that the schools, the hospitals, the relief centers, the initiatives directed towards service of the poor, the cultural and spiritual development of peoples not only preserve their relevance but, appropriately brought up to date, often are revealed as special places for evangelization, witness and authentic human promotion.

TEMPTATION OF INDIVIDUALISM AND RISKS OF DIVISION

5. Sometimes it may be necessary to abandon works or activities in order to be able to dedicate oneself to others, to create more limited communities in order to answer the most pressing needs of the poor in certain regions. I know your ardent desire to be present to the poor, and I appreciate your efforts in this regard. However, as I said recently to the religious of Sao Paulo (July 3, 1980), it seems opportune to recall here certain needs for new forms of presence.

First of all, these efforts must always be conducted in a climate of prayer. The soul which lives constantly in the presence of God and lets itself become permeated with the warmth of His charity will easily escape the temptation of individualism and the contradictions which risk division; it will be able to interpret in the light of the Gospel the option for the poor and for the victims of the selfishness of men, without yielding to socio-political radicalism which, sooner or later, produces effects contrary to those hoped for and engenders new forms of oppression. Finally, the person in touch with God will find the way to come close to people and to become part of their milieu, without losing her own religious identity, and neither hiding nor disguising the uniqueness of her vocation which is to follow Christ, poor, chaste and obedient.

Moreover, these experiences must also be prepared for by serious study in a constant dialogue in the heart of the institute, with responsible superiors and in collaboration with concerned bishops. In this way, the programs will be worked out after examining the possibilities of success (cf. Lk. 14:28ff.), without running risks, but always acting in conformity with the most urgent needs and according to the nature of the institute.

In conclusion, it will be important always to pursue such experiments in accord with the hierarchy, attempting humbly and courageously, if necessary, to correct them, to set them aside or to adapt them in a more suitable manner.

Above all, always and in everything, behave as loving daughters of the Church, generously and faithfully adhering to its authentic Magisterium—the guarantee of fruitfulness. The fidelity promised to Christ can never be separated from fidelity to the Church: "He who hears you, hears me" (Lk. 10:16).

PENANCE AND CONVERSION

6. The Holy Year which we have been celebrating since March 25, and the preparation for the Synod of Bishops next September, are of

invaluable assistance to you in carrying out your mission of evangelization.

The Holy Year invites us to rediscover the riches of salvation, and so it calls us to a personal commitment to renewal, through penance and conversion.

The celebration of this event is, for all Christians and therefore for religious, an earnest appeal to repentance and conversion. It makes us rediscover a sense of sin and become aware of the fact that we are sinners. It makes us rediscover a sense of God. This attitude of conversion will especially show itself in a more sincere approach to the sacraments, and it will impel us to practice a charity that is based on truth and that promotes justice. I would like to emphasize at this point the real and profound link that exists between the fraternal life of religious and the very theme of the Holy Year. This is perfectly highlighted by the new Code of Canon Law: "By their fraternal communion, founded and rooted in charity, religious will give an example of universal reconciliation in Christ" (Can. 602).

In this same spirit of communion and joy, I wish to repeat my cordial welcome to all of you who have come to Rome for this meeting. My contact with the members of the two international Unions of Superiors General is a valued way of reaching the religious of the world and of maintaining a continuing contact with the development of religious life. On Tuesday of this week I had the pleasure of meeting with the executive committee of the Union of Superiors General. Today I meet with you and I hope to have further contacts with both Unions in the future. When you go home, carry with you my special blessing to the sisters of your congregations.

The Blessed Virgin Mary, the first of the redeemed, the first to have been closely associated with the work of the Redemption, will always be your guide and model. Like Mary the Mother of Jesus, who was totally consecrated to the Person of her Son and to the service of the Redemption, so you and your sisters will learn to know nothing except the crucified Jesus, who became for us wisdom, justice, sanctification and redemption (cf. 1 Cor. 1:30; 2:2).

The World Thirsts
for the Good News

On May 19, 1983, in the Throne Room, John Paul II received in audience the participants in the one-hundred-sixth general chapter of the Third Order Regular of St. Francis, led by the new Minister General, Fr. José Angulo Quilis. The chapter, which began May 8, and ended May 21, was dedicated to the examination of the order's new rule, recently approved by the Holy Father, as well as the appointments to positions of responsibility.

After the brief greeting by the new Minister General, the Pope delivered the following address.

Beloved Fathers of the Third Order Regular of St. Francis,

1. I am very happy to receive you on the occasion of the one-hundred-sixth general chapter of the order, assembled both to elect the new Minister General and to examine the situation of the order in various parts of the world where the Lord calls you to work, in order to infuse into your apostolic activity a new thrust of vitality for the near future, and to review your religious life in the light of the charism of foundation.

I thank you for your visit and express my heartfelt greeting to each and every one of you individually. Encouraging you to go forward at an ever faster pace, I invite you to keep alive the bases of the Franciscan ideal within your communities and in God's holy Church.

2. Your presence here in the house of our common Father reminds me of St. Francis' arrival seven hundred seventy-three years ago when, after having gathered together his first disciples—twelve, like the number of the Apostles—and having drawn up the first rule of life, which was based on absolute poverty and inexhaustible charity, he wanted to come to Rome in person to present it for the approval of Innocent III.

The rule of the Poverello of Assisi is imbued with the evangelical spirit. And this is the fundamental reason for the irresistible fascination exercised over the centuries by the saint from Assisi; this is the explanation for that secret which from the first shoot of the twelve "Penitents" allowed the vigorous flowering of the great and varied Franciscan family, so praiseworthy in the history of the Church in the service of the People of God.

Your Third Order, beginning with the charismatic inspiration of the Seraphic Father, is directly connected with him, above all since it was St. Francis himself who promoted it with the purpose of ensuring necessary strength to the observance of the Third Rule.

Fervor for charity, depth in the difficult virtue of humility, joy in poverty. In other words: imitation of Jesus, love for the brethren, stripping of one's self, action and contemplation. These are the genuine principles of seraphic spirituality which bear the fruit of perfect happiness.

3. It has been repeatedly recalled by the Apostolic See that the directives regarding the renewal of religious life desired by the Second Vatican Council are primarily aimed at achieving a reform of an interior nature. The effort of religious institutes to update the objectives or methodologies would be futile if not inspired and accompanied by a deepening of and a new thrust to spirituality.

Beloved fathers, the modern world is thirsty for the Good News.

If the announcement of the extraordinary Jubilee, proclaimed to celebrate the 1950 years since the Redemption, intends to stimulate the generosity of all the People of God to a more personal and deeper encounter with its Savior, so much more is this goal expected from consecrated souls. It is the indispensable premise for the divine work of the evangelization of the world.

Thus the ceaseless search for the most authentic sources of your history, the commitment to revive them and to relive them in the spirit of the Gospel, following the example of the great saint from Assisi, become a support for the continual development of the Church of God.

With this wish, I impart my intercessory apostolic blessing to you and to your order.

Nourish Your Spirituality and Catechesis with Dogmatic Truths

On May 20, 1983, the Holy Father dedicated the first meeting of his pastoral visit to the Archdiocese of Milan to female religious. After receiving the welcome of the populace in the "Cinque Giornate" Square, the Pope went to the Sports Palace, seat of the meetings of the Twentieth National Eucharistic Congress, where more than twelve thousand sisters from the whole Lombardy region were gathered, along with representatives of religious from the Veneto and Piedmont regions.

In response to the presentation address by the Cardinal Archbishop of Milan, Carlo Maria Martini, the Pope delivered the following discourse to the religious.

Beloved religious from Milan and Lombardy!

1. My visit to this archdiocese on the occasion of the National Eucharistic Congress has a well qualified and significant characteristic: it is a journey of witness, of catechesis and of adoration of the most Blessed Sacrament of the

altar. Therefore, I could not omit a special meeting with you religious who are consecrated precisely to Christ, present in the Eucharist, and who have prepared for this great event with intense prayer.

I greet you cordially and express to you my gratitude and esteem for the enormous and careful work carried out by you and by your individual congregations in the service of this local Church and of the Lombardy region. How many spiritual and also social fruits your love for Christ and for the brethren has produced! An immense array of consecrated souls from century to century has spread goodness, love, charity, relief, joy, well-being, consolation everywhere. Children have been received and educated, parents helped and advised, young people loved and guided, the sick cured and comforted, the poor helped and consoled, those discriminated against and those gone astray have been lovingly taken in and cared for. Certainly, it has not been possible to relieve every suffering and eliminate all distress; perhaps there have been deficiencies and defects. But it is impossible not to recognize sincerely the immense work carried out in this land with love and with dedication, at times heroic, by the sisters of the various congregations, by you, who find strength and happiness, serenity and courage in the intimate union with the Eucharistic

Jesus. Wherever your love and your smiles pass, through the grace of God, good flourishes! For all of this, let us together thank the Lord, who has called you and chosen you for such dignity and given you such a noble and ever authentic mission. And at the same time let us pray that, also through your fervent witness, He give to today's Church numerous and holy vocations, so necessary for modern society, which above all needs love, understanding, mercy and hope.

My greeting therefore becomes a wish and an exhortation to be evermore fervent in the commitment to your sanctification and fraternal charity, and it is extended to all your fellow sisters who could not be present at our meeting because of unbreakable commitments and reasons of health. My greeting goes with special affection to the numerous cloistered nuns who, in continual prayer and self-giving, are an irreplaceable and fruitful part of the Church and of the social organism itself.

A DEEPLY DOGMATIC SPIRITUALITY

2. The important event of the National Eucharistic Congress which urged me to come as a pilgrim to Lombardy also suggests to me the recommendation I leave you this evening: that your Eucharistic spirituality may always be deeply dogmatic.

The Eucharistic dogma affirms the true, real, substantial presence of Christ who offers Himself to the Father as a sacrifice in our name and who is intimately united with us in Communion. The Council of Trent, recalling and interpreting with definitive authority the words spoken by Jesus both in the discourse on the bread of life (Jn. 6) and at the Last Supper, expressed itself in this way: "The Church of God always had this faith: immediately after the consecration, under the appearances of bread and wine there is the true body of our Lord and the true blood, together with His soul and His divinity. His body exists under the appearance of bread and His blood under the appearance of wine by virtue of the words of consecration. His body is under the appearance of wine, His blood under the appearance of bread and His soul under both appearances by virtue of that connection and natural concomitance which holds united all the parts of Christ the Lord, who rose from the dead never to die again. Finally, His divinity is found present through His admirable hypostatic union with His body and His soul. It is therefore very true that as much is contained under one of the two species as under both. In fact, just as Christ is whole and entire under the appearance of bread and under every part of the same appearance, He is also whole and entire under the appearance of wine and under its parts" (Sess. XIII, 3).

Then, interpreting the affirmations of the Apostles, of the letter to the Hebrews, and of the whole early Church, the Council of Trent affirms and explains that the Eucharist is the "sacrificial presence" of Christ in time, that is, the Eucharist is the renewal of the sacrifice of the cross.

The Second Vatican Council reaffirms the same truth: "As often as the sacrifice of the cross in which 'Christ our passover has been sacrificed' (1 Cor. 5:7) is celebrated on an altar, the work of our Redemption is carried on" (LG 3; cf. SC 47).

READ AND MEDITATE

3. Therefore, nourish your spirituality and your catechesis with dogmatic truths! Read and meditate on the great and fundamental doctrinal documents of the Church regarding the Eucharist, the encyclicals, and statements of qualified and authentic teachers, the experiences of the saints and mystics! There can be no confusion or mystification about the Eucharist!

St. Thomas Aquinas well said that the truth of the Eucharist "cannot be grasped with the senses, but only with faith, which is based on the authority of God" (S. Th. III, 75, 1). And St. Ambrose, the great Bishop of Milan (334-397), wrote: "Not without significance do you say

'Amen,' since now in your spirit you confess that you receive the body of Christ. Therefore, when you come up to request it, the priest says to you: 'The body of Christ,' and you answer: 'Amen,' that is, 'It is true.' One's inner conviction safeguards what the tongue confesses" *(De Sacramentis* IV, 5, 25).

The Christian is convinced that as a creature he must pray to and adore God, the Creator and Lord of the universe and of his life; but enlightened by faith he knows that true "adoration," perfectly valid, worthy of the infinite sanctity of God and of his own personal intelligence, is possible only through the Sacrifice of the Mass, to which every other prayer is linked. One cannot live without adoring, and therefore one cannot live without the Mass! The Christian knows that Jesus is present in the form of "food" and "drink," because He "gave Himself" totally to man and wants to unite Himself intimately with us to strengthen us in faith and will, to console us during tribulations, to transform us into Himself, to inflame us with love toward all creatures. Only from the Eucharistic dogma, precisely understood and totally lived, come the true meaning of Christian existence, the strength of the religious vocation, the authentic commitment to the transformation of society, the enlightened sense of unity in Christ, in truth and in charity.

In the same work on the sacraments, Saint Ambrose wrote: "Receive every day what must do you good every day!... Whoever has been wounded goes to be healed. Our wound is this, that we are under sin, and the medicine is the heavenly and adorable sacrament" (ibid., V, 4, 25).

CENTER OF YOUR LIFE

4. May the Eucharist, that is, holy Mass and Holy Communion, truly be the affective and dynamic center of your consecrated life and of each of your communities so that the very virtues of Christ may always shine in you: strength, patience, goodness, generosity, total gift of self, and supernatural joy. Sometimes this all means heroic and enduring sacrifice! But it also means always feeling more need for the Eucharist and a longing for heaven. In The Way of Perfection, St. Teresa wrote this of Jesus: "The soul which intensely desires to feed on this food will find in the most Blessed Sacrament spiritual delight and consolation, and as soon as one has begun to taste it there will no longer be trials, persecutions or toils which he cannot bear easily" (c. XXXIV, 2).

Beloved! May the most holy Virgin be close to you and sustain you. As St. Ambrose exhorts, may she be "the model for your lives" (cf. De virginibus, 1, II, 2, 6).

In one of her apparitions to St. Catherine Labouré, our Lady said to the young sister—frightened by the greatness and the difficulty of the mission which had been entrusted to her—"It is here at the foot of the tabernacle that you must seek strength and consolation!" The heavenly Mother addresses the same words to each of you. With the Eucharist, near the tabernacle, may you be holy and fearless sisters, today and for the rest of your lives!

With this wish, I impart to you my heartfelt apostolic blessing.

Index

Daughters of St. Paul

IN MASSACHUSETTS
50 St. Paul's Ave., Jamaica Plain, Boston, MA 02130; **617-522-8911.**
172 Tremont Street, Boston, MA 02111; **617-426-5464; 617-426-4230.**

IN NEW YORK
78 Fort Place, Staten Island, NY 10301; **212-447-5071; 212-447-5086.**
59 East 43rd Street, New York, NY 10017; **212-986-7580.**
625 East 187th Street, Bronx, NY 10458; **212-584-0440.**
525 Main Street, Buffalo, NY 14203; **716-847-6044.**

IN NEW JERSEY
Hudson Mall—Route 440 and Communipaw Ave.,
Jersey City, NJ 07304; **201-433-7740.**

IN CONNECTICUT
202 Fairfield Ave., Bridgeport, CT 06604; **203-335-9913.**

IN OHIO
2105 Ontario Street (at Prospect Ave.), Cleveland, OH 44115;
216-621-9427.
25 E. Eighth Street, Cincinnati, OH 45202; **513-721-4838;**
513-421-5733.

IN PENNSYLVANIA
1719 Chestnut Street, Philadelphia, PA 19103; **215-568-2638.**

IN VIRGINIA
1025 King Street, Alexandria, VA 22314; **703-683-1741; 703-549-3806.**

IN FLORIDA
2700 Biscayne Blvd., Miami, FL 33137; **305-573-1618.**

IN LOUISIANA
4403 Veterans Memorial Blvd., Metairie, LA 70002; **504-887-7631;**
504-887-0113.
1800 South Acadian Thruway, P.O. Box 2028, Baton Rouge, LA 70821;
504-343-4057; 504-381-9485.

IN MISSOURI
1001 Pine Street (at North 10th), St. Louis, MO 63101; **314-621-0346;**
314-231-1034.

IN ILLINOIS
172 North Michigan Ave., Chicago. IL 60601; **312-346-4228;**
312-346-3240.

IN TEXAS
114 Main Plaza, San Antonio, TX 78205; **512-224-8101; 512-224-0938.**

IN CALIFORNIA
1570 Fifth Ave., San Diego, CA 92101; **619-232-1442.**
46 Geary Street, San Francisco, CA 94108; **415-781-5180.**

IN WASHINGTON
2301 Second Ave., Seattle, WA 98121.

IN HAWAII
1143 Bishop Street, Honolulu, HI 96813; **808-521-2731.**

IN ALASKA
750 West 5th Ave., Anchorage, AK 99501; **907-272-8183.**

IN CANADA
3022 Dufferin Street, Toronto 395, Ontario, Canada.

IN ENGLAND
199 Kensington High Street, London W8 63A, England.
133 Corporation Street, Birmingham B4 6PH, England.
5A-7 Royal Exchange Square, Glasgow G1 3AH, England.
82 Bold Street, Liverpool L1 4HR, England.

IN AUSTRALIA
58 Abbotsford Rd., Homebush, N.S.W. 2140, Australia.